Intelligent Adapta[...]

Business Process Management
Adaptive Case Management

Foreword by
Sandy Kemsley

Excellence in Practice Series

Published in association with

Workflow Management Coalition

W f M
f C

23 Years of Thought-Process Leadership

Edited by
Layna Fischer

Future Strategies Inc., Book Division
Lighthouse Point, Florida

Intelligent Adaptability
Business Process Management / Adaptive Case Management

Published by Future Strategies Inc., Book Division

Lighthouse Point FL 33064 USA
954.782.3376 fax 954.719.3746
www.FutStrat.com; www.BPM-Books.com; books@FutStrat.com

Publisher's Cataloging-in-Publication Data

© 2076 ISBN 978-0-9863214-6-7

Intelligent Adaptability

/Fischer, Layna (editor)

/Kemsley, Sandy; Palmer, Nathaniel; Khoshafian, Dr Setrag; Webber, David RR; Winkler, Kay *et al* (authors)

p. cm.

Includes bibliographical references, glossary, appendices and index.

1. Adaptive Case Management, 2. Intelligent Systems, 3. Knowledge Work, 4. Business Intelligence, 5. Business Process Technology, 6. Business Process Management, 7. Big Data, 8. Predictive Analytics, 9. Business Process Innovation, 10. Internet of Things

Table of Contents

Appendices

Win an Award for *your* Case Management project

Get recognized for your vision and your team's superb efforts by entering the Global Excellence Awards:

Sponsored by WfMC and supported by BPM.com and Future Strategies Inc., these prestigious awards recognize user organizations worldwide that have demonstrably excelled in implementing innovative solutions.

The WfMC Global Awards for Case Management recognizes and focuses upon successful use cases within Adaptive Case Management. Case Management represents an adaptive approach to supporting knowledge workers in today's leading-edge organizations. ACM provides secure, social collaboration to create and adapt goal-oriented activities that enable informed decision-making using federated business data and content.

http://adaptivecasemanagement.org

Foreword: Machine Intelligence and Automation in ACM and BPM

Sandy Kemsley, Kemsley Design Ltd., Canada

INTRODUCTION

Last year in "Beyond Checklists" (Kemsley, 2016), I wrote about the need for intelligent ACM (adaptive case management) that augments human-powered case work with machine intelligence to drive innovation and maintain operational efficiencies. Intelligent ACM – incorporating rules, analytics, machine learning, and event processing – provides a platform to significantly enhance knowledge worker productivity by automating activities and decisions that don't require their level of skill. Freed from routine work, workers can focus on adding value through complex decision-making, problem resolution, collaboration and innovation.

Moving on a year, this chapter will look at how machine intelligence and automation technologies are emerging in ACM and business process management (BPM), the new capabilities that this provides, and the impact on organizations and the way people work.

THE IMPACT OF AUTOMATION

In 2013, two researchers from University of Oxford published a paper (Frey and Osborne, 2013) on the characteristics that make particular jobs more, or less, automatable. With its prediction that 47% of US jobs are at high risk of automation, this paper inspired many popular articles with titles such as "Will Your Job Be Replaced by A Robot?" that range between eye-opening and fear-mongering. This research categorizes work as either routine or non-routine, and either manual or cognitive, with the automation of routine tasks (both manual and cognitive) being relatively straightforward based on explicit rules and processes. Emerging uses of big data and machine learning are now enabling automation of non-routine tasks, changing the landscape of work and employment.

If we consider how ACM/BPM systems are used in the domain of cognitive tasks, automation has already greatly reduced the need for routine clerical and administrative roles. Now, increasing automation of non-routine tasks is beginning to replace people in decision-making activities such as insurance claims adjudication, legal research and medical diagnosis. In addition to the impact of job losses, knowledge workers have a radically altered role performing creative and social intelligence tasks that are still difficult to automate, while simultaneously using the automated systems to gather data, present aggregated findings and offer advice.

Just as business process reengineering did in the1990s, this new wave of process improvement is focused on eliminating tasks that do not add customer value, and increasing the amount of automation in what remains. This has the potential to eliminate many current job functions, radically change some of the remaining jobs, and hollow out business process outsourcing operations. Clearly, automation cannot be implemented independently from the human work that it augments: workers' goals and tasks will change, requiring different skills, performance models and incentives.

WHAT CAN – AND SHOULD – BE AUTOMATED?

Machine intelligence and automation in ACM and BPM are not a single technology, but a variety of technologies and techniques that can be combined in myriad ways. Below are typical uses of the most common technologies for adding intelligence to non-routine cognitive work.

Rules and Decision Management

Automated rules and decisions have two key roles:

- Ensuring that a knowledge worker doesn't violate regulations or compliance when they forget – or intentionally ignore – the standard operating procedure for a specific task. Declarative rules (constraints) can trigger when an action may breach compliance, preventing or requiring the worker to take certain actions. This is especially valuable in environments with rapidly-changing regulations, where staff turnover is high, or where the training time for a specific role is long.
- Replacing human decision-making to completely automate tasks, as has been done with the automation of routine work in the past. Decisions are invoked at specific points in a process or case, based on the information available at that point in time. An automated decision may have an associated degree of uncertainty and risk; if this exceeds a threshold, the task can be assigned to a knowledge worker for resolution. This is effective in non-routine adjudication scenarios, where many (but probably not all) cases can be completed without human intervention.

Automated rules, whether used to advise or replace workers, have an additional advantage: they provide clear evidence for why a specific decision was made for each case. This tends to remove individual biases and make more equitable decisions, although it may replace them with systemic biases of the decision designers.

When implementing automated rules, be aware that the new EU General Data Protection Regulation (GDPR) protects against potentially-damaging decisions made without human intervention, specifically related to personal profiling. From section 71 of the regulation (EU 2016): "The data subject should have the right not to be subject to a decision, which may include a measure, evaluating personal aspects relating to him or her which is based solely on automated processing and which produces legal effects concerning him or her or similarly significantly affects him or her, such as automatic refusal of an online credit application or e-recruiting practices without any human intervention."

Analytics

Analytics in ACM/BPM systems provide both insights and advice in non-automated scenarios:

- Aggregating and distilling information about a case to provide the knowledge workers with a more manageable set of information on which to base their decisions, while still allowing access to the underlying data sources.
- Predicting "what-if" scenarios, and recommending next best actions and decisions to assist the knowledge worker in decision-making. This reduces the learning curve and risk, and incorporates information that the workers may not have unearthed on their own.

These are both examples of analytics for use during the processing of tasks by workers, but analytics also have huge value for understanding and further improving the process. For example, when knowledge workers ignore automated recommendations, these instances become examples where either the analytics algorithm failed to understand the requirements, or the workers require additional training. For tasks where workers always (or almost always) agree with the recommended action, the task becomes a target for automation by using predictive analytics in combination with decision management.

Machine Learning

Supervised machine learning uses training examples – such as the actions and decisions of a knowledge worker – to derive automated methods of completing the same tasks. This is particularly useful for semi-skilled tasks such as the classification of unstructured content (e.g., contracts), and performing straightforward adjudication. Machine learning may completely replace some roles, but can also be used to automate some of the semi-skilled tasks now done by skilled knowledge workers, freeing them to focus on more complex or unstructured work.

Machine learning capabilities are now readily available since they no longer require a data scientist to configure and deploy: many analytics packages include pre-built machine learning building blocks that can be configured by an analyst with knowledge of business data, and called as services from ACM and BPM systems.

Robotic process automation (RPA), which automates desktop activities by emulating user interactions with software, also uses machine learning to monitor workers while they perform a task in order to derive an automated process. In scenarios using legacy systems without well-structured programming interfaces or service calls, RPA can be used in concert with ACM and BPM to automate a task or provide an accelerator for a knowledge worker, such as copying and pasting information from a legacy screen to a letter template.

Event Processing

Event processing listens for asynchronous events generated by other systems and devices, then triggers actions or updates data based on rules related to those events. Unplanned external events – ranging from a customer's actions to stock market fluctuations to the physical location of an order – can impact work to be performed by knowledge workers, or may be handled with an automated response.

Big Data

Although not, strictly speaking, considered intelligence or automation, big data is the driver behind all these intelligent technologies: without an accumulation of event data and other information, it would be impossible to derive rules, train learning algorithms, or make analytic predictions.

Not only are they all reliant on big data, there is a great deal of interdependence between the technologies: event processing uses rules to trigger actions; machine learning uses predictive analytics for supervised learning; rules may be derived from machine learning; and analytics are reliant on the data generated by events. Typically, they are not implemented singly, but as a suite of capabilities when automating business operations.

THE CHANGING WORK ENVIRONMENT

As discussed in the section on the impacts of automation, many workers may see their jobs disappear. The potential job losses predicted will cause societal changes beyond the scope of this paper, as automation begins to take over semi-skilled and skilled cognitive jobs, and the cost of automation undercuts business process outsourcing costs.

The jobs that remain will look quite different from what they do today, requiring a shift in the skills and mindset of both the knowledge workers and the organizations for which they work. Frey and Osborne assess that the skills that can't (yet) be automated fall into three categories:

- Perception and manipulation, particularly when there are many unidentified objects in an unstructured environment, such as navigating a robot within a home.
- Creative intelligence, primarily because we find it difficult to explicitly specify how creative works are conceptualized and valued.
- Social intelligence, particularly for tasks that combine social interaction with emotion and "common sense" such as negotiation and persuasion.

Considering the business environments within which ACM and BPM systems are typically deployed, knowledge workers need to improve creative and social intelligence skills, while learning to use intelligent systems to augment these human skills with automated data collection and processing. These new capabilities include:

- Goal-directed, rather than process-driven, work methods
- Customer interactions for exception handling and problem resolution
- Creative problem solving using methods and tools from multiple domains (i.e., "thinking outside the box")
- Improvement and innovation of business operations and processes
- Expertise with analytics, rules and machine learning tools
- People management and mentoring
- Training materials design
- Collaboration

In conjunction with these shifting roles and skills, organizations must change how work is measured and rewarded. Although research exists on incentives for social collaboration (Kemsley, 2014), most organizations still struggle to move past models that reward employees for individual transactional contributions. Since transactional work is what is being automated, these worker productivity metrics no longer apply. Instead, worker incentives must set expectations for collaboration and social participation, and provide rewards aligned with customer service and process improvement, not just transactional efficiency.

CONCLUSIONS

Machine intelligence and automation are fast encroaching on business activities that many still consider the domain of human intelligence, as new technologies are applied to non-routine cognitive tasks. The key technologies – rules, analytics, machine learning and event processing, underpinned by big data – are being integrated with ACM and BPM systems to replace workers in some tasks, and augment human capabilities in others.

As automation capabilities continue to expand, knowledge workers need to improve social intelligence skills that are difficult to automate in order to remain relevant, and learn to use the intelligent systems to support their work.

REFERENCES

(EU 2016) Council of the European Union. General Data Protection Regulation, Regulation (EU) 2016/679. http://data.consilium.europa.eu/doc/document/ST-5419-2016-INIT/en/pdf

(Frey and Osborne, 2013) Carl Benedikt Frey and Michael A. Osborne. The Future of Employment: How Susceptible Are Jobs To Computerisation? Oxford Martin Programme on Technology and Employment, September 2013.

(Kemsley 2014) Sandy Kemsley. Business Process Management and the Social Enterprise. Handbook on Business Process Management, Volume 1, Springer, 2015.

(Kemsley 2016) Sandy Kemsley. Beyond Checklists. Best Practices for Knowledge Workers: Innovation in Adaptive Case Management, Future Strategies Inc., 2016 https://bpm-books.com

Introduction and Overview

Layna Fischer, Future Strategies Inc.

Intelligent Adaptability describes how ACM is emerging in the era of machine intelligence and automation technologies, including Big Data, digitization, Internet of Things (IoT), artificial intelligence (AI), intelligent BPMS and BPM Everywhere.

WfMC Chair, Keith Swenson states; "A platform for digital transformation brings a number of different capabilities together: processes, agents, integration, analytics, decisions, and—perhaps most important—case management."

In this book, you will learn how support of adaptive, data-driven processes empowers knowledge workers to know in real-time what is happening at the edge points, and to take actions through the combination of rule-driven guidance and their own know-how. It is not a traditionally-automated system but *intelligent adaptability*, where technology doesn't replace human decision-making but extends the reach of the knowledge worker; making data actionable.

In award-winning case studies covering industries as a diverse as law enforcement, public safety, transportation, insurance, banking, state services and healthcare, you will find instructive examples for how to transform your own organization.

Leading industry analysts study the awards entries for emerging industry trends. Read the chapter, *The Seven Trends Impacting The Case Management Landscape* by Connie Moore, Digital Clarity Group.

This important book follows these ground-breaking best-sellers on ACM; *Best Practices for Knowledge Workers, Thriving on Adaptability, Empowering Knowledge Workers, Taming the Unpredictable, How Knowledge Workers Get Things Done,* and *Mastering the Unpredictable* and provides important papers by thought-leaders in this field, together with practical examples.

FOREWORD: MACHINE INTELLIGENCE AND AUTOMATION IN ACM AND BPM

Sandy Kemsley, Kemsley Design Ltd., Canada

Last year in "Beyond Checklists" Ms Kemsley wrote about the need for intelligent ACM (adaptive case management) that augments human-powered case work with machine intelligence to drive innovation and maintain operational efficiencies. Intelligent ACM – incorporating rules, analytics, machine learning, and event processing – provides a platform to significantly enhance knowledge worker productivity by automating activities and decisions that don't require their level of skill. Freed from routine work, workers can focus on adding value through complex decision-making, problem resolution, collaboration and innovation.

Moving on a year, this chapter will look at how machine intelligence and automation technologies are emerging in ACM and business process management (BPM), the new capabilities that this provides, and the impact on organizations and the way people work.

Part 1: Knowledge Work and Case Management

INTELLIGENT AUTOMATION DELIVERS INTELLIGENT ADAPTABILITY

Nathaniel Palmer, WfMC, USA

Adaptability is the key benefit enabled by Adaptive Case Management (ACM). As a framework enabler for driving adaptability, however, critical ACM solutions require the ability to receive signal data and apply this against rules and policies (e.g., decision logic) to drive optimal outcomes. The ability to adapt differentiates ACM from the process automation that came before it. For this reason, we have most often contrasted "automation" as being both limited and antiquated within the context of modern knowledge work and the inherent benefits of ACM. Yet might the benefits of ACM, and specifically the emergence of *Intelligent Adaptability,* extend also to a transformation of process automation?

In this chapter, we will explore how *Intelligent Automation* can be realized to deliver on the promise of Intelligent Adaptability, expanding the capabilities of ACM beyond what had previously been thought to be the limitations of automation.

PUBLIC SAFETY AND DYNAMIC BUSINESS PROCESS CONTROL

David RR Webber, Huawei Public Safety, China

Public Safety covers the complete spectrum of challenges across society and the ultimate goals are always the same; provide citizens with a trusted environment where they can prosper without fear of threats to property, personal wellbeing and life disruptions. The risks are ever-changing and can run the gamut from cyber security, financial security and physical security to emergency management.

This chapter describes why and how knowledge worker support for public safety applications is crucial. Channeling information feeds from both background analytic systems and real-time event management. Synthesizing these to provide alerts, insights and actionable intelligence, followed by invoking the most appropriate response and associated business process(es) to remediate the situation. This can include geospatial inputs on locations of resources and assets. Teams need to be able to respond and coordinate with accurate situational awareness providing an appropriate level of services from limited resource pools.

SMART ADAPTIVE BPM ENGINE

Pedro Robledo, BPMteca, Spain

Adaptive Case Management envisions processes that are not designed in advance, but are rather processes that respond moment-by-moment. In an agile environment, where all structured processes have predesigned their business behaviors in advance, they will need to be adapted depending on real-time circumstances. Disruption from Artificial Intelligence applied to BPM will provide a smart adaptive BPM engine that will cause fundamental changes for the structured processes because these could change their predesigned behavior as the BPM engine starts learning, so this new capability of BPM will provide the right tasks at the right moment for a customer. The fundamental idea is the automatic adaptation of the process models are defined by the automatic learning of the Workflow Engine that orchestrates the processes.

INTELLIGENT DIGITAL TRANSFORMATION WITH VSAAS

Dr. Setrag Khoshafian, Pegasystems Inc., USA and
Sushil Kumar, Pegasystems Inc., USA

The concept of Digital Value Streams within enterprises has evolved from the realization that each customer interaction, independent of the source or channel, needs to work harmoniously together to meet the customer need. Rather than having each channel work as an independent silo of customer interaction and information, the concept of a Digital Value Stream chains all of these interactions as links in achieving the overall customer objective. The notion of VSaaS (Value Stream as a Service), expands on this digital value stream concept within enterprises (intra) to go across business enterprises (inter), who can now plug in their business unit participants into the value stream, to contribute and achieve robust shared business objectives.

BUSINESS RULES DESIGN AS ENABLER FOR INTELLIGENT PROCESS SOLUTIONS

Kay Winkler, Negocios y Soluciones Informáticas S.A., Panama

Adaptive Case Management and Digital Transformation are trending terms used by most vendors in the field of BPM. The showcased platforms are acclaimed for their overarching premise—and capabilities—to more effectively and faster than ever before bridge the gap between customers and businesses. The ensuing propaganda also lends itself to create false impressions that there may be premade technological solutions available to the end users that would fit the criteria of a true adaptive case management (ACM) system. That, of course, is somewhat oxymoronic to the whole concept of knowledge worker enabling and supporting solutions itself. Smart processes that allow for adaptations are usually the result of iterative process enhancements within mature and scalable Business Process Management Suites (iBPMS) that earn their prefix "i", for *intelligent*, through strategic features, enabling the definition, storage, enforcement and discovery of business rules.

This chapter is dedicated to exactly these features and to the practical guidelines of how to leverage business rules throughout real-life BPM implementations.

TRANSFORMING COMPLIANCE REGULATIONS INTO USER EXPERIENCE

Christoph Czepa and Uwe Zdun, University of Vienna, Austria;
Christoph Ruhsam, ISIS Papyrus Europe, Austria

Compliance regulations are still often hard-coded in prescriptive, rigid business processes and perceived as a burden and obstacle for knowledge work, or even worse, they are simply evaluated *post ex* (i.e. through audits) without providing any prior IT tool support during case enactment. In this chapter, we discuss how compliance regulations, specified by a domain-specific business vocabulary and semantics (business ontology) can be leveraged to enable compliance by *supporting* the knowledge workers rather than interfering with their work. Support can be provided in form of a natural language compliance rule editor using the terms from the domain specific business vocabulary (ontology-based compliance rules). This way, reactive as well as proactive guidance can be offered that takes both the compliance rules and the knowledge workers' past decisions into account to enhance the users' working experience. This opens the stage for new ACM-based business applications that truly serve the needs of business users focusing on delivering value to their customers.

Part 2: Award Winning Case Studies

SEVEN TRENDS IMPACTING THE CASE MANAGEMENT LANDSCAPE

Connie Moore, Digital Clarity Group, USA

This chapter describes seven trends impacting the case management landscape in 2017 and 2018.

The Workflow Management Coalition (WfMC), a standards organization for workflow and business process technologies, announced the 2017 winners of its *Excellence Awards in Adaptive Case Management*[1].

The winners demonstrate the best of the best in workflow, business process management (BPM), digital process automation and case management. Case management projects are not being done in a vacuum or because some manager decides to bring in new technology to replace older solutions. Instead, digital disruption, which is pervasive across all industries, is driving companies to strategically transform their end-to-end processes.

The organizational and technological fallout from digital disruption touches every single industry, organization, and business process.

FEIN SUCH KAHN AND SHEPARD, P.C., USA

Nominated by Fujitsu America, USA

Fein, Such, Kahn, & Shepard, P.C. is a general practice legal firm providing comprehensive service to clients in New Jersey for over 25 years. A good legal firm that performs consistently with the trust of their clients is virtually guaranteed repeat business, but Fein Such wanted more. In 2013, Fein Such embarked on a daring initiative to reform the way they run their business. One of the firm's principals with high-tech experience in Silicon Valley convinced the Fein Such Executive team that the same legal talent could do much more, if the tedious manual information activities were digitized and automated.

GRINNELL MUTUAL, USA

Nominated by Hyland, creator of OnBase, USA

Grinnell Mutual, in business since 1909, is the 114th-largest property casualty insurance company in the United States and the largest primary reinsurer of farm mutual companies in North America. The company provides reinsurance for farm mutual insurance companies as well as property and casualty insurance. Its products are available in 15 states.

Grinnell Mutual, leveraging its longtime ECM vendor's case management capabilities, created a mission-critical application for managing the vital areas of policy underwriting and claims for all its clients. The case management application was built on an underlying content repository, leveraging native integration and workflow functionality. Rather than relying on traditional development or custom coding in IT, Grinnell Mutual's system administrator created the application via point-and-click configuration of the platform.

---

[1] http://adaptivecasemanagement.org

LEADING EUROPEAN BANK BANKING CORRESPONDENCE MANAGEMENT SYSTEM

Nominated by ISIS Papyrus Europe AG, Austria

This case study describes the implementation of an Adaptive Case Management system—Banking Correspondence Management System (BCMS)—in a leading European Bank (in the following named 'the Bank').

The Bank is one of the largest players in the world with roots anchored in Europe's economic history. With presence in more than 70 countries and over 180,000 employees, the Bank is a leader in the Eurozone and a prominent international banking institution. For the Bank, the existing solution to create mass business communication as online requested business documents had become slightly outdated and called for a complete remake to use more efficiently the human resources of the output management department dealing with document design, development as well as production.

MOLINA HEALTHCARE INC., USA

Nominated by Datum Solutions, United States

Molina Healthcare, Inc. (Molina), offers health plans, clinical care and health information management to families and individuals covered by Medicaid, Medicare and other government-funded programs. With data held in complex medical charts, Molina found it challenging to meet deadlines for evaluations and audits by the Centers for Medicare and Medicaid Services (CMS), risking millions of dollars in potential lost revenue and audit penalties. By centralizing medical records in a single repository with integrated case management, the organization can retrieve chart data 50% faster—helping it meet regulatory requirements, avoid penalties and potentially qualify for millions in bonus payments.

UNICREDIT LEASING CROATIA

Nominated by EMC, USA

UniCredit Leasing Croatia is part of UniCredit Group, which offers corporate and investment banking, small and midsize enterprise banking, retail banking, and other financial services. It is among Europe's leading commercial banks, with 155,000 employees serving 40 million customers in 20 European countries.

To address market-based and operational challenges, UniCredit Leasing Croatia needed improve efficiency, protect shrinking margins, and deliver high-touch service to more demanding customers. But inefficient and disjointed document-related processes made these goals difficult to reach. In response, UniCredit sought and successfully deployed a technology solution.

WPS HEALTH SOLUTIONS

Nominated by Naviant, Inc. & Hyland, USA

WPS Health Solutions is a Medicare Administrative Contractor (MAC). As a MAC, one of the services WPS provides is to credential and enroll more than 100,000 physicians and medical facilities that would like to offer services to Medicare patients. The credentialing process for provider enrollment is a labor-intensive process of research and validation of the 300+ pieces of information that are submitted in a standard application an effort to ensure providers follow industry standards, and to detect and minimize potential fraud and waste in the Medicare system. In addition to case management functionality and the components, WPS leverages the full range of native built-in capabilities within its solution, including data and document management, electronic forms, workflow automation and process logic, and security controls.

Win an Award for *your* Case Management project

The WfMC Awards for Case Management are the ideal way to be recognized by the industry worldwide, to publicly acknowledge and recognize the efforts of your team and to inject passion into your case management projects.

Sponsored by WfMC and supported by BPM.com and Future Strategies Inc., these prestigious awards recognize user organizations worldwide that have demonstrably excelled in implementing innovative solutions.

The WfMC Global Awards for Case Management recognizes and focuses upon successful use cases within Adaptive Case Management. Case Management represents an adaptive approach to supporting knowledge workers in today's leading-edge organizations. ACM provides secure, social collaboration to create and adapt goal-oriented activities that enable informed decision-making using federated business data and content.

Get recognized for your vision and your team's superb efforts by entering the Global Excellence Awards

We work with leading industry analysts such as Forrester, Gartner and Digital Clarity Group who use these award-winning case studies to analyze ACM technology users and suppliers, illustrate trends, industry growth, ROI and more.

Read more about the Awards here: adaptivecasemanagement.org

Section 1
Intelligent Automation

Intelligent Automation Delivers Intelligent Adaptability

Nathaniel Palmer, WfMC, USA

INTRODUCTION

Adaptability is the key benefit enabled by Adaptive Case Management (ACM). As a framework enabler for driving adaptability, however, critical ACM solutions require the ability to receive signal data and apply this against rules and policies (e.g., decision logic) to drive optimal outcomes. The ability to adapt differentiates ACM from the process automation that came before it. For this reason, we have most often contrasted "automation" as being both limited and antiquated within the context of modern knowledge work and the inherent benefits of ACM. Yet might the benefits of ACM, and specifically the emergence of *Intelligent Adaptability*, extend also to a transformation of process automation?

In this chapter, we will explore how *Intelligent Automation* can be realized to deliver on the promise of Intelligent Adaptability, expanding the capabilities of ACM beyond what had previously been thought to be the limitations of automation.

WHAT'S WRONG WITH AUTOMATION?

How did automation get its bad rap to begin with? Today's process automation looks a lot the package-handling picture below, with a complex set of conveyor belts designed for optimal efficiency and consistency. Industrial engineers designed the ideal routes to move packages in the most efficient way possible, and indeed these pathways are fixed. They do not change or adapt their paths based on what is in the package.

Figure 1: Today's process automation looks a lot like conveyors, with fixed pathways and process flows designed by architects and engineers, not adapted according to the context of work and business events

Most process automation systems and indeed many BPM initiatives were designed and built in the same manner. However, that rigid model of automation of following fixed pathways is inconsistent with the way we work. We *do* care about what's in the package. We cannot fully script out in advance the sequence of steps and end-to-end processes without knowing the exact context of any given task we will be performing. For this reason, process automation to date has been limited to repetitive and relatively simplistic process areas. Yet when we combine case management and data-driven intelligence with process automation, we can expand the range of what can be automated or otherwise managed. This combination of capabilities enables "intelligent automation."

Figure 2: Intelligent automation leverages the efficiency of automated actors with data-driven intelligence that leverage rules and analytics to enable goal-seeking optimization and decision making.

What does intelligent automation look like? Using the same metaphor as before, see above one of Amazon's fulfillment centers where its Kiva robots have replaced the fixed conveyor belts. Just as we do in our own work, the robots do care and, in fact, do know what is in the package. Using this awareness of context (what's in the package and where it's going) the robots determine the best pathways and placement of products to enable the fastest possible fulfillment process. The robots leverage process, rules and data to define pathways which adapt to the context of work at that moment, just as we need to adapt to successfully complete our human work.

It is the combination of case management and data-driven intelligence that delivers the ability to manage work while dynamically adapting the steps of a process according to an awareness and understanding of the content, data and business events that unfold. This is the basis of intelligent automation, enabling data-driven processes to adapt dynamically to the context of the work, delivering the efficiency of automation while leveraging rules and policies to steer the pathway toward the optimal outcome. This also highlights the focus on goal achievement as a key focus of case management. The case management system collects data and content, then correlates these to rules which prescribe the steps needed to the achieve goals. When a case is launched, *what* we know, and often *all* we know, are the goals of the case; what defines successful completion for closure of the case. The process of the case is defined by the underlying policy and rules combined with the information that we gather along the way.

ROBOTS ENTER THE WORKFORCE

Robotic Process Automation (RPA) is one of the fastest-growing sectors of business technology, yet one which is often misunderstood; "But it's just screen-scraping[1] on steroids..." No, it is far more powerful than that. Don't waste any time listening to those nattering nabobs of negativism who would describe it that way. RPA is indeed entirely new and, as part of a broader strategy for workflow technology, can enable levels of efficiency and digitalization previously out of reach.

This advance is every bit as powerful, with an equivalent potential for disruption, as adding physical robots into the enterprise workforce. Unlike solutions whose function is to coordinate and sequence tasks for humans to perform, RPA specifically acts on behalf of humans to perform work; e.g., RPA automates human tasks (manual work) rather than only machine tasks, as previously with traditional software automation. This fact underscores both the growing interest in RPA and the confusion with

---

[1] https://en.wikipedia.org/wiki/Data_scraping#Screen_scraping

screen-scraping. Existing user interfaces can remain intact, and the software robots can perform the same functions just as a human user would do, in passing security credentials as well as entering and/or accessing data from the application into which it is logged.

Automating Knowledge Work

Intelligent Automation bridges the "islands of automation" where humans are the integration points among systems that otherwise cannot communicate. This is work that cannot be automated any other way. By definition, the task requires logging in and out of different systems to complete the process (or even a single task) and these are often third-party systems or otherwise environments which cannot be integrated through a programmatic interface. Instead, people must do the integration, with swivel chairs and sticky notes, and as a result the design of the related rules and workflows are based on how the applications were built, rather than the actual objectives of the end-to-end process which span them.

Introducing a New "Stack" for Supporting the Knowledge Worker

RPA, by itself, most often has no interface. It acts on behalf of the knowledge worker, rather than serving as the core system with which they interact. This underscores the fact that "intelligent automation" is not necessarily a category of software but rather a design pattern for leveraging best of breed components for delivering a powerful set of capabilities. At the foundation of any solution for intelligent automation or otherwise, case management in general is a data layer. This includes an Operational Data Store (ODS) for driving the actions and operations with which the knowledge work is engaged. In addition, there are necessarily one or more Systems of Record (SoR) which stores the data comprising each case record and its supporting context.

Above the data services record are three distinct, but synergistic, components which provide the "brains" of intelligent automation. These components are RPA combined with a BPM System (BPMS) and a Decision Automation package for defining and managing decision logic. On the latter, Decision Automation (or Decision Management) should be understood as more than Business Rules Engine (BRE). The engine is merely the execution, but Decision Management is a relatively new category of software which facilitates the definition and on-going management of rules and policies as distinct artifacts and business assets.

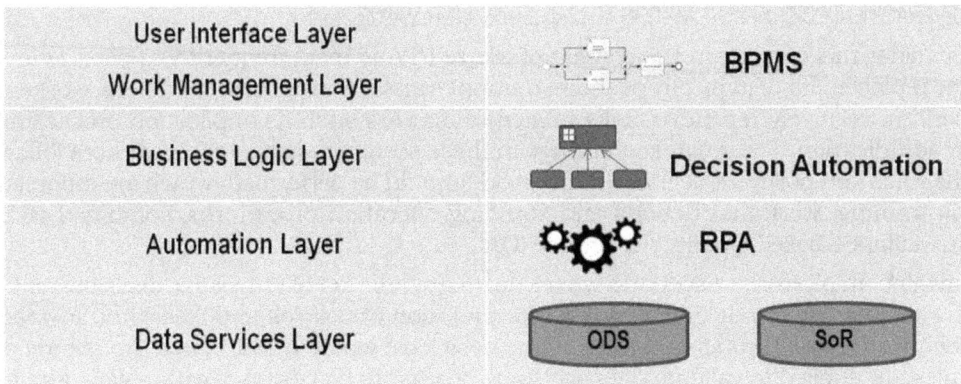

Figure 3: Intelligent Automation Starts with a COTS Stack

WHERE TO BEGIN WITH INTELLIGENT AUTOMATION

This is why the value proposition of RPA can be so compelling. It is the ability to integrate *processes*, rather than systems and applications, and the ability to deliver work closer to holistic or comprehensive automation rather requiring (far more expensive) humans to perform this work manually. What is the best starting point for leveraging RPA? Look first at repetitive human tasks, where users are bogged down performing tedious work, repetitive steps, or work without requiring any meaningful analysis. Also look for where users are shifting back and forth among different application interfaces as part of the task or process step. These scenarios are where the low-hanging fruit will be found and offer the logical starting point for RPA.

Placing Your Bets

Yet your plans shouldn't begin with only the easy targets (the low-hanging fruit.) Rather, your strategy should lay the groundwork for horizontal scale, tying together discrete moments of automation within a more comprehensive, end-to-end process. To support this, have a clear model for the separation of concern between BPM and RPA. Understand that BPM was never designed to fully *replace* the work done by human beings, but rather to *facilitate* that work by assigning tasks, sequencing steps, enforcing rules, and other means of work management. In contrast, RPA in fact is purpose-built specifically to *replace* work otherwise less efficient and effective when performed by humans.

BPM and RPA work in concert to enable far more efficient and effective coordination of both knowledge work and automated tasks. Yet while the synergy of this combination offers great potential, realizing this value does not happen by default. There is not yet an established standard or methodology which prescribes the ideal interplay between BPM and RPA, and indeed some of the greatest pitfalls lie in the poorly-defined separation of concern between the two.

For example, one of the common mistakes is to create rules within the RPA definition (the configuration of software robots) which are complex, and thus miss the opportunity for separately managing decision logic (business policies and rules) from the procedural logic necessary to the automated task. No RPA platform is designed for decision management, yet a well-architected approach can and should leverage best-of-breed capabilities. As part of a broader automation or digital transformation strategy, we use decision management to ensure both consistency business rules, as well as to enable workers to make better informed, data-driven decisions.

LEVERAGING DECISION AUTOMATION TO DRIVE GREATER VALUE

Consider this concept in the context of where RPA is most frequently applied today; the replacement of (typically offshore) manual transaction processing. There, workers perform relatively repetitive tasks related to matters such as application processing or adjudication. The greatest challenge in these scenarios is to ensure workers follow the rules and policy guidelines for how work should be performed, which are enforced via training, work instructions and standing operation procedures, combined with surveillance-based Quality Assurance (QA).

Imagine an alternative scenario where users are relieved of subjective decision-making (i.e., having to rely on their own interpretation of policies and rules) and instead their work flows through a library of business logic where hundreds or thousands of rules are applied to validate data accuracy, to ensure consistency with policy, and to present a data-driven recommendation for the best next action. This provides an objective measure (actual reportable data and analytics) to demonstrate that work is performed according to established policy. It also lowers the training burden, by removing the need to understand exactly what to do at each point, while ensuring greater accuracy and consistency because each and every transaction, process step, and data element are checked automatically (rather than applying Quality Assurance to only a small sample).

Tackling the End-to-End Process

Expand the aperture on this scenario, and imagine BPM doing what it does best by coordinating the end-to-end process, managing the sequencing of steps and state of process as it advances the span of control from one step to the next. Now with the much finer-grained definition of how work must be performed, consider that many of the steps which had previously required human intervention can now be performed by software robots, coordinated by the master process, with the instructions provided not by an automation script, but a complete set of rules and policies able to scale to the complexity of your business. Over time the scope of the scope of this automation can grow to encompass an increasing number of erstwhile human tasks, as performance data are captured and more is understood about how the work should be performed.

This is the promise of intelligent automaton for supporting knowledge workers, and ultimately enabling intelligent adaptability, by leveraging RPA, AI, Machine Learning, Decision Management and BPM to drive greater quality and efficiency.

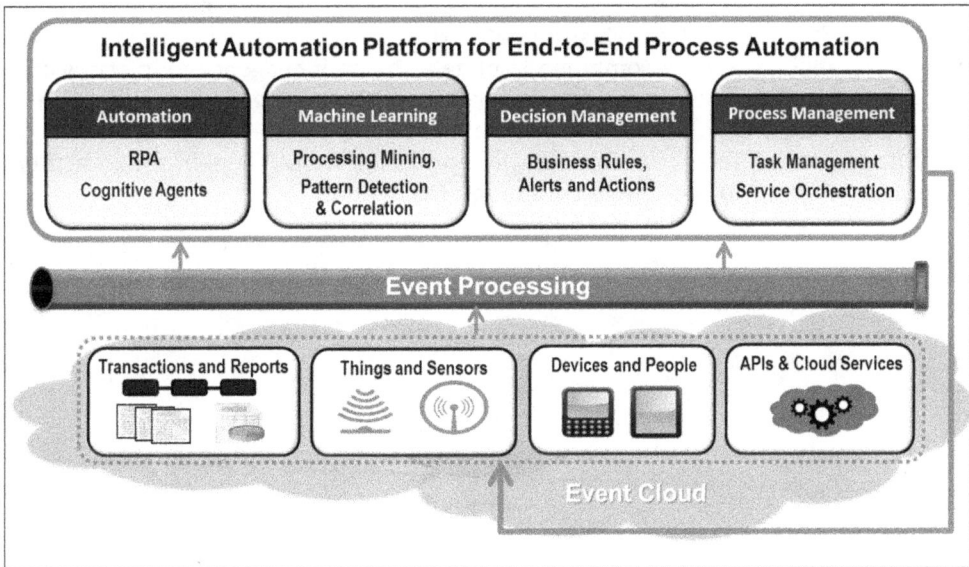

Figure 4: Intelligent Automation as an Integrated Digital Platform

This chapter has, so far, avoided reference to *digital transformation* yet it should be evident that these capabilities for intelligent automation and intelligent adaptability extend beyond the traditionally-siloed focus of case management and have the potential to transform every aspect of the enterprise. There is an immensely powerful set of "digital benefits" to be realized through leveraging automation in a way which enables not only improved work management practices, but also increased accuracy, efficiency and quality of work performed. Using standard rules with less reliance on subjective judgement, improves data quality with more accurate analytics while delivering the ability to understand the impact on rule and policy changes *before* they are implemented.

That Dickensian[2] sentence captures each goal of digital transformation and frames how the "whole" of a digital platform as illustrated in Figure 4. The goals of *going digital* are to bring the efficiencies of the digital medium to matters which do not scale or readily adapt in their physical form. Imagine, for instance, transforming the thousands of policy pages and the multiple days of training required to support your current knowledge work with a manageable and measureable set of decision models owned and controlled by business stakeholders, and which are not otherwise dangerously locked inside application code. Sound digital to you?

How about gaining rich new sources of analytics and audit data based on actual decisions made and actions taken, rather than surveillance-based Quality Assurance? Or worse, first learning about negative outcomes from disgruntled customers and business partners.

The Promise of Intelligent Adaptability

A key benefit of the Intelligent Adaptability approach to supporting knowledge work and knowledge workers is that it allows users the ability to leverage a very robust set of process- and decision-automation while using a user-centric interface (through the BPMS tier). One of top priorities for supporting adaptability for workers means they stay within the environment that suits them best and in which they feel the most productive. The elements of automation should be opaque and are most subtly represented in the interface. This ultimately defines the heart of intelligent adaptability as the ability to offer a combination of data-driven intelligence to inform workers on context and facilitate sound decision-making. By ensuring "guard rails" to prevent them from violating policies or laws, you elicit efficiency automation thus also reducing the burden of "busy work" and system-jumping without constraining their environment or ability to apply their own unique know-how.

---

[2] Relating to or similar to something described in the books of the 19th-century English writer Charles Dickens, especially living or working conditions that are below an acceptable standard.

Public Safety and Dynamic Business Process Control

David RR Webber, Huawei Public Safety, China

UNDERSTANDING THE PUBLIC SAFETY DOMAIN

Public Safety covers the complete spectrum of challenges across society and the ultimate goals are always the same; provide citizens with a trusted environment where they can prosper without fear of threats to property, personal wellbeing and life disruptions. The risks are ever-changing and can run the gamut from cyber security, financial security and physical security to emergency management.

Operationally, Public Safety is viewed as four phases; Prevention, Detection, Response and Recovery. Across these phases there are literally hundreds of business processes and this chart shows a selection of the general categories.

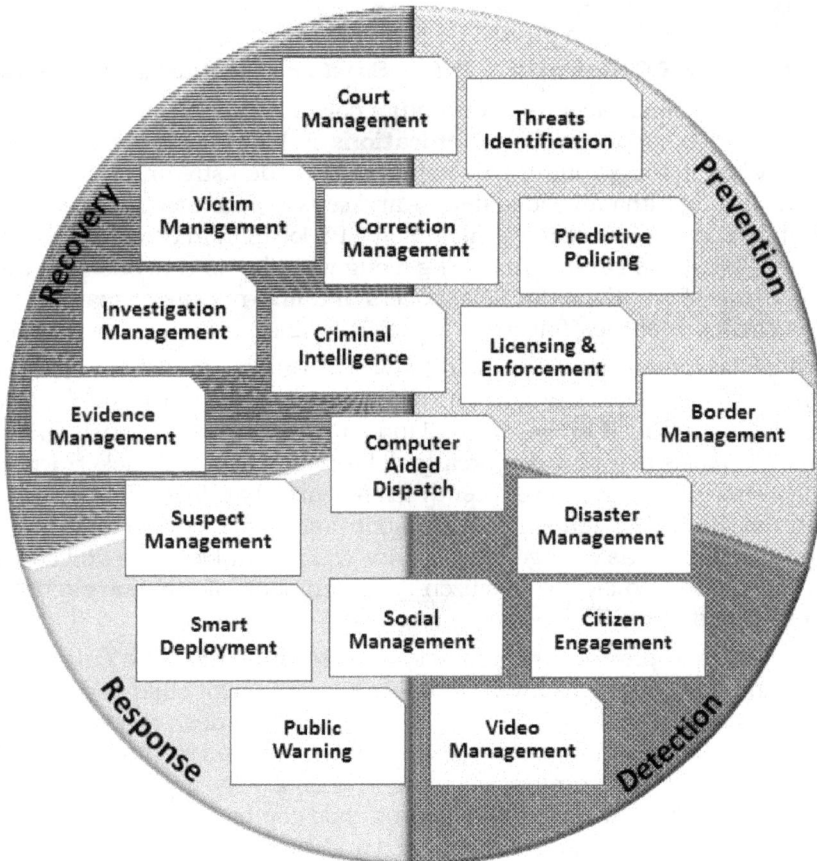

Figure 1 Public Safety 4 Phases with associated Business Process Areas

To meet these challenges, modern public safety organizations are using completely digital infrastructures including converged collaborative operational command and control centers. This collaborative environment combines digital technologies with infrastructure for Communications, Cloud, Command and Control, Intelligence, Surveillance and Reconnaissance (C4ISR) to provide as complete a picture as possible for organizing public safety.

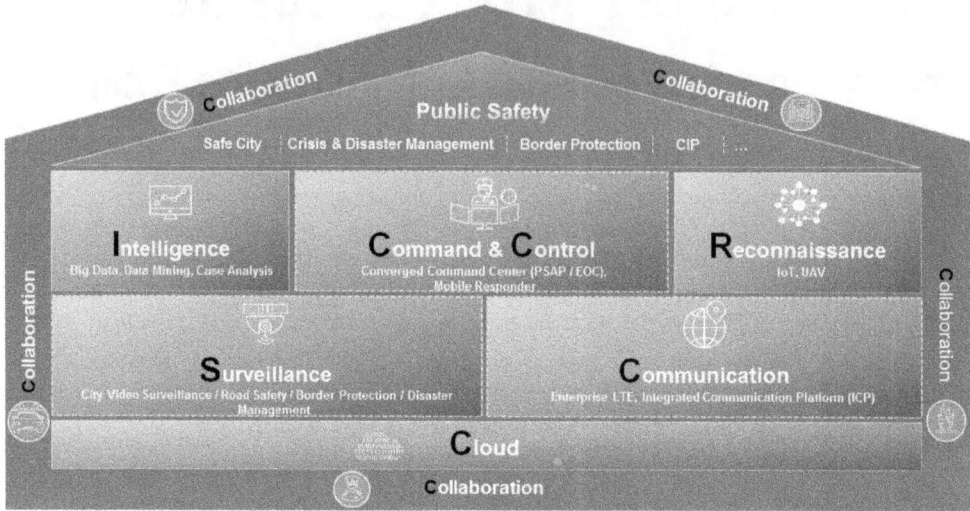

Figure 2 C4ISR Collaborative Public Safety conceptual components

The diagram above illustrates this conceptual collaboration environment and next we examine each component. **Communications** is high-speed digital broadband trunking capable of supporting the demands of live video streams with secure dynamic routing along with embedded device- and sensor-generated traffic flows. Then secure digital voice communications including GPS location information plus handheld device applications running mapping along with day-to-day business applications. This is transformational for field officers and first-responder teams ensuring critical information is at their fingertips and collaboration is happening in real time.

The **Cloud** infrastructure provides the distributed platform for information sharing and computer resource accessing across a regional area. So, for example, video information can be uploaded to the Video Cloud for further analysis, such as tracking movement of vehicles across a city area to determine where a vehicle travelled. An example is a DUI[1] driver may have recently left a nearby bar. In addition to video, the Cloud can distribute GIS mapping information and share government-to-government applications such as emergency response equipment locations and case management. The Cloud also facilitates citizen-to-government information such as vehicle registration and driver license databases.

Leveraging the Cloud provides the ability to drive **Intelligence**. Particularly the use of Big Data and Deep Mining software tools. An example is for child abduction cases where patterns can be deduced. Nearby hotel registration desk records may reveal persons leaving close to the time of the abduction, followed by purchase of travel tickets for adult and child. Through scanning of video footage in the travel station for facial, size and clothing matches to the missing child combined with witness descriptions of the adult, suspects can be determined and located.

Surveillance is the main real-time digital toolset providing the eyes and ears into particular incidents and events. Ranging from body-worn cameras to fixed and mo-

---

[1] Driving Under Influence (of alcohol).

bile video cameras including UAV (unmanned aerial vehicle) mounted cameras. Combined with scene analysis software, facial recognition and vehicle automated number plate recognition (ANPR) extraction. These capabilities allow for automated analysis beyond what the unaided human is able to do. For example, thousands of hours of video footage can be scanned for specific matches to vehicle make, model and color around a crime scene and event time threshold.

Completing the picture is **Reconnaissance** to which sensors and devices contribute. For example, a perimeter fence with breach detection, a pipeline with contact point detection sensors or manhole covers with access sensors. These are Internet of Things (IoT) devices that provide point or area information of events and triggers. Included in this is Critical Event Processing (CEP) rules software that is configured to analyze and generate alerts and alarms while ignoring false alarm situations. It allows broad monitoring of areas while saving physical security staff resources.

Next, we consider how this technology mix interacts with the actual business processes entailed in Public Safety.

OPERATIONAL PROCESSES AND ACTIONABLE INTELLIGENCE

Part of the command and control is the computer-aided dispatch center (CAD) functionality. The diagram here shows how a network of dispatch centers provides the regional, city and then locality dispatching and control.

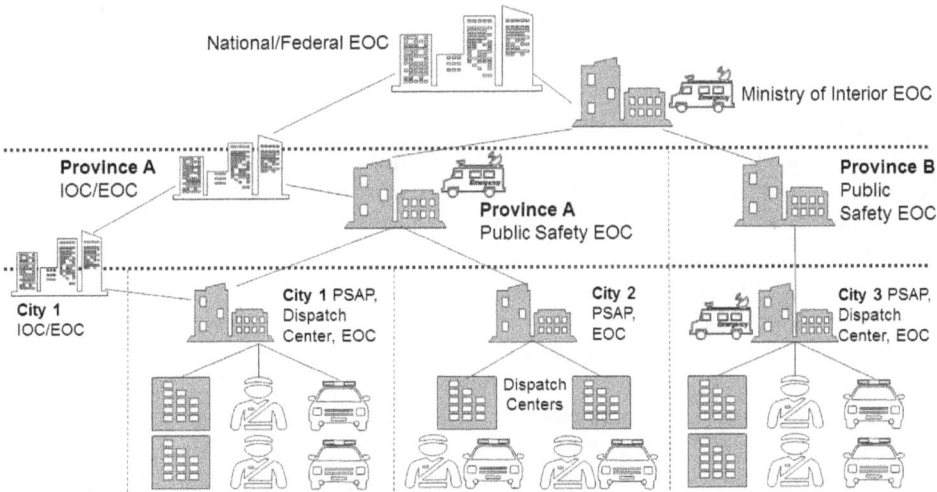

Figure 3 Network of Dispatch Centers

Typically citizens can call their single national centralized emergency number or call a local area emergency in addition. Alternatively, through a mobile device application this offers on-screen selections that automatically pick the best process option based on the seriousness and the location of the user.

Intelligence is required throughout this process. Firstly at the centralized facility filtering occurs for prank calls, repeat calls and erroneous calls. Then dispatch is determined on the type of service needed, location and severity. Combined with this is situational awareness; is the event known and what are live video feeds showing the command center directly? The citizens themselves may be providing live picture streaming and photographs from the scene, or social media feeds, or live media broadcasts which are similarly contributing. Public safety resources may already be at the scene or local citizen volunteers who are trained in early response.

What happens next is a combination and synthesis of all this information. Public Safety is driven by operational procedures. These business processes are tailored and honed from years of experience and how their operational needs respond and collaborate in different scenarios. All services have their own; fire, ambulance, police, emergency and community responders. In a digitally-converged collaborative world these no longer work independently, they must support each other and, more critically, share information directly so there is a common understanding of the **actionable intelligence**.

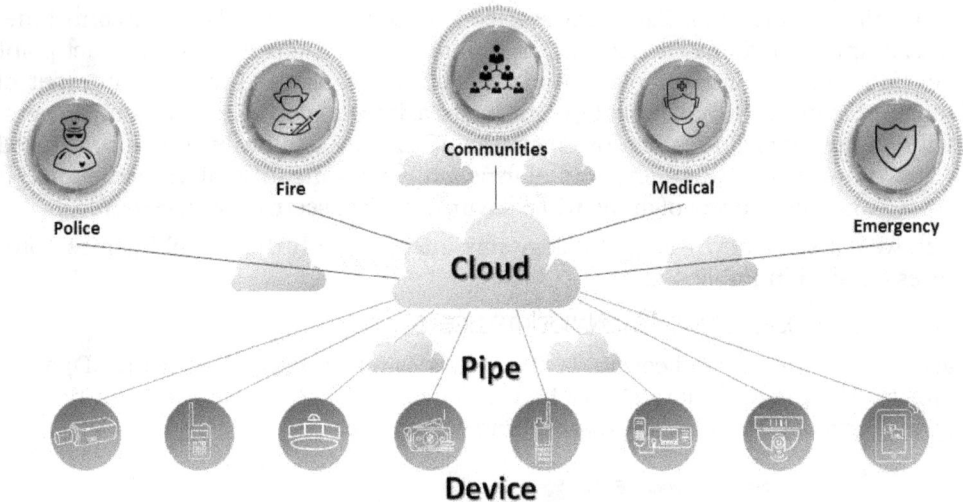

Figure 4 Services collaboration network

The Cloud technology provides the central and secure means to collect and share intelligence. **The Pipe** is the communications channel, which can be public networks, security networks or wired infrastructure connections. **The Device** is the host of possible devices and sensors that connect and capture information, video and raw analytic data.

The actionable intelligence can then be drawn from a range of sources including case management history, personal profiles (medical, judicial, social), location knowledge including geospatial, historical experience and live video images. In addition, machine-generated analytics insights from **Big Data** associated with information from the makeup of the scenario can provide crucial knowledge. For example, in a typical home dispute call, responders may know that the suspect involved recently purchased a firearm and video analysis of vehicle tracking shows the weapon being placed in a vehicle that is now at the scene. Video scene analysis of objects, vehicles and the person's movements and tracking away from the immediate scene can reveal critical details, such as the person at the scene was met by a known suspect earlier in the day.

The timeframes for processing all this intelligence is usually under five minutes which is what the typical response times are for emergency responders reaching a live scene or incident.

Similarly, an emergency response call to a fire outbreak requires knowledge of the location; the firefighting resources on hand, potentially hazardous materials stored nearby, the best access route to reach the location, the nearest responders with the equipment needed (e.g. ladder trucks) and the size and scale occurring. Collaborating police resources need to know where to stop traffic to facilitate access and also prevent risk to people nearby while medical services need to know if persons have been injured or require attention. Notice that traffic control is a whole separate process. For example, a police officer may have authority to stop traffic on a local side street, but what if smoke from a fire is blowing across a major highway? This requires a separate response team and formal process and authorization to close traffic on the highway, create a detour to divert traffic around the incident and do impact assessment.

Emergency responder business processes are designed to cope with these real-time demands and to guide the responders themselves to take appropriate actions locally. Next we consider how automation can provide dynamic process control.

DYNAMIC BUSINESS PROCESS CONTROL

Predicting the Unpredictable

The Public Safety challenge is about handling the unpredictable to produce the best outcomes given the available resources. Business processes exist for handling given typical scenarios. For example, detaining illegal immigrants at border control points and properly processing those persons to meet the provided legal and humanitarian rules, both nationally and internationally. In disaster response situations ,things can be much less clear in situations such as in a flood disaster. There the first priority is to notify responders themselves that an event is in progress, in addition to setting off broadcast warning systems that alert communities to threats and provide evacuation notifications. These responders and communities themselves need to have established ways to acknowledge that alarm messages are received and that alarm systems triggered properly. That is one example of a business process.

The European Union has funded work on this through its Seventh Framework Programme for advanced technology. The stated aim is to develop a profile-based Emergency Interoperability Framework for effective management of emergencies, crises and disasters. They have determined 14 areas where such process action profiles are needed.

Table 1: Emergency Process Action Profiles

Situation Reporting	Alert	Sensor Measurement	Enterprise User Authentication and Authorization (EUAA)
Mission Plan	Hospital Availability Communication	Sensor Management	Audit Trail and Node Authentication (ATNA)
Scheduling	Tracking of Citizens	Situation Analysis	
Resource Management	Emergency Situation Map	Permission	

Within each of these profiles, users naturally can include their own business processes to achieve the information exchanges to provide the necessary shared intelligence.

Command and Control Center

Within a Command and Control center, the central display provides the unified situation map view of the active event. In scrolling windows are situation updates and live camera views from the scene providing insights and reports.

We can see that in an active flooding scenario Response phase there are a range of aspects including warnings, evacuations, hospitals, and missing persons. While for the Recovery and Prevention phases there are Contingency and Practice Coordination.

The Command Center needs to be able to trigger phase-appropriate processes and also to see the current status for those teams that are involved. Typically they will assign separate situation managers to work on these with their own local display and communication resources within the center that then feed into the main control display. An example would be missing person coordination, and for each person there is an active process determining the current situation and working toward outcomes along with the master list of missing people that is then a feed into the command center display. Contrasting that is the hospital availability where formal automated information exchange feeds are happening in real time between each of the hospitals involved that detail their current situation and facilitates that they can provide.

Providing Dynamic Process Control

Previously within the business process domain we implemented adaptive process control. Similarly, dynamic process control for public safety needs to be able to stop, pause or divert a current process, or add new processing. An example would responding to a disturbance at a shopping mall. Responders may be helping customers and staff vacate the scene, but then there is a potential explosive device located. Suddenly the opposite needs to happen. People should be sheltering in place and avoiding moving through the area where the device is located. An additional team needs to be deployed and a new process for neutralizing potential explosive devices coordinated.

Such dynamic process control provides significant challenges to software design and implementation. Within a dynamic process, each step needs to include the ability to check external control. This is akin to the interrupt-driven processing metaphor used in device control.

The formal Business Process Modelling (BPM) approach can be extended to represent these dynamic relationships. The dynamic processes can be linked to create a collection of process models that can then be invoked either separately, together or mutually exclusive. Similarly, the traditional gateway decision steps may reference a linked process model with related named process flow blocks. This avoids processes restarting from the beginning if those named steps have already been accomplished by another process; essentially flow-pooling across dynamic processes with named blocks sharing context and content. Similarly, once a new process has completed, control may be returned to the original process to complete and check its named blocks to ensure everything has been done.

In our shopping mall example, a close process step may include screening the mall and ensuring that there is sign off on all non-essential staff and customers having vacated the premises.

The best visualization medium is clearly the highly graphical "video wall" large screen environments available in the command center where physical team positions can be visualized overlaid on to maps with live video streams from the scene. Meanwhile local teams can have their own user interfaces that can alert team members to specific process tasks, such as the cleanup needed from a hazardous material spill on a highway and that process itself will be dynamic, based on the type of hazards present.

CONCLUSIONS

Business process control continues to evolve and respond to new and challenging environments. Some of the most challenging are provided by Public Safety applications. A large part of public safety involves routine procedures that can be handled easily. These can be well scripted using the profiles techniques exampled by the European Union funded work for emergency response profiles. A key aspect to notice is the need for information exchange interoperability. This is often overlooked, but is a critical need in cross-service operations and well-understood within the public safety domain. Ensuring that systems and devices work together and can share information seamlessly is critical for operational success.

Broadband communications services combined with Cloud computing environments with information sharing API (Application Programming Interface) support have transformed the ability to collaborate consistently. Having a dynamic means to scale and provide computer system resources that can be accessed via any operating internet connection gives unprecedented collaboration capabilities to public safety organizations.

Similarly the provision of large screen graphical display "video wall" capabilities in Command and Control centers provides the critical ability to comprehend simultaneous situational information and manage remote processes in the field from the common central view. Linking centers across regional jurisdictions provides opportunities for collaboratively working and sharing resources and process skills across distributed locations.

This environment provides new opportunities for business process specialists to document and implement. It also provides challenges in being able to manage dynamic process control, including stopping, pausing and diverting active processes to respond to new situation awareness, along with triggering new processes based on that actionable intelligence becoming available. Sharing that actionable intelligence between process models through pooled knowledge.

The use of knowledge tools becomes important in order that an existing process may suddenly need to be changed based on information that now is available either from a direct physical event, or from new information discovered by knowledge mining tools. An example would be Video Cloud information being scanned for matching and tracing patterns may suddenly detect a match and alert an existing process. The process owners can now react to this new knowledge. Modern data cloud environments provide the ability to continually glean a common view of knowledge in real time.

The world is entering a new age of information use for Public Safety. This is driven by the availability of nationwide high-speed broadband communications services and cloud computing systems. Combined with high-definition video surveillance systems, together they can provide unprecedented levels of information to assist public safety services to understand and even anticipate, then reach and respond to citizens' safety needs in daily life.

DISCLAIMER
The views expressed here are those of the author and may not also reflect those of Huawei Technologies Ltd.

Smart Adaptive BPM Engine

Pedro Robledo, BPMteca, Spain

INTRODUCTION

Adaptive Case Management envisions processes that are not designed in advance, but are rather processes that respond moment-by-moment. In an agile environment, where all structured processes have predesigned their business behaviors in advance, they will need to be adapted depending on real-time circumstances. Disruption from Artificial Intelligence applied to BPM will provide a smart adaptive BPM engine that will cause fundamental changes for the structured processes because these could change their predesigned behavior as the BPM engine starts learning, so this new capability of BPM will provide the right tasks at the right moment for a customer. The fundamental idea is the automatic adaptation of the process models are defined by the automatic learning of the Workflow Engine that orchestrates the processes.

STRUCTURED AND UNSTRUCTURED BUSINESS PROCESSES

From the emergence of workflow systems, until now under the BPM paradigm, we have sought the automation of business processes seeking continuous improvement. As Peter Morris says, "Most process applications used guided processing to force work down the happy path and are not interpretive and the goal in most BPM deployments is to standardize the process in order to automate and derive business value through the elimination of defects or process steps." When looking for non-variability through SixSigma, the execution of instances of structured processes (predictable and deterministic) with optimum and expected performance is achieved. The flows of structured processes can be very complex, however. Decision points, business logic, business rules are all attributes that determine how the process can flow are predefined.

Robotic Process Automation (RPA) is used to automate repetitive processes that do not require human intervention, that is, to replicate an employee's activity on the desktop of their computer to process complex operations in the same way as a human. For both, structured process with BPM and repetitive process with RPA, the sequence of tasks is known.

The power of using BPM for structured processes is not debatable and it is required to be implemented in all companies, but in practice, few workers spend much of their time responding to unstructured and unpredictable work patterns which are difficult to automate because each process instance is not repeatable, being necessary to respond ad-hoc to each event that is happening until solving the process. In these cases, we talk about unstructured and unpredictable processes, where the exact sequence of tasks and activities cannot be determined in advance.

In unstructured processes, the end point is known, but the way to achieve the result is finished by each stage, each milestone in the management of that case. The particular circumstances of each case will imply a specific sequence of activities and predefined results. Hence, in order to solve these unstructured and unpredictable processes, ACM (Adaptive Case Management) is applied and this capability has been included by the main suppliers of BPM systems, normally in the BPMS called Intelligent BPMS.

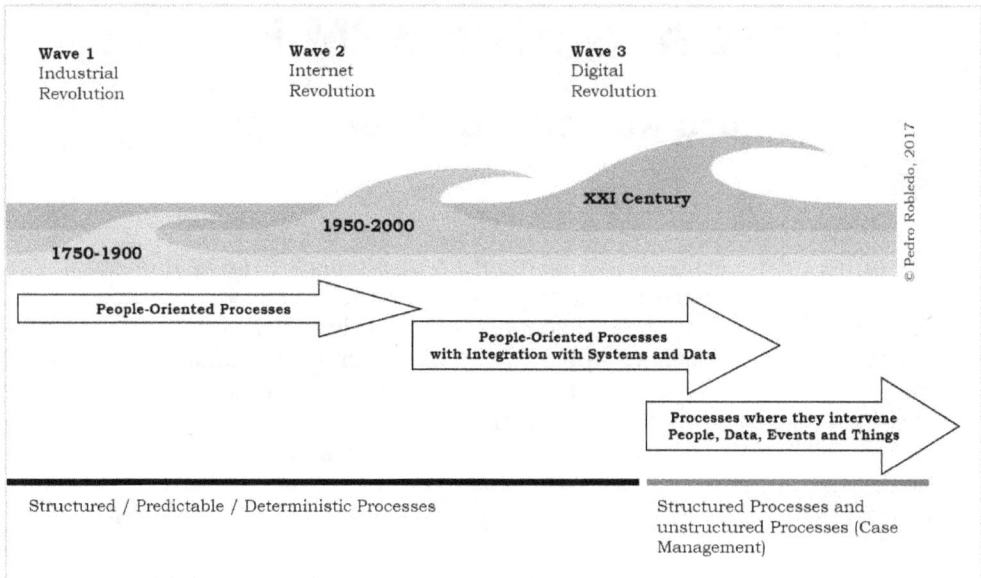

Wave 1	Wave 2	Wave 3
Industrial	Internet	Digital
Revolution	Revolution	Revolution

XXI Century

1950-2000

1750-1900

© Pedro Robledo, 2017

People-Oriented Processes

People-Oriented Processes
with Integration with Systems and Data

Processes where they intervene
People, Data, Events and Things

Structured / Predictable / Deterministic Processes

Structured Processes and
unstructured Processes (Case
Management)

Figure 1: Structured and Unstructured Processes during the Three waves

THE POWER OF DISRUPTIVE TECHNOLOGIES FOR BUSINESS PROCESSES

Artificial Intelligence

It has been 60 years since illustrious John McCarthy introduced the term "Artificial Intelligence" in 1956, referring to "... the science and ingenuity of making intelligent machines, especially intelligent computer programs."

The application of Artificial Intelligence (AI) can be seen in all sectors: bed allocation in a hospital, optimization of financial investment, robotics, virtual assistants, work schedules, video games, aircraft simulators, predictive maintenance of machinery, estimation of electrical consumption, detection of clinical patterns, autonomous cars, facial or voice recognition, natural language processing ... therefore, would it not be convenient to apply the full potential of Artificial Intelligence to Business Process Management? The answer must be in the affirmative; to apply artificial intelligence at any stage of the BPM life cycle, but I think where it has a disruptive power is in the execution of structured and unstructured processes.

Consider the real case of the use of the IBM Watson machine, which, through the application of AI, diagnosed a rare leukemia type of a 60-year-old woman in only 10 minutes comparing information of 20 million cancer papers. If Watson could correct the diagnosis of human doctors, and provide a precise diagnosis for the appropriate treatment for the recovery of the patient, think what could the application of the AI in the automation and execution of business processes. Imagine the value of receiving the most accurate decision in terms of the next activity to be performed in the flow of a process. If our companies are evaluating only 0.5 percent of available information, we can imagine the value we could get by analyzing the remaining 99.5 percent. We will need technological assistance, of course, because humans do not have enough time to process so much data, and much less to do it with the necessary speed to make decisions in seconds during a process.

Every day, more than 2.5 billion gigabytes of data are generated on a global scale given the digital era and the proliferation of data. Each gigabyte of data would be equivalent to sending from our cellphone for a month between half a million and a million text messages. There are more varieties of unstructured information (video, audio, images, text ...), more speed to process them and more storage volume with less cost, and are needed ensure the accuracy of captured information, extract value from all available information, maintain processes with the variability of the environment and visualize results clearly, simply and truthfully. According to Harvard Business Review; "Eighty percent of organizations believe that the inability of different professionals in a business to work with data in common is a key factor in not being able to meet their business goals on time." The problem lies in not being able to have a global and coherent view of all the information available in the different IT systems that they use and of all the data sources to which they can connect, beside not having enough time to invest in the intake and debugging of all the data. Traditional companies have to start a journey to lead data-driven businesses to be able to make better decisions, with the goal of becoming companies driven by artificial intelligence. In this way companies will not work analyzing the past, but solving daily problems in real time and forecasting their future, allowing them to react and not to lament.

It is also worth reflecting that only one percent of the enormous amount of data circulating (according to IDC) is being analyzed, therefore, the disruptive and transforming challenge of companies is how to be able to process (evaluate, select, analyze, implement, change, relate ...) that complex information, and in real time (the time necessary for that information to be useful for our business).

This challenge is magnified when realizing that, as Peter Whibley discusses in *The Internet of Things Will Be Invisible*, it is estimated that more than 26 billion devices will be connected to the Internet (Internet of Things, IoT) generating information, which in turn, must also be processed.

Thanks to increased efficiency in the processing of high data volumes (Big Data), increased computer capacity and advanced analytical systems, companies can make better use of data to become more competitive and make the best decisions for its business, with agility and time saving. The streaming analytics technology enable us to identify complex patterns and provide rapid and accurate results without human intervention. In addition to identifying patterns, the system can review data and predict specific behavior, thus becoming an automatic learning system.

Machine Learning

Machine learning is a scientific discipline of artificial intelligence whose aim is to develop algorithms that allow computers (machines) to learn. The machine-based data analysis generalizes data through a sophisticated process of knowledge induction and solves complex problems. Everyone who has made a purchase online has instantly received recommendations for products that may interest us, so who or what is behind this action? Machine Learning (ML) is being used for this purpose. Other applications focus on predicting machine failures, detecting business opportunities, detecting fraud in transactions, selecting the best candidate resumes, attracting potential customers, predicting urban traffic, predicting potential disease based on symptoms, store chemical compounds correctly to avoid possible chemical reactions, visual recognition, predictive robotics, generate reports or automatic response letters and so on. Machine learning thus provides intelligence to business environments by freeing workers from more routine tasks and time-consuming processes. According to analyst Gartner, smart machines will trend from 2021, achieving a 30 percent adoption by large companies.

Deep Learning

Deep Learning algorithms allow us to extract knowledge from huge volumes of data (images, videos, texts and conversations) by automatically building hierarchies of concepts that range from the most basic to the most complex to create a neural network of many layers. The neural network created in BPM allows us to interweave all the necessary knowledge to focus in the right direction to all the processes and therefore to its workers towards the business objectives.

Cognitive Systems

Cognitive Systems are systems of discovery and counseling, which are characterized by facilitating communication between people and technology by using natural language processing (understands grammar and context, recognizes the voice), makes informed decisions very quickly (millions of data in a matter of seconds and answers complex questions almost in real time). They also provide reasoning (before a question, formulate hypotheses and choose the answer with the highest level of confidence) and analyze millions of structured data (business system data) and unstructured data (articles, videos, audio, posts, text books, sensors, research reports, content social networks) in real time. They learn continuously, accumulating value and knowledge of each experience, making them increasingly intelligent.

Peter Fingar notes in *Cognitive BPM*, "Cognitive computing systems can understand the nuances of human language, process questions akin to the way people think, and quickly cull through vast amounts of data for relevant, evidence-based answers to their human users' needs."

When Cognitive Systems are combined with the discipline of Business Process Management, "intelligence" is added in the execution of a company's business processes which is facilitated by chaining the execution of processes in response to decisions which have been taken by the cognitive system. For example, the customer service mailbox processes all communication received (voice, email, SMS, text ...), understands natural language, identifies the intent of the message, automatically respond in seconds to the client (without human intervention). Depending on circumstances, the system activates a task to the most appropriate person in the organization for further action. Through cognitive counseling, unstructured processes can be solved, which are defined in the execution itself (the system indicates which tasks to perform and who should perform them, learning the sequence to be able to repeat it in the future).

Blockchain

Blockchain relies on mathematics and cryptography (to ensure privacy) and, by using decentralized systems that share digital events among many different parties, updating content requires the consensus of the majority of the participants of the system. Once entered, information cannot be erased. The use of Blockchain within an organization and in transactions with customers and suppliers permits the introduction of a machine-readable and verifiable transaction log.

SMART ADAPTIVE BPM ENGINE

The Smart Adaptive BPM Engine interprets a structured or unstructured process flow diagram by organizing, controlling and supervising the work of the participants during the execution of a process instance using intelligent systems that adapt in real time to the context in the pursuit of objectives business. The engine orchestrates dynamic and static interaction patterns among people, intelligent objects, information systems, and other resources, based on metadata, process flow, and the possible states of a case. This includes patterns of deterministic and non-deterministic processes, such as dynamic collaboration. The engine maintains the stat- of-the-process instances, activities and interactions. The engine also records all state changes to manage a process, such as activities, flows, events, data, rules, roles, and other process artifacts. The engine has the ability to execute process instances and execute business rules when necessary based on cognitive data to decide for the best next task in real time.

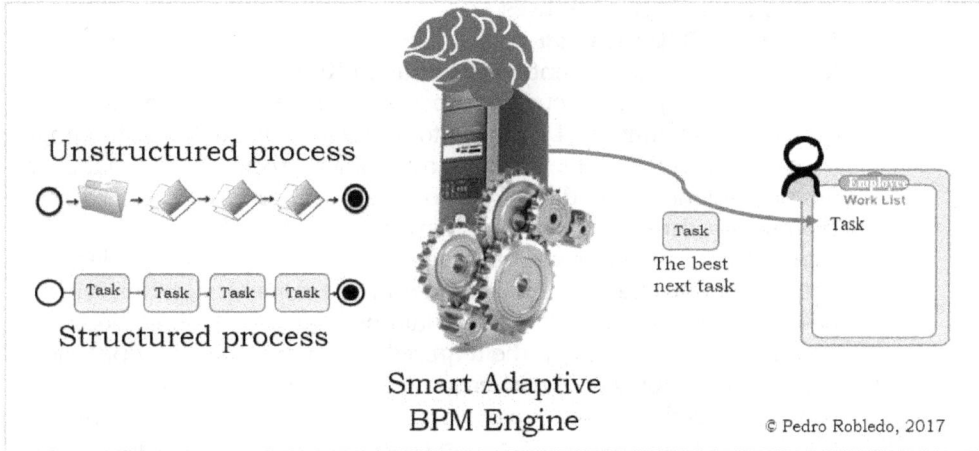

Unstructured process

Structured process

Task

The best next task

Employee
Work List

Task

Smart Adaptive BPM Engine

© Pedro Robledo, 2017

Figure 2: Smart Adaptive BPM Engine provides the best next task

MAIN FEATURES OF THE SMART ADAPTIVE BPM ENGINE

The 10 main components necessary for an intelligent BPM suite when incorporating "smart adaptive" features are:

1. An **intelligent process orchestration engine** that manages structured processes and unstructured processes or cases, and it is able to orchestrate the required tasks or sub-processes (stored in a repository) in any circumstance depending the context and real-time data.

2. **Analytical Technology** which allows the detection of large data volumes (Big Data), Natural Language Processing (NLP), Contextual Analysis and Active Analytics (sometimes called continuous intelligence or operational intelligence) to monitor the progress of activities, and analysis of activities and changes around processes aligned to KPIs and strategic objectives.

3. **Artificial Intelligence** that evaluates all the available information to provide the best decision for the next task to do during the execution of any process instance. AI technologies provide sentiment analysis and the possibility to convert unstructured data to something more organized.

4. **Machine Learning and Deep Learning** from which the system continuously learns the workflow information being captured when process instances are executed in order to improve performance, effectiveness and efficiency of the processes.

5. **Process Automation using Cognitive Systems** which acts according to the most correct decisions, based on the previous or real-time analysis.

6. **Complex Event Processing** (CEP) technology that allows Complex Event Management in a specific time period: filtering by criteria, event correlation, statistical calculation of event data, detecting patterns, enrichment by combining reference data from external systems, providing sufficient context, multidimensional analysis and situational analysis. We can consider CEP as the key technology necessary for the real-time processing of large volumes of events that allows predictive decisions by the BPM engine to decide the best task to perform.

7. **Balanced ScoreCard** (BSC) to keep organizations flexible, prepared for different changes, but always oriented to their strategy, to align the behavior of people (through the correct activity) towards the achievement of defined strategic objectives.

8. **Predictive Optimization** suggestions are based on continuous monitoring. This includes identifying trends in KPIs that highlight inefficiencies or opportunities in current processes, so the engine provides the required or recommended changes to fix them. This ability of the engine assesses the relative efficiencies of automated processes and makes recommendations for modifications to business logic and even processes, themselves, thus continually escalating process efficiency.

9. **Blockchain** which introduces a machine-readable and verifiable record of transactions enabling verification and decisions by algorithms not possible earlier because the input data necessary for the decision was not previously available at the required level of trust and completeness.

10. **Internet of Things** (IoT) has features that allow use of any object to which is added a sensor capable of collecting and transmitting information. Therefore, the information collected will start processes in the BPM engine.

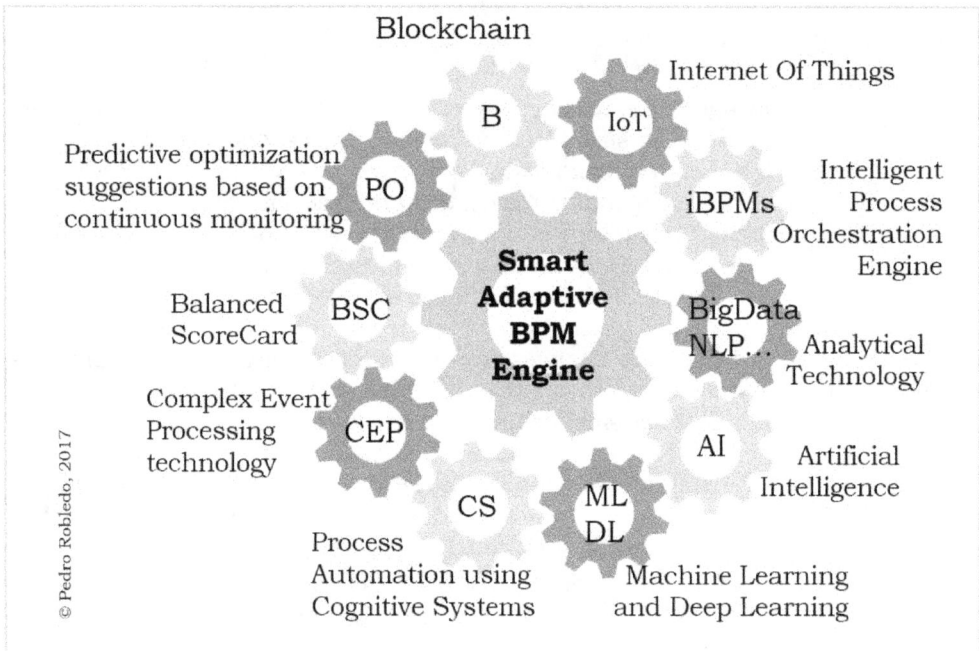

Figure 3: Ten Main Features of Smart Adaptive BPM Engine

CONCLUSIONS

As companies face unprecedented dynamism, in an environment where innovation must be continuous to be competitive and where analysis of maximum information is crucial, intelligent BPMS are essential in order to meet the needs of customers with agility and flexibility.

Unfortunately, the BPM Suite does not integrate machine learning algorithms with our processes. The idea is to run the BPMS in parallel with the machine learning algorithm in order to take the control in any step of the workflow. This intelligent component will provide the best next task to execute according to the presence of complete information.

In both deterministic (structured) and non-deterministic (non-structured) processes or cases), the BPM engine should make the decision that is best for the strategic objectives to be achieved. Even though the flow is predetermined (in the deterministic case) or will be decided by a worker in an open case, the Smart Adaptive BPM Engine will determine or suggest the most appropriate activity to perform in context to continue the flow of the process. Through this system the user has the opportunity to improve the productivity of the job immediately without having to wait to analyze the business processes and perform simulations with new process scenarios. In real time, the necessary knowledge is available that allows workers to make smart decisions and dedicate themselves to value tasks by applying the best practices that relate to their objectives.

In the next months, many vendors will talk about the challenges and opportunities involved in the shift toward the use of AI technologies in BPM as key role in digital transformation in all organizations. BPM will see a new disruption from the inclusion of machine learning and new AI features.

REFERENCES

[Campbell 2017] Jamie Campbell. BPM in the rise of deep learning. Virtusa's Blog 2017. http://blogs.virtusa.com/2017/05/bpm-in-the-rise-of-deep-learning/

[Charme] Leonard du Charme. Responsive Low-Code BPM Meets AI (Artificial Intelligence). AgilePoint's Blog http://agilepoint.com/responsive-low-code-bpm-meets-ai-artificial-intelligence/

[Fingar 2014] Peter Fingar. Extreme Competition: Cognitive BPM. BPTrends 2014. http://www.bptrends.com/cognitive-bpm/

[Fingar 2015] Peter Fingar: Cognitive BPM, published in *BPM Everywhere*. Future Strategies Inc. https://bpm-books.com/products/bpm-everywhere-print

[Gartner 2016] Press Release. Gartner Says Smart Machines Will Enter Mainstream Adoption By 2021. http://www.gartner.com/newsroom/id/3545017

[Koplowitz 2017] Rob Koplowitz with Christopher Mines, Allison Vizgaitis. Artificial Intelligence Revitalizes BPM. New Features Will Drive Deeper Customer Engagement in Core Processes. Forrester 2017. https://www.forrester.com/report/Artificial+Intelligence+Revitalizes+BPM/-/E-RES136829

[Morris 2015] Peter Morris. Artificial Intelligence & BPM. LinkedIn 2015. https://www.linkedin.com/pulse/artificial-intelligence-bpm-peter-morris

[Potrzeba 2016] Megan Potrzeba. Machine Learning Contributing to BPM Innovation. Appian Blog 2016. https://www.appian.com/blog/bpm/machine-learning-contributing-to-bpm-innovation

[Pucher 2016] Max J. Pucher. Artificial Intelligence and BPM. Pucher's Blog 2016. https://isismjpucher.wordpress.com/2016/12/15/artificial-intelligence-and-bpm/

[Sonntag 2016] Andreas Sonntag. An approach for semantic business process model matching using supervised machine learning. Twenty-Fourth European Conference on Information Systems (ECIS) İstanbul, Turkey, 2016. http://disi.unitn.it/~pavel/OM/articles/2976.pdf

[Qian 2017] Albert Qian. 3 Ways AI is Transforming BPM. Perficient's Blog 2017 http://blogs.perficient.com/integrate/2017/06/27/3-ways-ai-is-transforming-bpm/

[Wasser 2012] Avi Wasser and Maya Lincoln. Semantic Machine Learning for Business Process Content Generation. Springer 2012. https://link.springer.com/chapter/10.1007/978-3-642-33606-5_6

[Webster 2017] Charles Webster. A guide to AI, machine learning and new workflow technologies at HIMSS17 Part 1: Machine learning and workflow. Healthcare IT News 2017. http://www.healthcareitnews.com/blog/guide-ai-machine-learning-and-new-workflow-technologies-himss17-part-1-machine-learning-and

[Whibley 2016] Peter Whibley. "The Internet of Things Will Be Invisible" published in *BPM Everywhere.* Future Strategies Inc. https://bpm-books.com/products/bpm-everywhere-print

[Wilson 2017] H. James Wilson, Allan Alter and Prashant Shukla. Companies Are Reimagining Business Processes with Algorithms. HBR Press 2017. https://hbr.org/2016/02/companies-are-reimagining-business-processes-with-algorithms

Intelligent Digital Transformation with VSaaS

Dr. Setrag Khoshafian, Pegasystems Inc., USA
Sushil Kumar, Pegasystems Inc., USA

INTRODUCTION

Cloud computing is one of the hottest technology trends of the decade. Software platforms and infrastructures in "the cloud" (which usually means accessed via the public Internet through a browser or mobile device) are fast becoming the preferred mode of provisioning enterprise software. One of the other significant trends in digitization has been the automated collaboration of various stake-holders in end-to-end digitized value streams. Digital Transformation is about execution and increasingly the context of the execution is achieved through end-to-end digitized value streams involving a whole ecosystem of active collaborators and participants on the Cloud. Digital enterprises are getting robust visibility and collaboration with their customers and trading partners. Artificial Intelligence (AI) is now starting to play a tremendous role in the adaptability of services as well as collaboration, for the digital enterprise.

This is a significant and underemphasized potential of the cloud; the Cloud as a foundation for intra- as well as inter-enterprise business collaboration for specific business objectives. The trend toward ubiquitous connectivity is unstoppable. This connectivity includes the emergence of IoT (Khoshafian, 2015) for cyber–physical connectivity and it includes connectivity among enterprises for inter-business transactions. More importantly it includes both, not only for connectivity but for collaboration and orchestration to achieve shared business objectives.

Digital Transformation is primarily about collaboration and also about getting things done at digital speeds. This paper covers transformational value stream digitization approaches, various Cloud architectures and will explain how digitizing value streams and offering Digital Value Streams as a service, truly helps transform businesses. We will also go through a number of examples, including digital prescriptive maintenance, connected healthcare, and connected cities.

The concept of Digital Value Streams within enterprises has evolved from the realization that each customer interaction, independent of the source or channel, needs to work harmoniously together to meet the customer need. Rather than having each channel work as an independent silo of customer interaction and information, the concept of a Digital Value Stream chains all of these interactions as links in achieving the overall customer objective. The notion of VSaaS (Value Stream as a Service), expands on this digital value stream concept within enterprises (intra) to go across business enterprises (inter), who can now plug in their business unit participants into the value stream, to contribute and achieve robust shared business objectives.

DIGITIZING THE VALUE STREAM

Digitization is having a tremendous impact on all industries. From a technology perspective digitization means disruptive mega-trends in connectivity; Social, Internet of Things, Analytics, Cloud, AI and Mobility. However, the success or survival rate of enterprises will very much depend upon the robust digitization of their *value streams*. Borrowing a compelling perspective from Theory of Constraints (Goldratt, 2004): "a chain is no stronger than its weakest link."

What does that mean for a digital enterprise, especially the ones that are attempting to evolve, improve, and transform customer experiences (actually, most, if not all)? Well, it means customer interactions are not optimized just by focusing on the call center or self-serving customer channel interactions. The intersections could be through Web or mobile or customer service representatives (CSRs) or increasingly intelligent interactive voice response systems (IVRs) and intelligent virtual agents. Optimizing the front channel customer interaction is, of course, critical and important.

However, the customer-promotion scores (an objective assessment of the customer experience) will depend on the aggregation of tasks that involve multiple business units to resolve the customer request. For instance, fixing a broken appliance might involve the CSR, the warranty department, the field service and finance. Unfortunately, even in this current era of digitization, most organizations are siloed. It is not enough to just focus on the responsiveness of the CSR, the elegance of the Web or mobile app for customer service or just the front-end customer interaction channels. These are, of course, important. But they are part of the end-to-end value stream that needs to be strong and responsive through all the stages of the value chain. It becomes even more challenging if the value stream needs to involve different digital enterprises, which is the focus of this paper.

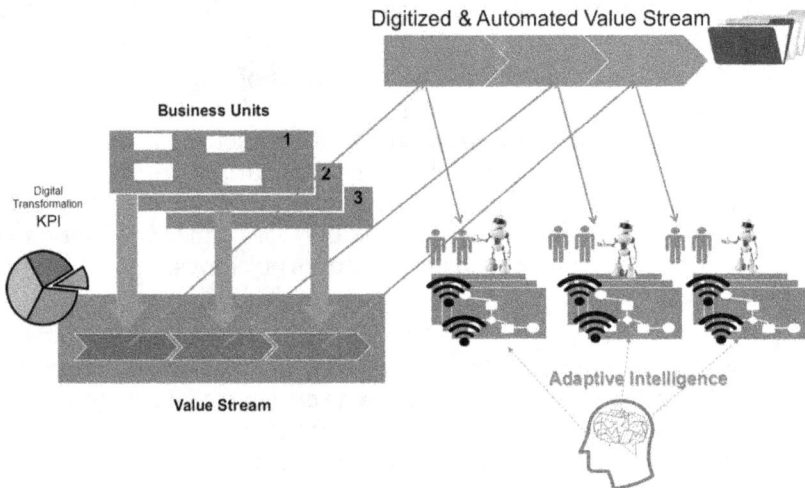

Figure 1: Digitizing Value Streams

Therefore, in reality, each customer interaction—independent of the source or channel—typically ends up involving multiple business units that need to work harmoniously to respond to the customer. The *entire* stream needs to be digitized and optimized; not just individual links within business units. Dynamic Case Management (DCM) (Khoshafian, 2014) automation that supports stage-based design and automation is a powerful enabler of value-stream optimization and governance. Therefore, business value is achieved through digitizing and automating the value stream through *intelligent* DCM.

The speed by which KPIs and end-to-end value streams are associated with dynamic cases is critical. Automation and business activity monitoring allow the digital enterprise to be responsive to potential weaknesses and take corrective actions in *real-time*. DCM connects the front office to the back office and runs across all channels to deliver a consistent, end-to-end experience. Sub-cases handled by different teams or organizations are all aggregated through the holistic case to meet a specific customer objective. All the links or stages can be kept in control in real-time with digitized policies for escalation as needed. Artificial Intelligence (AI) drives the digitized value streams and machine learning can be leveraged to continuously learn and adapt.

EXAMPLE: END-TO-END PRESCRIPTIVE MAINTENANCE

Here is a robust example that brings home the value proposition of VSaaS. Prescriptive Maintenance (Khoshafian and Rostetter, 2015) involves collaboration among various entities; the connected device, the customer who owns the device, the customer service representative (CSR), the Field Service Dispatcher, the mobile, skilled Field Service Technician, and others such as billing and warranty operations. It could also potentially involve suppliers for parts that are needed to resolve the service case.

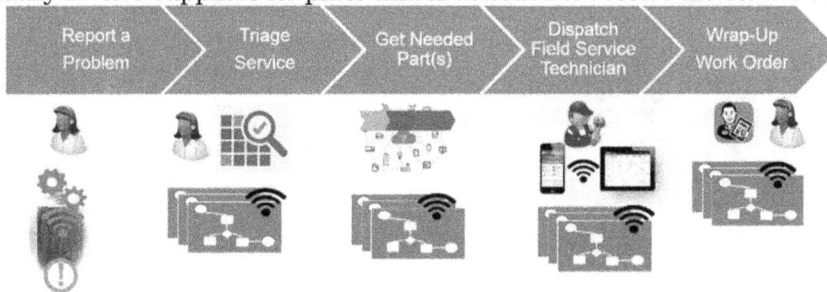

Figure 2: Digital Prescriptive Maintenance Value Stream

The various stages or milestones of the end-to-end field service value stream could be described as follows:

- *Report a problem:* In this scenario, a problem could be reported to the customer service representative. Increasingly, with connected devices, the device itself could detect and communicate to the servicing organization, which is typically the manufacturer.
- *Triage service:* The next stage is the triaging to determine if the problem can be diagnosed and fixed remotely or via a service call. The triage might involve business rules, predictive analytics, as well as machine learning adaptive analytics. Potentially human decision-makers may be involved in accepting the course of action to resolve the problem.
- *Get needed parts:* In some cases, the service issue could be resolved remotely. Manufactured edge devices often have sophisticated software that can be updated remotely by the manufacturer. Devices can also be viewed, pinged or otherwise controlled remotely.

The value stream also illustrates the parts acquisition stage. The supply chain process itself involves multiple stages and decisioning for the best supplier as well as the overall Internet of Things enabled logistics, tracking and on-time delivery.

- *Dispatch field service technician:* The next phase is the dispatching of the field technician. Business rules in conjunction with analytics and connectivity are leveraged to dispatch the best-suited field technician. While servicing, the technician uses mobile devices for the servicing tasks. Optionally the technician could leverage augmented reality to view potential issues that may need additional servicing.
- *Wrap up work order:* Finally, the wrap-up of the work order could involve warranty payments, customer surveys, and overall resolution of the case.

A key takeaway here is that there are different digital enterprises and resources involved in the resolution of the end-to-end dynamic case that automates the value stream. This could involve for instance, the manufacturer of the device, the dealer that sold the device, the supplier of the part, the field service provider, and various business units (finance, warranty, procurement) that are also involved in the case.

When different organizations are involved in the digitized and automated value stream (through DCM), it becomes necessary to deploy the value stream on the Cloud, making it easily accessible for all.

CLOUD COMPUTING

By some estimates, the cloud computing market will reach $241 billion by 2020. The cloud software market is growing extremely fast—by some estimates five times faster than the software market as a whole (Mahowald and Sullivan, 2012).

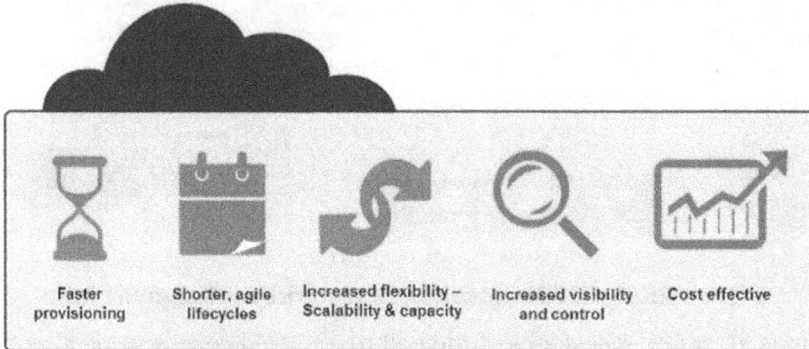

Figure 3: Advantages of Cloud Computing

There are distinct advantages to cloud computing:
- Provisioning is much faster, whether you are provisioning hardware or business applications.
- The lifecycles of updates or changes to the resources, such as new versions of the software or application, are shorter and more agile.
- Cloud computing enables you to easily scale and add more capacity to handle larger number of concurrent users for a business application deployed on the cloud.
- Cloud computing provides increased visibility and control, especially for the business. The business is empowered to select specific business applications and start using them, almost instantaneously.
- Cloud computing can be highly cost-effective since you pay for what you use. The subscription-based, pay-as-you-use model is very attractive to organizations attempting to control up-front costs of servers, data center rental space and o-premise software licensing.

Cloud computing can be categorized by using two primary characteristics; **deployment model** and the **service model**.

CLOUD COMPUTING DEPLOYMENT MODELS

There are various cloud deployment models that can be leveraged to meet the needs of specific business applications.

Public Cloud: is a type of cloud deployment in which the cloud services are delivered over a network which is open for public usage. The public cloud service provider provides infrastructure and shared services to various customers. Customers can leverage these services but have no control over the location of the infrastructure.

Public cloud is better suited for business requirements which require managing the load; the host application is SaaS-based and manages applications that many users consume. Due to the shared nature of this model, the operational cost and capital expenditure are quite economical. The cost is shared by all the users, thus public cloud profits the customers more by achieving economies of scale. Public cloud facilities may be availed for a fee as in Amazon, Azure and Google.

Private Cloud: probably better known as an internal cloud. In the case of the private cloud, the cloud computing model is implemented on a cloud-based secure environment, protected by a firewall, and is under corporate governance within an enterprise. This provides the corporation greater and direct control over their data. It could be constituted by a set of physical or virtual computers that are hosted internally or externally and offered up as a distinct resource pool. Businesses that have dynamic or unforeseen needs, assignments which are mission-critical, security alarms, management demands and uptime requirements are better suited to private cloud. Obstacles with regards to security can be avoided in a private cloud, but it is susceptible to natural disasters and internal data theft.

Hybrid Cloud: is a type of cloud computing model that combines workloads from both public and private cloud components, based on need and demand and is reasonably well integrated. It can be an arrangement of two or more cloud servers, i.e. private, public or community cloud that are bound together but remain individual entities. Benefits of the multiple deployment models are available in a hybrid cloud hosting and allow the user to increase the capacity or the capability by aggregation, assimilation or customization with another cloud package / service. In a hybrid cloud, the resources are managed and provided either in-house or by external providers and includes features like flexibility, scalability, performance and security.

Non-critical resources like development and test workloads can be housed in the public cloud that belongs to a third-party provider, while the workloads that are critical or sensitive are housed internally. Businesses that have more focus on security and demand for their unique presence implement hybrid cloud as an effective business strategy. When facing demand spikes, the additional resources required by a particular application can be accessed from the public cloud. This is termed *cloud bursting* and is available with the hybrid cloud.

There are some inherent complexities such as API compatibility issues, higher costs and more complex network connectivity issues.

Community Cloud: is a type of cloud hosting model, wherein the infrastructure setup and configurations are mutually shared among corporations, such as healthcare conglomerates, banking institutions etc. It is usually a multitenant setup of several organizations that belong to a specific group which have similar computing needs, privacy and security concerns. The primary goal of a community cloud is to be able to share and attain common business goals and objectives. It can be hosted externally or internally. Because the cost is shared across multiple corporations within the community, a level of cost optimization is achieved, in addition to the shared interests and platform objectives. The community cloud is typically appropriate for businesses that work on joint ventures or research that need a centralized cloud computing ability for managing, building and implementing similar projects.

'Value Stream' Cloud to host VSaaS: We could define this new concept as an evolutionary model from the community cloud model, shared among enterprises with mutually-beneficial business objectives or value streams. This could be a multi-tenant setup shared among several enterprises, across industries. This is somewhat akin to the EDI (Electronic Data Interchange) transaction mechanism that originated in the 1970s, used to exchange business transactional data among partners, except that now we are leveraging unique cloud-based features and functionality. More importantly, the participants in the Value Stream are coordinating and cooperating to resolve cases or get collaborative work done. There are specific inter-digital enterprise objectives. Service levels and process efficiencies as well as optimizations are achieved end-to-end with various participants. Intelligence (business rules, analytics, machine learning) and dynamic adaptability are essential in driving the completion of the value stream.

CLOUD COMPUTING SERVICE MODELS

As mentioned in our description of cloud computing characteristics, there are many categories of services with IaaS, PaaS and SaaS being the three most common and important.

- **IaaS:** Infrastructure as a Service is used to deliver infrastructure as fully outsourced services. Rather than purchasing servers and network equipment and worrying about data center space, clients usually associate IaaS with *virtualization*[1]. Virtualization allows multiple operating systems to run on the same hardware server. It also applies to other types of infrastructure resources such storage.
- **PaaS:** Platform as a Service is a SaaS types of service. Clients can use a PaaS offering to build complete business applications on the cloud. A PaaS offering can be extensive and include a development environment, testing, deployment, and hosting of the developed application on the cloud. The entire lifecycle of development is provisioned on the cloud, including collaborative design of processes, business rules, decisioning, reports for activity monitoring, UI, integration, as well as application versioning. The solutions that are tested, designed, and developed on the cloud can target various types of channels, including mobile devices.
- **SaaS:** Software as a Service is perhaps the most popular type of service on the cloud. Complete business solutions are accessed on the cloud by clients using web browsers as well as mobile devices such as tablets or smartphones. The cloud has become a common delivery mechanism for many applications for collaboration, content management, accounting, human resource management and customer relationship management.
- **VSaaS:** Value stream as a Service is a new service concept on the cloud. Enterprises plug-in to collaborative value streams with specific roles and tasks automated through intelligent and dynamic cases, as part of the digital ecosystem. Through this transformational approach involving multiple organizations, there will be mutually-beneficial application-functional components, that are additive and would enhance the end-to-end value stream. All participants will benefit, including potentially target-end customers (e.g. patients in healthcare value streams). Organizations leverage the cloud to

---

[1] http://en.wikipedia.org/wiki/Virtualization

gain visibility into the end-to-end work processes across digital enterprises and accomplish their shared objectives in an optimal, collaborative manner.

ADAPTIVE INTELLIGENT COLLABORATION ON THE CLOUD

Collaboration involving various participants on networks has itself gone through quite a journey. In 1995, I wrote a book (Khoshafian and Buckiewicz, 1995) titled "Introduction to Groupware, Workflow, and Workgroup Computing." In the 1980s and 1990s local and wide-area networks were used to realize both synchronous and asynchronous collaboration especially within the enterprise. In fact, workflow was a workgroup collaboration to achieve specific departmental task orchestration objectives. Now with the emergence and—as we saw in the last two decades with the explosion of the Internet—the "collaboration" of the previous decades became social networking and social interaction; the most successful of those being Facebook with more recent ones such as Instagram, Snapchat, Instant Messenger and others. The numbers are astounding and the explosion is exponential.

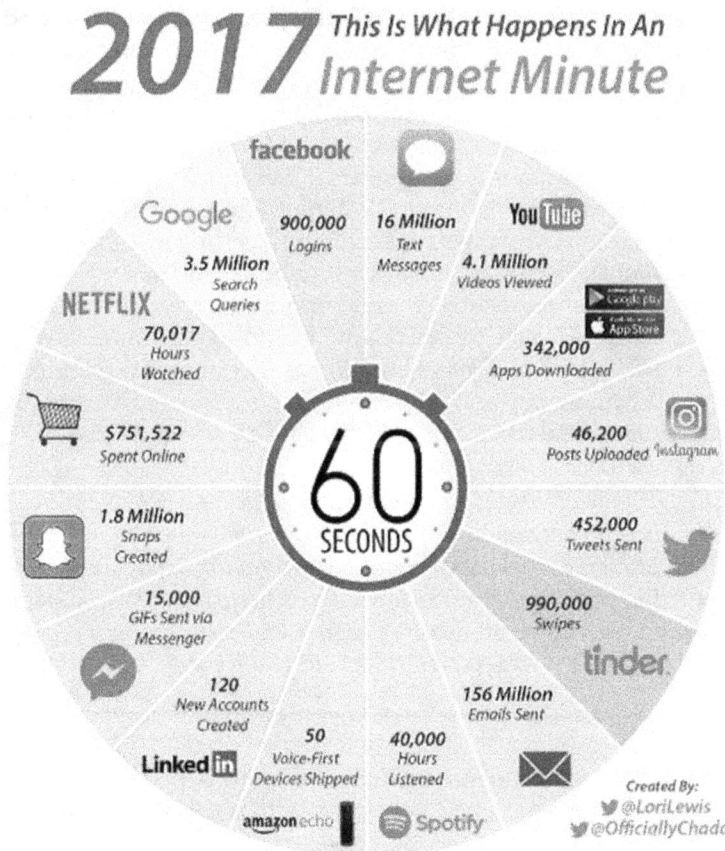

2017 This Is What Happens In An **Internet Minute**

Google — 3.5 Million Search Queries
facebook — 900,000 Logins
16 Million Text Messages
YouTube — 4.1 Million Videos Viewed
NETFLIX — 70,017 Hours Watched
342,000 Apps Downloaded
$751,522 Spent Online
46,200 Posts Uploaded Instagram
1.8 Million Snaps Created
60 SECONDS
452,000 Tweets Sent
15,000 GIFs Sent via Messenger
990,000 Swipes — tinder
120 New Accounts Created
156 Million Emails Sent
Linked in — 50 Voice-First Devices Shipped
40,000 Hours Listened
amazon echo — Spotify
Created By: @LoriLewis @OfficiallyChadd

Figure 4: 60 seconds on the Internet

The article "Voice of the Network through Social BPM" (Khoshafian et al. 2011) elaborated on the digital transformational impact of social networking. As indicated, the collaboration especially for business value needs to involve orchestration of tasks and activities. The enterprise needs to be responsive and act upon its discoveries. Digitized values streams automated through dynamic case management (Khoshafian, 2014) leverages real-time decisioning to enable organizations to operationalize various tasks, policies, content, and interactions – *all in the context* of a case. Unlike pre-determined structured processes, dynamic processes are collaborative, ad-hoc, and can respond contextually. DCM maps and supports end-to-end value streams. Cases connect social networks, front offices, and back offices cohesively. With advances in case management, including real-time decisioning, organizations can generate, interpret and dynamically respond to events.

With value streams, the ecosystem extends beyond the boundaries of the enterprise and helps achieve tremendous efficiencies through collaboration – social networking or otherwise.

Collaboration on the Cloud is an essential enabler for digital transformation. The *participants* in this collaboration can involve:
- *People:* from various enterprises involved in contributing value to the value stream but potentially also end-customers who are the ultimate beneficiary. Within digital enterprises, there will be specific roles or skills and tasks will be dynamically assigned based on the qualifications and availabilities.
- *Business Ecosystem:* This are the end-to-end trading partners involved in the value streams, each contributing specific capabilities to achieve the overall objectives of the value stream.
- *Enterprise Applications (aka Systems of Record):* Systems of Record such as Enterprise Resource Planning (ERP) applications are here to stay for at least the near-term. Increasingly, ERPs are also getting migrated to the cloud and often digital enterprises deploy a hybrid cloud strategy, depending upon their security, reliability, and performance requirements. These systems of record are active participants in end-to-end value streams.
- *Connected Devices and Internet of Things:* In almost every industry, connectivity is becoming pervasive. As discussed in (Khoshafian and Roeck, 2016) there are four core use cases of connected devices participating in end-to-end digitized value streams:
    - *Things as Participants in Digitized Process & Cases*
    - *Events activating DCM to respond to the event.*
    - *Stream of Events: to correlate and handle complex scenarios*
    - *Big Data and Predictive Analytics to detect patterns & Act*

Thus, collaboration on the cloud involves both social collaboration (synchronous and asynchronous) as well as work collaboration to resolve the end-to-end value stream case.

Adaptive Intelligence

The "intelligence" within value streams can emanate either from knowledge in the heads of cognitive workers or mined from data. With intelligent and machine learning digitized value streams, the overall value stream can continuously learn and adapt. These are often operationalized through business rules. There are many types and categories of rules: decision trees and tables are the most popular. Others include constraints and expressions to calculate, for instance, payments or discounts.

Intelligence can also be mined from data. With end-to-end digitized value streams involving customers, social networking, IoT and digital enterprises the data is "Big Data." Predictive and machine-learning models can be used to discover models from the value stream data and act upon it within the context of automated dynamic cases.

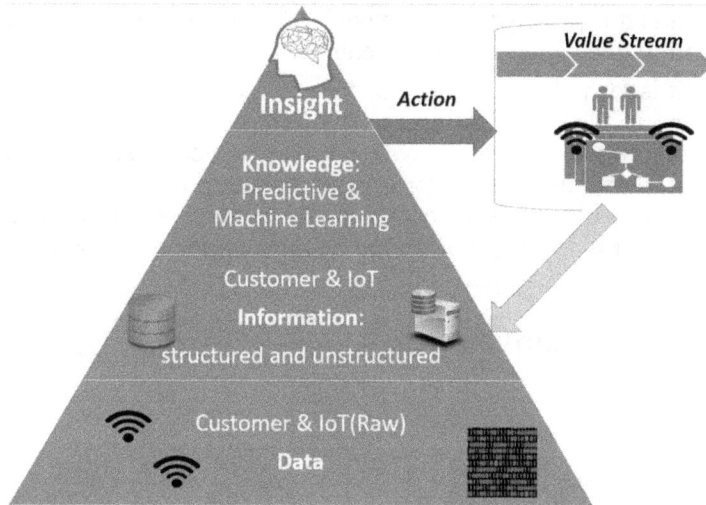

Figure 5: Insight to Action with Value Streams

There are many different types of predictive models including classification models, regression models, clustering models, and others. In addition to aggregating and mining models from heterogeneous data, another benefit of AI is to opt for a system of continuous learning within the system itself. The need-to-know when the historic data is used for modeling is no longer representative of current circumstances. With traditional predictive analytics, once the predictive model has been inferred from the data, it will not change anymore. In that case, the model will get 'tired' and should be replaced by a new model based on more recent data. The model is derived from a snapshot of the data and immutable thereafter. Any organization that is responsibly using static predictive models will want to ensure that those models are continuously monitored.

Enter self-learning (aka machine learning or adaptive) approaches. Instead of looking at a snapshot of data, this model looks at a moving window of data as it enters the self-learning adaptive system. It is still about predictability but now it is much more dynamic with continuous adjustments as sentiments or customer interactions or customer device behaviors change. A popular use for self-learning includes digital customer marketing space and the decision strategy which adapts to changes in customer behavior or market dynamics. Customer behavior can change because of demographic trends, legislation, interest rates or myriad other factors such as how the customer is using their wearables or connected devices.

Static or more dynamic self-learning systems can leverage either a single source of data (e.g. customer inbound transactions) or more importantly an aggregation or fusion of data multiple sources of data capturing customer behaviors, sentiments, or activities. The latter provides better assessment and opportunities for optimized customer engagements. The whole purpose of, and motivation for, analytics—static predictive or self-learning—is to discover these patterns (predictive models), use them to predict future behavior, and then *act* on the insight.

Example: Connected Healthcare

The following example illustrates the end-to-end value stream collaboration of healthcare providers, emergency services, payers, and patients. Wearables and connectivity throughout patient care generate enormous amounts of data that can be analyzed and mined for predictive models. The action part can leverage these models within end-to-end digitized value streams.

Whether it is for patient wellness or for emergency life-threatening scenarios, with VSaaS, any of the participating entities (Provider, Payer, Emergency, Patient) can plug in and cooperate. Once the value stream is modeled and deployed as a service, various tasks with intelligence for escalation and routing of the work are assigned to the participants across the extended digital healthcare enterprises. The patient and other participants leverage connected healthcare devices which also become part of the end-to-end value stream.

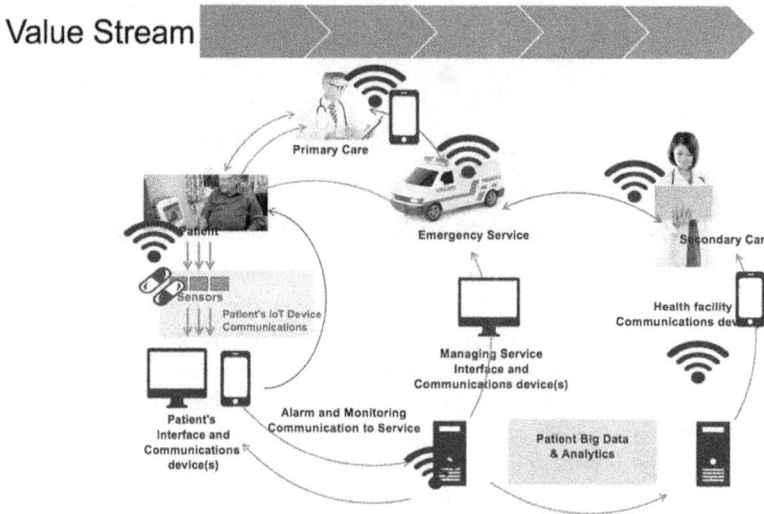

Figure 6: Healthcare Value Stream

CONCLUSIONS FOR VALUE STREAM AS A SERVICE

Collaboration on the Cloud is already a real possibility for digital enterprises. Evolving from infrastructure, platform and software as a service, the VSaaS offers digital transformation opportunities for many industries. The digitization and automation of the value stream are realized through intelligent dynamic cases. The intelligence emanates from business rules as well as predictive and machine learning models that drive the value stream. There are many dimensions for "dynamic" (aka adaptive) capabilities of this emerging category of Cloud offering. All the constraints, service levels, and the overall performance requirement of the value stream can be continuously monitored and responded to.

The adaptive intelligence of automated value streams involving multiple digital enterprise participants is a powerful enabler for digital transformation using a 'pluggable' value chain model. It provides:

- *End-to-end visibility of the value streams:* clearly identifying the potential weakest links and remedying potential bottlenecks in real-time.
- *Unprecedented collaboration among various stakeholders and business partners:* The Cloud has matured from a mere option for businesses to purchase software or IT to facilitate deployments to an environment of digital business interactions.
- *IoT OpeEx Service Offerings:* In addition to business interactions within the context of *value* streams, digital enterprise partnerships can offer various operational service products on the cloud that leverage the automation as well as the intelligent analytics and adaptability of their value streams.

This chapter described some of the advantages of VSaaS; there are many more. VSaaS is the next stage in the overall evolution of "XaaS" offerings on the Cloud. Implementation may be challenging from a setup, security, and reliability perspective because it involves different organizations. Digital enterprises have already challenges in capturing and digitizing their own value streams. VSaaS adds more complexity, but at the same time, it provides opportunities for innovation and rewards for all the participants.

REFERENCES

Goldratt, Eliyahu M., (2004). *The Goal: a process of ongoing improvement.* Great Barrington, MA: North River Press.

Mahowald, R. and Connor, S. (2012). "Worldwide SaaS and Cloud Software 2012-2016 Forecast and 2011 Vendor Shares," *International Data Corporation.* http://www.idc.com/getdoc.jsp?containerId=236184

Khoshafian, S. (2015). "Digital Transformation with Internet of Things in Intelligent BPM." In *CIOReview,* March 2015, pp. 26-27, https://magazine.cioreview.com/March-2015/BPM/

Khoshafian, S., and Buckiewicz, M. (1995). *Introduction to Groupware, Workflow, and Workgroup Computing.* New York: John Wiley and Sons.

Khoshafian, S. et al. (2011). "Voice of the Network through Social BPM." Co-authors Patrick Tripp and Steve Kraus. Published in Social BPM: Work, Planning and Collaboration under the Impact of Social Technology, *2011 BPM and Workflow Handbook* Published by Future Strategies Inc., in association with the Workflow Management Coalition (WfMC). Edited by Layna Fischer.

Khoshafian, S. (2014). *Intelligent BPM: The Next Wave for Customer-Centric Business Applications.* Pega eBook publication. https://www.pega.com/insights/resources/intelligent-bpm-next-wave-customer-centric-business-applications

Khoshafian, S., and Rostetter, C. (2015). "Digital Prescriptive Maintenance." *In Internet of Things, Process of Everything, BPM Everywhere* published by Future Strategies, Inc., Lighthouse Point, Florida.

Victories, V. (2015). "4 Types of Cloud Computing Deployment models you need to know." https://www.ibm.com/developerworks/community/blogs/722f6200-f4ca-4eb3-9d64-8d2b58b2d4e8/entry/4_Types_of_Cloud_Computing_Deployment_Model_You_Need_to_Know1?lang=en

Business Rules Design as Enabler for Intelligent Process Solutions

Kay Winkler, Negocios y Soluciones Informáticas S.A., Panama

INTRODUCTION

Adaptive Case Management and Digital Transformation are trending terms used by most vendors in the field of BPM. The showcased platforms are acclaimed for their overarching premise—and capabilities—to more effectively and faster than ever before bridge the gap between customers and businesses. The ensuing propaganda also lends itself to create false impressions that there may be premade technological solutions available to the end users that would fit the criteria of a true adaptive case management (ACM) system. That, of course, is somewhat oxymoronic to the whole concept of knowledge worker enabling and supporting solutions itself. Smart processes that allow for adaptations are usually the result of iterative process enhancements within mature and scalable Business Process Management Suites (iBPMS) that earn their prefix "i", for *intelligent*, through strategic features, enabling the definition, storage, enforcement and discovery of business rules.

This chapter is dedicated to exactly these features and to the practical guidelines of how to leverage business rules throughout real-life BPM implementations. The key questions that will be answered throughout this section cover:

- What is the significance of rules in business processes?
- Why is it important to differentiate between process rules and business rules?
- What practical approaches exist for rules discovery?
- How can rules be effectively managed as part of BPM?
- How can embedded business rules lead to intelligent processes?

The chapter will put emphasis on providing applied insights to accomplishing the feat of progressive process improvements to the point of obtaining adaptive business solutions. Most of this can be achieved without having to replace your tried and proven technologies but by rather complementing them with a mix of rule-driven solutions and accompanying implementation strategies.

THE IMPORTANCE OF RULES

Setting boundaries

In one of the latest discussions over at BPM.com, the authors pondered about the importance of defining BPMS as an overarching and unifying concept that should not embody any or only the least number of possible borders among features, technologies and users versus delimiting certain aspects of such a platform to achieve an elevated level of control and clearer ownership (Schooff, 2017).

There seem to be two general schools of thought. On one hand, there's the assumption that due to the encompassing nature of end-to-end processes, resulting from successful BPM initiatives, the BPMS, as the underlying technology, has also to be completely boundary-less. Contrary to this impression is the understanding that the aspect of technology, the BPMS in this case, doesn't necessarily equal the solution it is hosting (the different business processes). From this point of view, experts agree that while it is the aim of BPM to connect people and departments with an uninterrupted value stream toward the end-customer, a clear segregation of BPM platform components and assigned owners is not only something to be desired but something necessary for a long-term strategy of the company's Business Process Management initiative.

This consideration can also be extended to the process component-level itself. Typical processes that are centered and organized around humans and human activities usually contain two macro operational components; one being a commercial component (sales, negotiation and decisioning: "time to yes") and the other being the actual execution itself (post sales: e.g. contracts, disbursements and other paperwork: "time to cash").

A simplified view of an end-to-end process, assigning responsibilities to different process components:

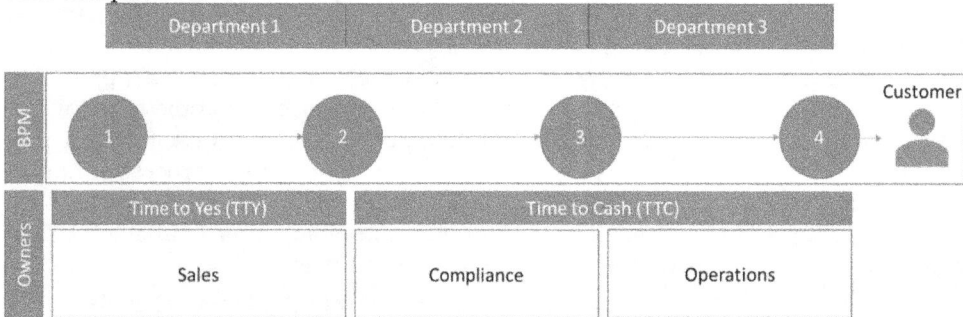

Figure 1 – End-to-End process, covering company value chain with different process component owners; Winkler, Kay; 2017

While both components describe indispensable parts of an integral value stream for the company, most likely, both will have different owners, KPIs and SLAs.

In that sense, not only would one have to segregate the technical scope of a BPM implementation (not to duplicate legacy or ERP functions, for instance) but the business processes themselves, which should be segregated too by their core functions and goals.

That allows for clear ownership, associated project management control and focused KPI measurements. Of course, that does NOT mean process isolation or silos. Through methodologies, process frameworks, standardization (such as BPMN, CMMN, DMN etc.), even APIs, conceptual as well as technical integrations will be achieved. It is of absolute importance that processes are horizontally and vertically integrated and "talking" to each other. However, in the capacity of highly-standardized pieces of the bigger BPM puzzle and not as a huge "process blob."

The Association of Business Process Management Professionals (ABPMP) has listed a total of 10 different roles that at some point would be responsible for the company's process management (Andrew Spanyi, 2013). The final quantity, types and levels of dedication of those roles in any given organization will end up depending on a variety of factors, from budgetary constraints over process maturity to the overall BPM strategy in place.

As will become apparent during the later paragraphs, the process and business rules occupy a special place in terms of ownership and management, demanding singular attention from all stakeholders.

This is simplified visualization of an end-to-end process, assigning responsibilities to different BPMS components:

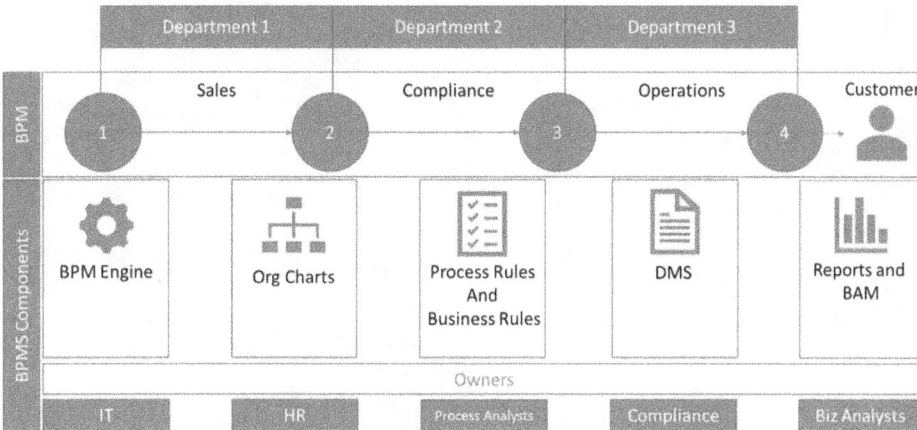

Figure 2 – End-to-End process, covering the company value chain with different BPMS component owners; Winkler, Kay; 2017

What can Rules do for You?

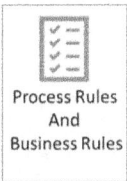

On an elementary level, rules in business processes are the elements in charge of handling all the logical sequences of the tasks and assignments themselves. BPM engines, in that sense contain, as part of their design interfaces, tools that allow the business process owners and designers to embed the different pathways a workflow can take, depending on defined conditions that may occur during runtime. These features, permitted to enhance the logical definitions of a business process, have been an integral part of process platforms for over a decade now.

As the following graphic shows, there has been an important evolution of workflow tools advancing to BPMS and beyond, thanks to technologies that provide not only more transparency but also more granular capacities of designing, visualizing and executing processes. The capability of being able to visualize and putting into action conditional process rules has been pivotal for that step.

A principal overview of technological components of an BPMS, compared to an iBPMS and the correspondent role of BREs:

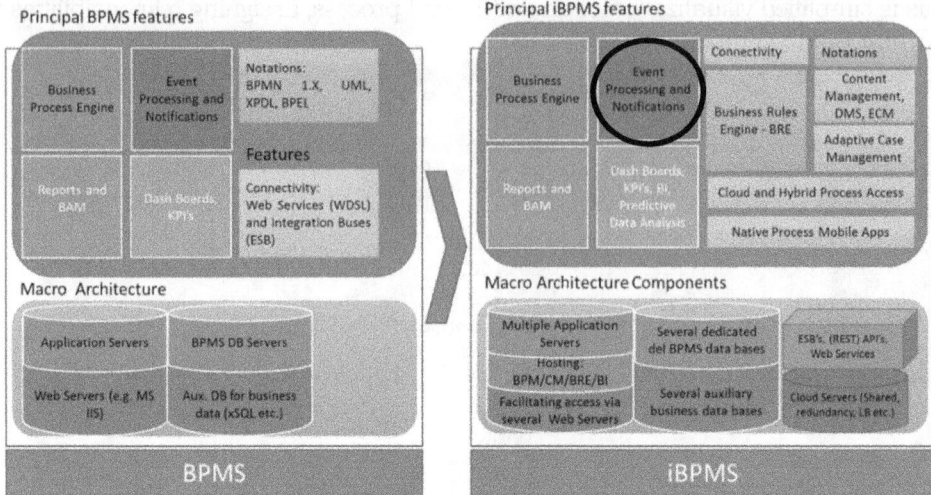

Figure 3 – From BPMS to iBPMS with BRE and other components;
Winkler, Kay; 2017

These advancements in BPM have been further leveraged by standardizations through notations that reduce ambiguities during design, communication and technical translations of logical process designs. These ultimately boil down to the design of conditional, logical and event-driven sequences for the workflow to follow.

Basic flowcharting, in that sense, has been around for even longer than BPM and workflow tools have themselves. However, one of the most important value propositions of standardized modeling within a BPMS is overcoming the limitations of being able to only create very simple process diagrams, evolving toward process models. Standards such as the BPMN 2.0 (Business Process Model and Notation) and UML (Unified Modelling Language), set forth by the Object Management Group (OMG), have enabled business stakeholders to visually design and to define dynamic models with rich icon sets and even very complex processes that contain sequential rules (Object Management Group, 2011).

Relying on dedicated tools for the definition and execution of the process "if-then-else" furthermore enhances the underlying notion of everything BPM: the continued improvements of process implementations through evolving iterations. Having established the standardized, basic rules framework that enforces the process routing in an initial implementation (baseline), results now can be periodically measured and correlated to these basic rules. For example, if we face a bottleneck in production during a seasonal high, we can establish and put into production a process enhancement with a conditional rule that detects slow response times or elevated market demands. This condition then can assure a more distributed task allocation, dynamically leveraging multiple resources for a limited period.

Back in 2003, Will van der Aalst founded the Workflow Patterns (WFP) initiative whose contents still represent most of present-day business process conditions that must be optimized and automated by BPM professionals. On the process flow level, van der Aalst differentiates between four major pattern groups: The control flow, resource, data end exception perspective of a business process. The WFP also provides a basic level of comparison and evaluation of the major, commonly used notations among these four perspectives, providing a business analyst with a comprehensive overview of typical scenarios to cover with BPM and which criteria to apply when evaluating competing notation methods (Aalst, 2010).

In practice, most of these logical sequences are still either designed in code or in BPMN as part of a self-contained platform. This of course, enormously limits the integral application, control and collaboration throughout the whole organization in terms of an integral process rules implementation. The lack of exposure of business rules, even on that very simple level, inhibits the formation of a clear business ownership over the implemented processes and naturally, the formation of process centers of excellence, which in turn forecloses the organization to enhance its BPM maturity level.

Administrators sharing access to multiple components within a typical BPMS:

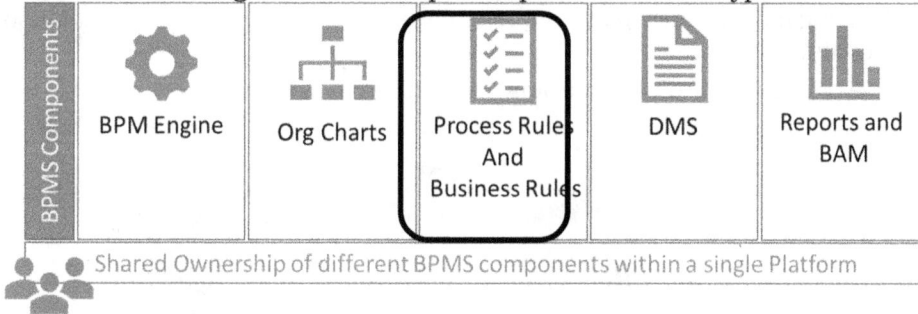

Figure 4 – Shared BPMS component administration; Winkler, Kay; 2017

Intelligent Design

It is primarily this step, coming from simple process flow rules and going to a full-fledged business rules engine (BRE), that enables BPMS to call themselves "intelligent."

In the previous paragraphs we described how logical sequence rules as part of the BPM, be it leveraged by BPMN or something else, help to define and to automate the conditional paths the process can take, confronted with different sets of circumstances (external data triggers, real-life market events or even something as simple as a specific form output). This "rules dimension" can be coined as horizontal business process rules as it describes the process behavior on the horizontal level.

Example of Process Rules describing the logical workflow sequence:

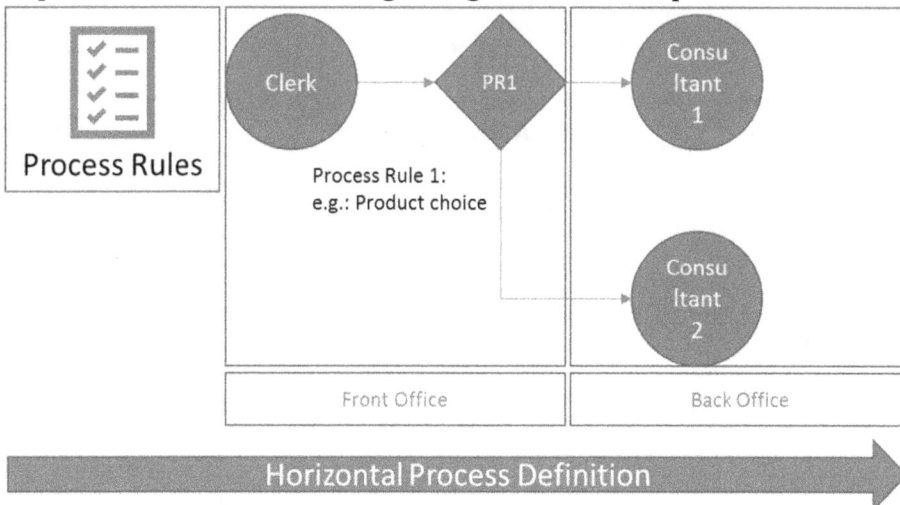

Figure 5 – Horizontal flow charting with process rules; Winkler, Kay; 2017

Drilling down on the process definition, you will always find components such as case evaluations, calculations, risk analysis or credit scoring. These rules are equally as important as the horizontal rulesets.

However, compared to process rules, do these process definitions rather describe the logical process design on a vertical level, without directly altering the process flow itself? A specific set of rules, for instance, may identify the validity of applying a discount to a specific purchase by one of our customers and then proceeds to calculate the amount of such a discount automatically, displaying the result in a specifically designated form field. The subsequent workflow step in this example process would remain being the customer payment, regardless of the application and calculation of the discount.

Example of Business Rules describing "internal" workflow logic:

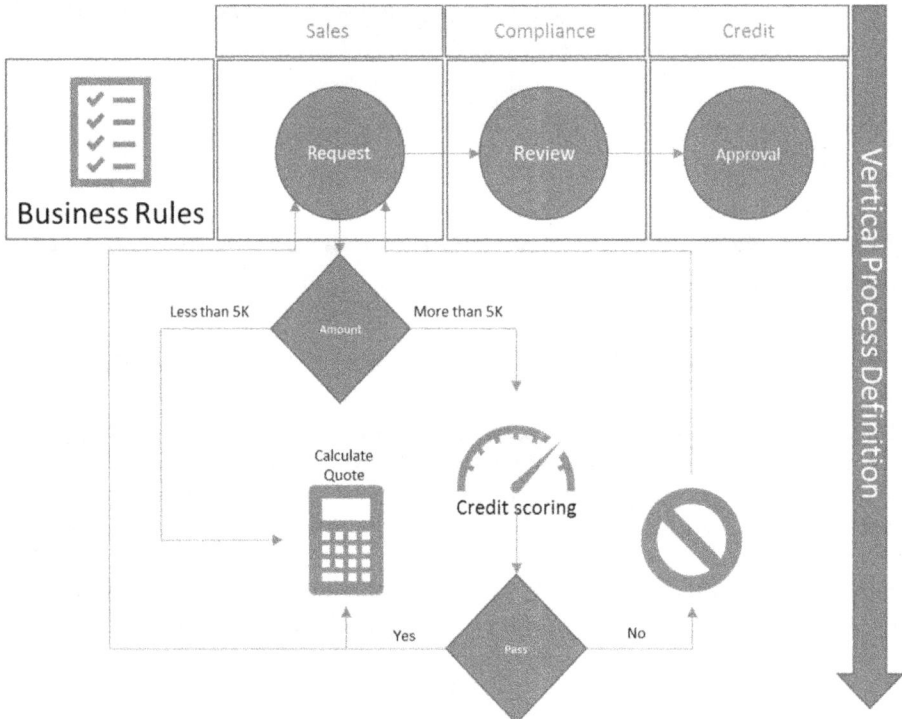

Figure 6 – Vertical process definition with business rules;
Winkler, Kay; 2017

Modern rules engines can combine and manage the definitions that detail both, the horizontal as well as the vertical process sequences, based on the evaluation and interpretation of internal and external data entries, including the integration of data sources that are completely independent from the automated process itself.

The biggest differentiator that would define a BRE over a simple set of rules that have been hard-coded into scripts (web services or BPMS definitions in BPMN) is the consolidation of all process-relevant policies and validations within the unified and dedicated repository that interacts with one or several processes at once. In addition, a BRE would be tightly integrated into all the organization's processes but be also completely exposed and independently manageable by the company's designated business analysts.

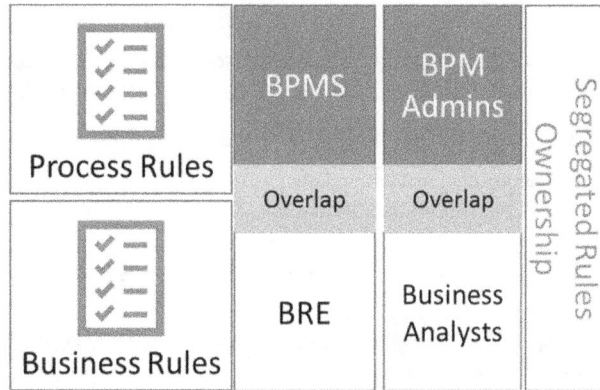

Figure 7 – Segregated ownerships per rules type, Winkler, Kay; 2017

Such an architecture supports and leverages a broad collaboration of all the business process stakeholders alike, beginning from the end-customer all the way to the back-office resources. Rules can be jointly designed, tested, validated during run time, measured and finally continuously improved with the appropriate versioning that such a lifecycle management would imply, as visualized in figure 7.

Several aspects must be considered by the BPM stakeholders, though. Firstly, as with most of all the other rules components that are mentioned throughout this chapter, BRE is accompanied by a certain level of redundancy. Because the rules engine can manage complex vertical calculations such as loan applications, it also is suitable for defining the conditions and resulting pathways a process can take, a function that normally would fall under the responsibility of the BPMS design utilities. The business process administrators will have to analyze variables including cost, ease-of-use and accessibility to define where to consolidate what kind of process logic.

Furthermore, an organization would have to decide also on when to implement a component such as a business rules engine. That way, a company could start automating business processes with a typical BPMS and later complement this architecture with a BRE, versus acquiring from the very start an iBPMS platform that contains such an engine by default. More details and guidelines on leveraging existing BPM technologies for this and other purposes can be found in the book "Digital Transformation with BPM" (Winkler, *BPM Farming: Reap Benefits by Nurturing Your Existing Platforms*, 2017). Finally, there are several new and alternative technologies within the realm BPM that can pose a substitution or a complement to a BRE (depending on the company's requirements). For example, users now have access to the very intuitive and visual rules notation standard known as Decision Model and Notation (DMN - currently in its version 1.1) as a native part of several leading Business Process Management Suites (Object Management Group, 2016).

In short, DMN will have an important contribution to the world of BPM, bringing concepts and technologies of BPMS and Business Rules Engines closer together.

With BRE, DMN and simple rules definitions utilizing BPMN, a more complete, standardized and actionable blueprint of business processes can be achieved as part of a single framework – and yes – sometimes even within a single suite.

That concept naturally extends also to the Case Management Model and Notation (CMMN) for BPMS with an "ACM flavor" or for pure ACM players.

PROCESS RULES VERSUS BUSINESS RULES

As seen above, the rules that define the process on a horizontal level describe how the workflow pathways branch out, given different internal and external stimuli. In each given process, there are multiple sets of vertical rules that describe the "micro-logic" of cases within the different workflow steps.

Depending on the technologies used for designing, evaluating and finally implementing those different logics, the first reason for differentiating between process rules and business rules become apparent. A typical scenario for hosting the workflow sequences on the process level would be the use of the design tools that are provided with utilities such as BPMN which, in turn, will for most BPMS vendors also be the place where the related rules are going to be stored. It is also still very common that none of the process designs and their corresponding rules are segregated and exposed from the BPMS engine, but instead are still a tightly-integrated part of the process repositories. In that relation, the users with access to the BPM design tools will also end up having access to the embedded process rules. For smaller organizations and initial automation initiatives this may not represent a challenge. It can become cumbersome however, once a company achieves a higher BPM maturity level, having optimized and automated the principal part of its end-to-end processes and value chains.

Not having a dedicated team in charge of monitoring, managing and improving over the long haul all the business logics, vertical and horizontal, will in fact prevent the company from achieving sustainable competitive advantages from its BPM solutions.

Having progressed with the implementation of complementary technologies like a business rules engine or DMN utilities, it is only logical for the company, from there onward, to also designate responsible users for each component; on one hand, the team in charge of managing the process rules that remain being part of the BPMS design tools and on the other hand the team that will be responsible for the contents of a BRE and/or DMN.

Business rules are, by nature, far more complex in design and interpretation than process rules. While process rules depict only logical flow sequences, business rules contain much of what the end-users tend to brand "the brains of the process." That is also the reason why, for certain process types, especially in the financial industry (Winkler, *Benefits of Policy and Rules Driven Processes in LatAm Retail Banking Automation*, 2017), a business rules engine can become a synonym for credit scoring systems (ref. see the example case "Example for Business Rules in Banking", below).

So, it's not surprising to observe even in mid-sized companies that teams of three or more resources are assigned full time to the management of a BRE. It is also very common for BRE knowledge workers to combine rules management with (big) data analysis.

Business rules include the validation of very simple data entries, like date selections, customer identification validations and socio-demographic categorizations. In the request step of a process, for example, the general inquiry section of the form may ask for the customer ID number (passport, driver's license, SS number etc.). Based on that number, a rule of the BRE is being triggered and executed, invoking a web service to check in the company's CRM and billing systems if the requester already exists as a customer and/or if he exists as a previous requester from a prior date. If that would be the case, the invoked web service would then populate all relevant information from the organization's correspondent systems back to the BPM front end form. Contrary, the end-user will have to fill out the process forms from scratch.

From there, business rule types grow exponentially more complex and can involve standardized components, such as in the case of the DMN where you would define and apply value expressions, boxed expressions (including decision tables), business knowledge and decisions.

From a practical point of view, one usually encounters the following types of business rules: business rules that approximate and therefore potentially conflict with process rules (basic routing), data validations and calculations. Normally, each rule either triggers a furthering rule or provokes an action within the form (micro level) or the process (macro level).

Business rules can enrich the automation of a business process in a variety of ways: system integrations can be more balanced out, products and services can be tailored closer than ever before to the very specific needs of a potential customer and complex calculations can be embedded into processes without coding, using natural and logical expressions.

For the latter, it has proven helpful to structure formulas by using fixed expressions together with variables, as part of mathematical equations.

Example: $Y = C1a + C2b + C3c$. Y in that case can represent an expression of "income" for a prospect customer that is comprised of income type 1 through 3 (C), while the factors a, b and c stand for eventual penalties or rewards the company may apply for different income types (for example, a devaluation of elevated-risk income types).

Example scenarios for Business Rules

A particular usage scenario for business rules that enrich the practicality of processes, is the dynamic control of document checklists.

For human-centric workflows, as part of the validation and approval portion of activities, usually different documents are required for the customer to procure, sign and to deliver to the company. A dedicated set of business rules can be employed for associating a dynamic checklist of documents to the process that identifies per case (risk determination) how far the customer can advance, without having to comply with determined documents of said list. Being adjustable, parameters of the document types, points of hard stops in the process and risk levels (e.g. decision tables), a great deal of flexibility and agility can be added to the BPM solutions, without to having to adjust the process models or any code.

For the financial industry business rules are especially relevant, complex and very common to be combined with business process management solutions.

A typical process here would describe the commercial activities of a bank as part of its consumer loan activities, selling products like credit cards, personal loans, car loans and mortgages. In all these cases, the classification of process components into the categories of the "time-to-yes" and the "time-to-cash" portions apply as well, to which the business rules are aligned respectively.

Often, the business rules or policies can turn out to be the most complex piece to the "retail banking process puzzle" and which usually will have to be automated to an important degree. Some of these automations will take place within credit scoring systems (integrated into—but independent from—the BPM implementation) while some of the other rules will reside on the very process flow and form level.

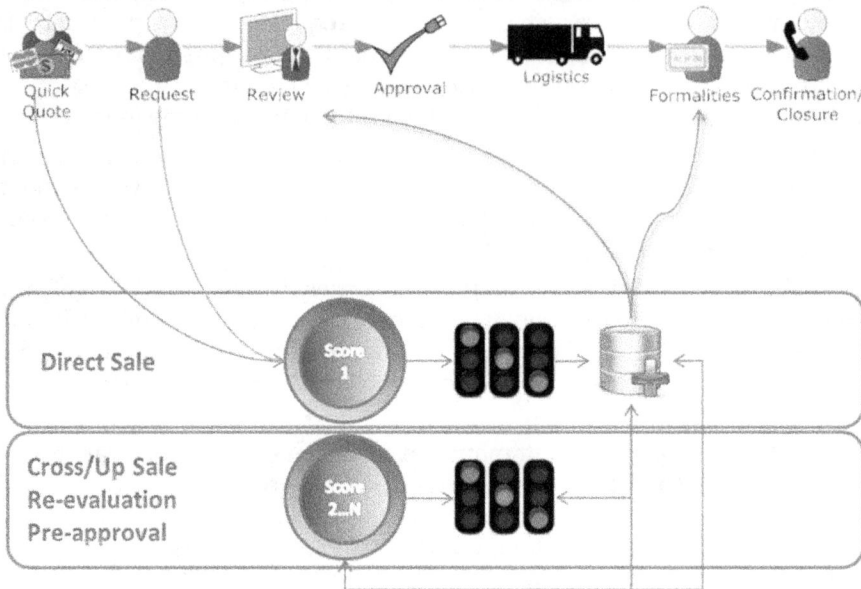

Figure 8 – Vertically embedded business rules in retail banking process; Winkler, Kay; 2017

As the figure above shows, the evaluation of retail banking policies doesn't only take place within different layers of the solution (within forms, process flow and third-party applications like credit scoring systems, such as Experian) but also among different process steps with gradually increasing levels of severity and rigorousness the further the process progresses, being the disbursement steps at the point of no return.

Vertically, the (simplified) policy validation of a retail banking process distributes as follows:

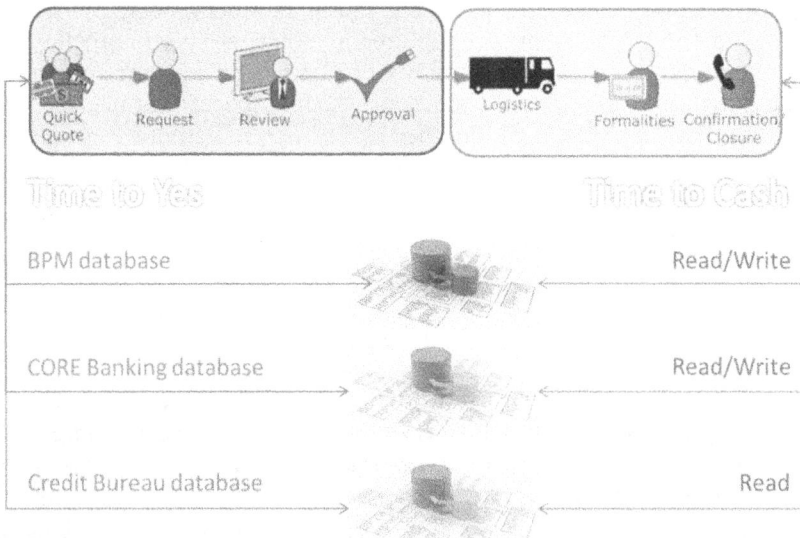

Figure 9 – Vertically embedded business rules in retail banking processes; Winkler, Kay; 2017

The most complete, complex and thorough policy validation of those processes usually occur in the first two process steps:

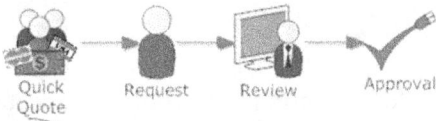

Filters	Inputs	Results from
Demographic data	BPM Process Form	BPM Database
Client profile	BPM Database*	BPM Database*
Debt level	BPM Process Form**	BPM Database*
Calculation of exposure limits	BPM Process Form	BPM Database*

* Can be alternatively obtained from the Core Banking database.

** Alternatively, the Credit Bureau can be consulted from this point forward.

Figure 10 – Business rules that serve as a pre-credit bureau filter in retail banking processes; Winkler, Kay; 2017

Building upon previous evaluation results, using compound business rules that stretch multiple process steps, we see:

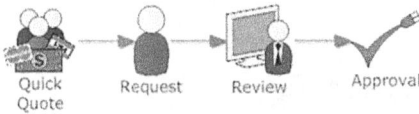

Filters	Inputs	Results from
Demographic data	BPM Process Form	BPM Database
Client profile	BPM Database*	BPM Database*
Internal References (KYC, Blacklists)	Core Banking database	Core Banking database
External References (Bureau, Blacklists)	External databases	BPM Database
Debt Level	BPM Form and Core Banking database	BPM Database*
Calculation of exposure limits	BPM Process Form	BPM Database*
Validation of physical and virtual documents	BPM Process Form and ECM/DMS integration	BPM Database*

* Can be alternatively obtained from the Core Banking database.

Figure 11 – Business rules that combine internal process data and external bureau credit scorings in retail banking processes; Winkler, Kay; 2017

In this example, it can be observed that a great deal of automated business rules is being sequentially executed in a vertical manner within the process, especially during its initial few steps. As for all rule evaluations, it is important to keep in mind that the data inputs and triggers do not only stem from parent processes, but also from integrated data sources within the company and from external sources.

RULES DISCOVERY AND MANAGEMENT

Discovery

Just as with pretty much everything else in BPM, process and business rules must abide to the very same lifecycle as continuously-improved business processes do.

The DMAIC (define, measure, analyze, improve and control) methodology perfectly fits the BPM discipline and applies on the micro level to the rules that define the process logic. This data-driven process improvement strategy is also responsible for linking the expected process results not only to its different rules but more importantly, also to the responsible human resources behind the design and instrumentation of the process assets.

In that sense, it has been a proven practice to team up all the relevant stakeholders when it comes designing, measuring the results and improving upon the process business logic. It is not really a viable scenario, yet a still commonly-committed mistake, to isolate data and statistical experts during the rules design phase from the customer facing resources and process owners who experience firsthand the day-to-day results of these "contraptions." This reasoning encompasses also the iteration of any rules in BPM. So, naturally, rules discoveries and their later management must go hand-in-hand by obligation.

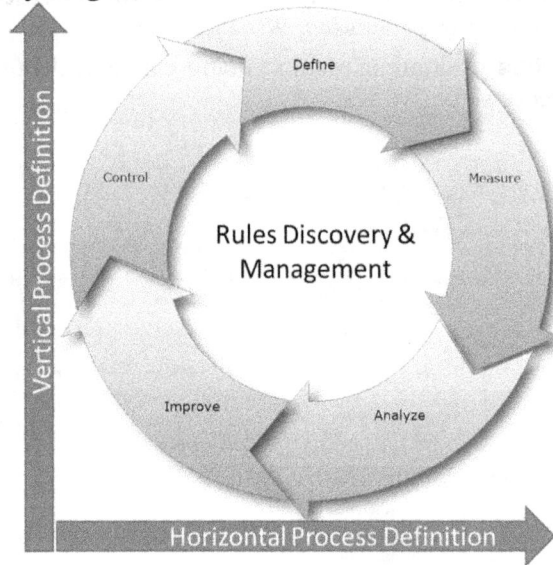

Figure 12 – Rules Discovery and Management within the DMAIC life cycle; Winkler, Kay; 2017

Understanding rules as enforcing elements for the business process to achieve the company's strategic goals, then these must be perfectly aligned to said strategy. This means any rule, be it a process or a business rule, should be formulated as a measurable expression that caters toward a numeric KPI that in turn directly contributes to achieving the company's strategic goals.

Example:

Strategic goals	Goals	KPIs (inputs)	Rules (Output generation)	Decision
Be a regional leader in customer	Each credit evaluation (CE) per	Time-to-yes per request measured in business hours.	If CE =< 1.5bh then Output = A;	B – Normal process flow.

service experience (CSX)	purchase request < 2 business hours (bh).		Else then Output = B.	A – Expedited process flow and email notification to superior.
	Each customer spends less than 0.25bh in branch per request.	Process Step Time T(step) (e.g. In Store Quote Step) in working hours, per request.	If T(step) =< 0.167bh then Output = C; Else then Output = D.	C - Normal resource pool. D – Assign from queue to additional resource pool.

Table 1 – Examples of rules designing, based on the company's strategy; Winkler, Kay; 2017

Analog to the design of indicators for process performance management (PPM), *the underlying rules* can be created with several levels of details and complexities in mind.

David McCoy from Gartner Inc., for example, suggests the differentiation of at least two levels when *designing performance indicators;* the workflow level (a more detailed view of the different variables) and the process level (representing the macro indicators) (McCoy, 2013). This can be translated to the design of rules as well, in which case the business analysts can define all-encompassing guidelines (rule books) that are comprised of different sets of individual process or business rules.

Technologies that have been identified as being disruptive to the BPM landscape will play a key role of how the rules discovery will take place in the future (Winkler, BPM.COM, 2017).

Big data analytics, predictive statistics and specific process scenario forecasting in conjunction with AI will allow that modern BPM platforms are going to be able to procure their own sets of rules which automatically will align to the organizations' goals. For the moment though, the biggest recognition for technological advancements in the BPM rules space seems to be the introduction of the previously-mentioned decision model and notation (DMN), becoming part of the standard design tools for some of the BPMS (or, alternatively, external and complementary DMN toolkits).

Management

For effective rules management, in addition to establishing the described links among rules designers and the customer facing resources, and making sure that these rules are designed with the company's strategy in mind, one of the most pivotal factors to acknowledge, in reality, is that the rules landscape is anything but homogeneous.

In truth, you will have different rules of different natures all over the place. There will be rules between the hand-off points among different processes. Within these processes, there will be a considerable amount of process rules describing most of logical workflow sequences. Then, there will be rules on the step level that define how the form interacts with the end-user, depending on different inputs (example: dynamic form elements that are either displayed or hidden, depending on a specific field value). In addition, you will most likely have also the micro rules that take care of all the business policies and calculations that the process embodies.

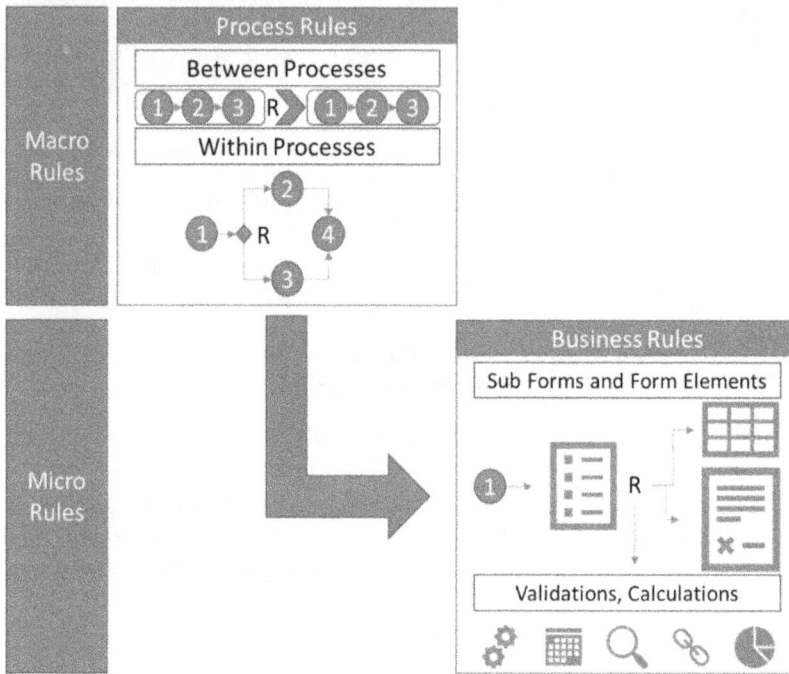

Figure 13 – Distributed BPM rules landscape; Winkler, Kay; 2017

In that relation, before assigning the owners for the rules administration, creating a graphical blueprint is recommended. Such a blueprint should preferably contain a visual representation of the different processes, their KPIs and associated rules.

Using this graphical layout, owners of rules can then consider the impacts of macro rules from one process to another, aligning to the company's end-to-end value stream, but it also makes it easier to segregate these ownerships among themselves. While macro and process rules most likely will be managed by BPM administrators, which can be process owners or department heads for instance, micro and business rules on the other hand, will be more likely to be managed by business analysts (if there is a BRE in place) and/or IT resources in charge of maintaining all the complementary scripts of policy validations and calculations.

Recognizing the diverse nature that the "brains of the process" really represents, it is only logical to also make sure that the subsequent diverse owners of the different rules are unified under one roof. This can be accomplished by either assigning a governing figure, acting in competence of a Chief Rules Office (CRO), or a broader governing body, like a Center of Excellence for rules.

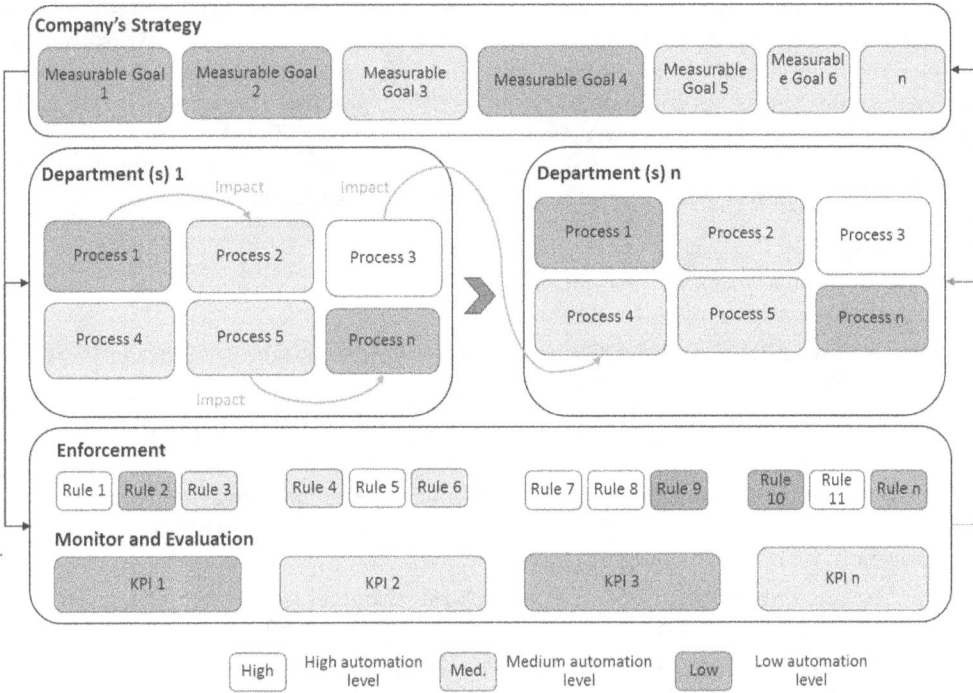

Figure 14 – Process and Rules Blueprint; Winkler, Kay; 2017

Another significant aspect to consider for the rules administration, would be the periodicity of revision cycles. It is quite typical to see at least 2-5 process improvements per year for successful BPM implementations year (Winkler, BPM.COM, 2017). Because it is the very nature and one of the core purposes of BPM as a discipline to encourage frequent improvements, these changes are not only to be expected but also necessary to ensure long-term success. Each iteration cycle, by obligation, must include the revision of the rules and their correlation with the obtained process results (through KPIs). The Center of Excellence will have to ensure the corresponding incorporation of the rules evaluation as part of the overall process revision procedure.

The adequate technical design of the business and process rules is one of the most determining factors that define the velocity and complexity (hence the level of effort) of their ongoing adaptation and improvement. For example, it would require a considerable higher level of effort (LoE) to change a scripted and hard-coded mortgage calculation each time a simple parameter of the formula changes, compared to simply changing the determined parameter within a database, leaving the rest of the formula untouched.

Rules equal Intelligence?

Neither the goals nor the effects of Business Process Management, for the most part, have been the substitution of the human element but rather its empowerment and its repositioning toward creative and strategic tasks within the value chain. Through successfully implementing BPM, businesses have been enabled to free up and to invest into R&D resources, even within the long tail of its products and services. That certainly holds true also for business and process rules.

Initially discovering, designing and implementing rules does not necessary mean that they are automated. As a first step, many companies consciously map and implement, but still manually execute these different rules. From there, there's a long way to begin automating the rules assets within the different technology layers that we summarized previously. That, in turn, is a stepping stone to start data-driven policy and rules discoveries. At some point these steps provide the user with a truly intelligent BPMS that produces its own rules within the threshold of the company's goals and policies, and which, at the same time, are based upon a well-structured and populated data universe, which allows for meaningful statistical analysis.

REFERENCES

Aalst, W. v. (2010). *Workflow Patterns*. Retrieved from http://www.workflowpatterns.com/

Andrew Spanyi. (2013). Process Organization. In A. International, *Common Body of Knowledge v3.0* (p. 323). ABPMP International.

McCoy, D. (2013). Process Performance Management. In A. International, *CBOK v3.0* (pp. 223-224). ABPMP International.

Object Management Group. (2011, January 03). *Object Management Group*. Retrieved from Documents Associated With Business Process Model And Notation: http://www.omg.org/spec/BPMN/2.0/

Object Management Group. (2016, June). *Object Management Group*. Retrieved from Decision Model And Notation: http://www.omg.org/spec/DMN/

Schooff, P. (2017, March 23). *BPM.COM*. Retrieved from Does Every Business Process Need to Have Boundaries?: https://bpm.com/component/easydiscuss/4823-does-every-business-process-need-to-have-boundaries?Itemid=#reply-4829

Winkler, K. (2017). Benefits of Policy and Rules Driven Processes in LatAm Retail Banking Automation. In L. Fischer, *BPM in Financial Services*. Future Strategies, Inc. http://bpm-books.com

Winkler, K. (2017). BPM Farming: Reap Benefits by Nurturing Your Existing Platforms. In L. Fischer, *Digital Transformation with BPM* (pp. 43-56). Future Strategies Inc. http://bpm-books.com

Winkler, K. (2017, April 04). *BPM.COM*. Retrieved from What Will Be the Top 3 Most Disruptive Technologies to Impact BPM (Specifically BPMS Platforms and BPM Vendors) Over the Next 12-18 Months, and Why?: https://bpm.com/bpm-today/in-the-forum/4873-what-will-be-the-top-3-most-disruptive-technologies-to-impact-bpm-specifically-bpms-platforms-and-bpm-vendors-over-the-next-12-18-months,-and-why#reply-4874

Winkler, K. (2017, May 18). *BPM.COM*. Retrieved from What Is a Clear Sign That a Company Has Been Successful with BPM?: https://bpm.com/bpm-today/in-the-forum/5021-what-is-a-clear-sign-that-a-company-has-been-successful-with-bpm#reply-5030

Transforming Compliance Regulations into User Experience

An Ontology-based Compliance Support Framework for Adaptive Case Management

Christoph Czepa and Uwe Zdun, University of Vienna, Austria, Christoph Ruhsam, ISIS Papyrus Europe, Austria

ABSTRACT

Compliance regulations are still often hard-coded in prescriptive, rigid business processes and perceived as a burden and obstacle for knowledge work, or even worse, they are simply evaluated *post ex* (i.e. through audits) without providing any prior IT tool support during case enactment. In this chapter, we discuss how compliance regulations, specified by a domain-specific business vocabulary and semantics (business ontology) can be leveraged to enable compliance by *supporting* the knowledge workers rather than interfering with their work. Support can be provided in form of a natural language compliance rule editor using the terms from the domain specific business vocabulary (ontology-based compliance rules). This way, reactive as well as proactive guidance can be offered that takes both the compliance rules and the knowledge workers' past decisions into account to enhance the users' working experience. This opens the stage for new ACM-based business applications that truly serve the needs of business users focusing on delivering value to their customers.

INTRODUCTION

Many knowledge-intensive business domains (such as healthcare and banking sectors) are subject to a large amount of compliance requirements stemming from sources such as regulatory laws (e.g., Sarbanes-Oxley), standards (e.g., ISO 45001 - Occupational health and safety), best practices (e.g. ITIL) or company internal regulations. The classical approach for integrating such compliance requirements in the enactment of business processes are flow-driven, predefined business process models that become instantiated and executed by the business users. Assuming the business process model is defined correctly and the business users follow it exactly, we can be sure that business process instances are compliant. However, deviations from those predefined business processes become frequently necessary in reality. Collaborative case handling can simply not be prescribed because it must assess every situation of a case as it evolves among all involved parties and thus, has to allow the users to define the most appropriate next actions to optimally satisfy the customer needs. That situation empowers business users, respects them as knowledge workers and leverages their tacit knowledge and experience. This has led to flexible business process management approaches that enable business users to actively shape the enactment of business processes by skipping activities, performing ad-hoc activities, and defining and changing goals. *Adaptive Case Management* (ACM) is a major approach that enables knowledge workers to gain full control over the business process execution (cf. Tran Thi Kim et al. 2013, Pucher 2011; Swenson 2010).

Compliance regulations are often hard-coded in prescriptive, rigid business processes and thus, not available in a language that is understandable to business users. Consequently, they are perceived as a major obstacle for knowledge work ("the system does not allow me to do that"). Long maintenance cycles of the involved process models might cause a delayed support of new compliance requirements while outdated ones are still enforced. As a result, knowledge workers might be forced to conceal actions from the IT system to circumvent an outdated compliance implementation, and for relevant compliance requirements, knowledge workers do not get any automated support if the new requirements have not yet been implemented. The situation might be even worse when no compliance rules are implemented at all and compliance is just evaluated *post ex* (i.e. through audits) without providing any tool support for users to become aware of compliance violations during case enactment. In such a case, the knowledge workers are on their own and compliance violations are discovered when it is often too late to react and compensate. Insufficient compliance or non-compliance might have severe negative impact on a company and its employees (e.g., legal prosecution) as well as customers (frustration and bad customer experience).

In this chapter, we introduce a framework approach to enable compliance regulations in a positive context. Particularly, supporting compliance regulations in the right way has the potential to provide a better working experience for knowledge workers and a transparent quality measure for their work results. There are several aspects that are important for a meaningful compliance support in ACM:

- Firstly, compliance rule authoring and management must be the responsibility of the business user and not the responsibility of the IT department. By empowering the knowledge worker to understand and maintain the compliance rules, long maintenance cycles caused by software development can be avoided, and knowledge workers will no longer have the feeling of being constrained by the IT system.
- Secondly, for the practical success of business-driven compliance rule maintenance, a business user-friendly way to describe compliance regulations must be provided.
- Thirdly, the ACM system must leverage the introduced compliance rules to provide proactive as well as reactive guidance to the knowledge workers.

In summary, we discuss a compliance support framework for ACM that empowers the business user to gain full control over the implemented compliance rules by shifting the responsibility and control over implemented compliance rules from the IT department to the business domain. This way, compliance is positioned as a supportive rather than a prescriptive measure. The knowledge workers' user experience will be positively affected and the customer's experience will be increased which is the only reason for a business to deliver value to their customers. This is possible by providing support for a business ontology-driven compliance rule authoring tool. This tool offers a structured natural language grammar, based on the business-specific concepts and relationships that are present in the domain ontology, and it makes suggestions to complete user inputs based on the ontology. Behind the scenes, the structured natural language rules are transformed to technical representations that the ACM system uses to support the knowledge worker during case enactment. This support focuses both on suggestions to react to existing compliance violations and to pro-actively avoid compliance violations. The framework does not only take the specified compliance rules into account but it also leverages the past decisions made by knowledge workers for providing guiding recommendations for specific appropriate next actions.

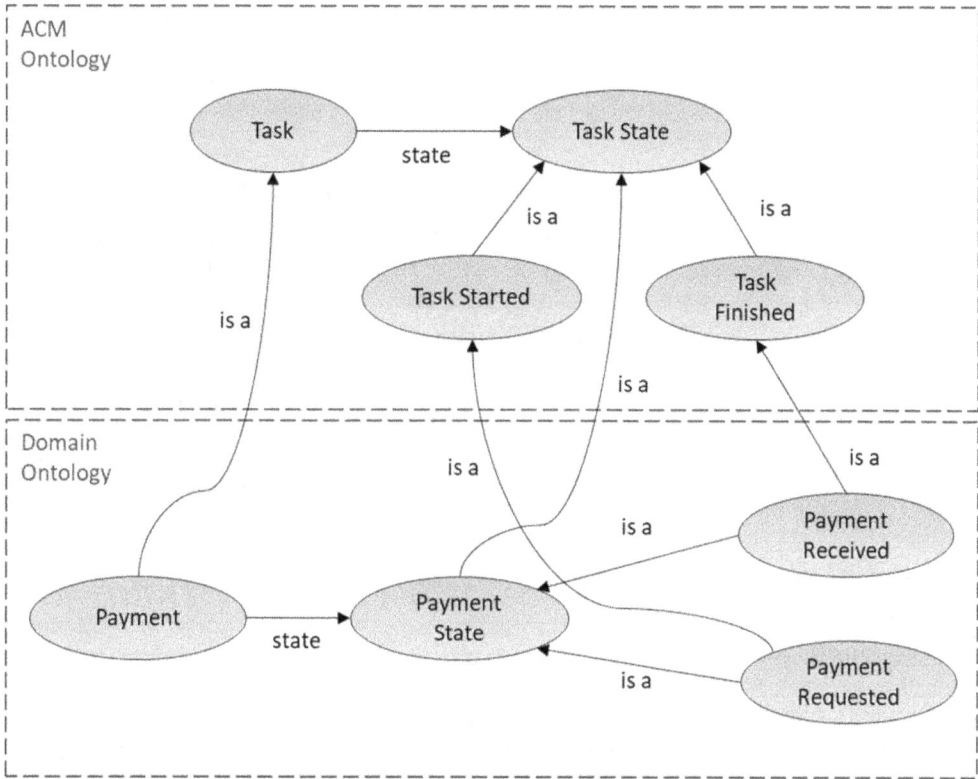

Figure 1: Mapping business domain concepts to ACM concepts

SPEAKING BUSINESS LANGUAGE: ONTOLOGY-BASED COMPLIANCE RULES

Ontologies represent the business vocabulary and semantics used in the context of a specific domain and thus, are an efficient method to organize information in a way that comes naturally to knowledge workers. The components of an ontology include concepts, attributes, relations and instances. They represent the domain specific entities which fully describe the knowledge of a specific business domain and thus, are being defined by the business people to match their daily experiences. The domain concepts refine the core concepts of ACM.

By this, the ACM system, for example, can be made aware that the domain concept "Payment" is in ACM terms a "Task" (cf. Figure 1). The example given in Figure 1 illustrates conceptually how the business domain specific ontology can be connected to the ontology of the ACM system. This architecture makes it possible to define compliance rules on basis of higher-level business concepts. For example, there could be a company policy; "Shipped orders must eventually be paid" which can be represented in a compliance language as "Shipping finished leads to Payment started". There are concepts derived from Payment, like Payment by Credit Card that are also covered by this compliance rule. Even a tighter integration of the business ontology is possible: Consider that not only concepts can be mapped to ACM elements but also larger structures of the domain ontology. For example, consider two concepts, "Order" and "Customer", and their relation "placed by". This would make it possible to derive a task "Place Order" with performer "Customer" directly from the domain ontology and to use this domain knowledge not only during case enactment but also for the definition of compliance rules.

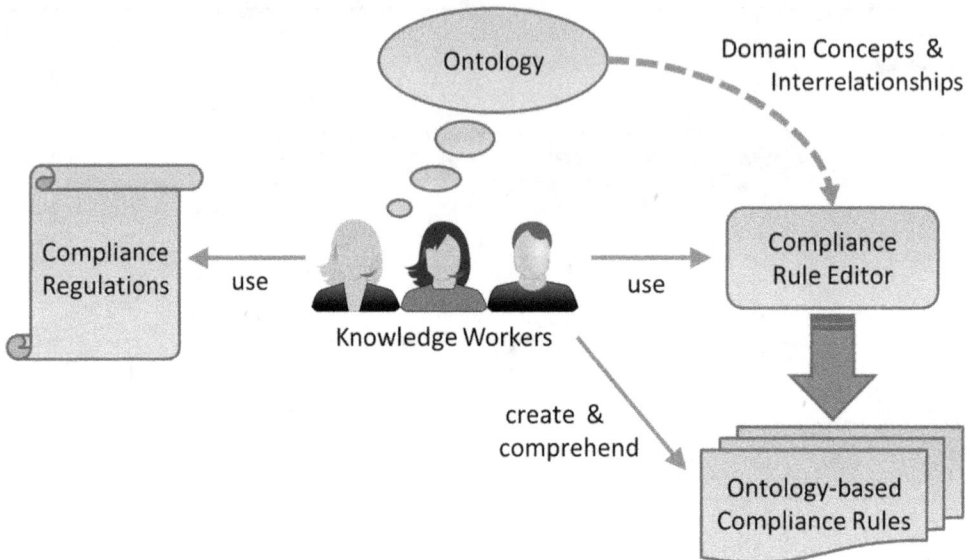

Figure 2: Ontology-based compliance rule language

Figure 2 shows schematically how compliance rules can be authored in a business user-friendly way. Knowledge workers can use the *Compliance Rule Editor* to author compliance rules. Moreover, they can define the *Ontology* of their business domain on which the rule creation is based upon. By using the *Compliance Rule Editor* knowledge workers can create *Ontology-based Compliance Rules* and define the scope they shall apply to (e.g. a specific case template). These rules consist of parts stemming from a compliance pattern-based grammar that abstracts underlying formal verification techniques and of other expressions that reflect the concepts and relations defined in the *Ontology*. The compliance rule language supported by the editor offers a simple interface to underlying complex technical representations that become completely abstracted.

Compliance rule patterns are used to express, for example, a qualitative time relation between events (e.g., "Payment finished precedes Shipment started") or to specify occurrences of events (e.g., "Shipment finished occurs only 1 time"). Compliance patterns stemming from different sources such as the Property Specifications Patterns (cf. Dwyer et al. 1999), the Compliance Rule Language CRL (cf. Elgammal et al. 2016) and the DecSerFlow language (cf. van der Aalst and Pesic 2006) can be integrated as they are used in the context of the compliance framework described in this chapter. Furthermore, the compliance pattern catalog (from which specific compliance rules can be defined by business users) can be extended by technical personnel (cf. Czepa et al. 2016a,b). Also the RuleSpeak and ConceptSpeak approach described by Ross (Ross 2013) and SBVR (Haarst 2013) can be taken.

For example, the *Response* pattern describes a temporal cause-effect compliance rule which can be expressed as

> ***Expression I* leads to *Expression II***

where *Expression I* is the cause and *Expression II* is the effect.

The *Precedence* pattern describes a temporal precondition and can be expressed as

> ***Expression I* precedes *Expression II***

where *Expression I* is the precondition that must be met before *Expression II* is allowed to happen.

An *Expression* is defined based on the ontology and enables leveraging domain-specific knowledge for the creation of compliance rules. The following ontology elements can be used to define such an ontology-based expression:

- *Concepts*: Concepts are the anchor for defining ontology expressions, so every ontology-based expression must start with a concept. If a concept is derived from a goal or activity, then the runtime state can be specified directly after the name of the concept.
- *Relations*: Once the context of a concept is defined, the relations of this concept to other concepts become obvious and usable.
- *Constraint Concepts*: Constraint concepts are specialized child concepts that allow defining specific constraints that determine whether an instance of the parent concept is also an instance of the constraint concept. These constraints may be related to attributes and/or relations of the parent concept.

During case enactment, ontology expressions are evaluated based on the actual instances and relations that are present in a case instance. That is, a concept expression is matched if there exists an instance of the concept. A relation expression is matched by a case instance if there exist two instances which have this relation.

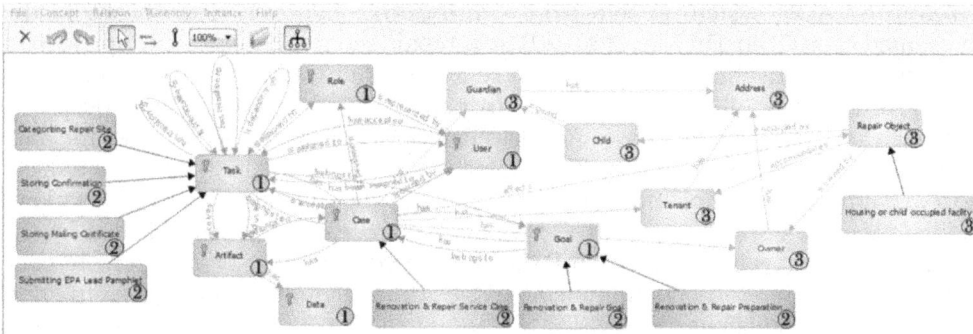

Figure 3: Ontology of a repair service management case

The compliance rule editor makes extensive use of the ontology while the business user types a rule. In the beginning, the business user starts typing and the compliance rule editor requests ontology concepts matching the (incomplete) user inputs (e.g., by matching the starting string of concepts or by computing the Levenshtein distance (Levenshtein 1966)). The response is a set of concepts which are proposed to the business user. The user either selects a proposed concept or continues typing. Eventually a proposed concept must be selected. Once the business user has selected a concept, it becomes possible to use the *context* of the specific domain concept. Thus, further auto-completions can be based on the set of relations of the concept. If appropriate, the editor makes not only proposals based on the ontology, but also proposes the possible elements of the compliance rule grammar to the user. When the user selects a specific relation, the context for suggesting further inputs is narrowed down to concepts that are potential targets of this relation originating from the already selected concept. Creating the compliance rule continues with processing user inputs to update the set of possible target concepts in the current relation context. Once the user has selected a target concept, the next part of the compliance rule could be either an element of the compliance rule grammar or a relation. For concepts that are derived from the application concepts *Goal* and *Activity*, the specific runtime state of these concepts can be directly specified after the name of each concept. For example, standard runtime states of goals are *Active* and *Completed*.

Figure 4: Creating a repair service management rule

A possible implementation for maintaining an ontology and for creating compliance rules in an ACM system is shown in Figure 3 and Figure 4, respectively. In the presented case (Tran Thi Kim et al. 2015), a repair service management application is in focus (for reusability ontologies can be grouped into sub-ontologies: (1) denotes the ACM ontology; the renovation & repair ontology (2) contains the concepts of activities for a repair service case and the repair object ontology (3) describes the data needed for a repair service case). The building and construction industry is subject to a vast amount of compliance rules stemming from sources such as regulatory laws and standards. For example, in the US, a compliance document published by the EPA (United States Environmental Protection Agency) in 2011 defines how to cope with potentially lead-contaminated paint during renovations, repairs and maintenance of buildings (cf. EPA 2011). The compliance guide applies to all activities that disturb painted surfaces in residential houses, apartments and child-occupied facilities such as schools and day-care centers built before 1978 in the US. Thus, an important activity is the categorization of the repair site before any kind of renovation work is performed. In Figure 4 the knowledge worker creates the ontology-based compliance rule

Categorizing Repair Site Completed <u>precedes</u> Renovation & Repair Preparation Goal Completed

which encodes exactly this requirement and assigns it to the case type *Renovation and Repair Service Case* that shall be affected by it.

"Oops, something went wrong": Detection and Notification of Compliance Violations

What good would the created compliance rules do if they could not be evaluated automatically? A major strength of the presented framework is exactly this capability. Every compliance rule is based on the concrete ontology of the business domain and a set of compliance patterns. As a result, it can be automatically transformed to technical representations and leveraged for detecting compliance violations automatically.

In general, ACM is non-prescriptive, so how do compliance rules and ACM fit together?

- Firstly, the knowledge worker has full control over the compliance rules.

- Secondly, the framework does not enforce compliance, but informs the user pro-actively and reactively of pending and existing compliance violations.

Figure 5 shows the automated compliance checking approach. The *Compliance Checker* is a framework component that observes the events happening in *Case Enactment*. If a situation is encountered that violates an *Ontology-based Compliance Rule*, the checker updates the runtime state of the compliance rule. Runtime states of compliance rules are integral parts of case enactment, so the compliance checking component reports these states to the case instance. On basis of this information, the user interface of the ACM software notifies the business user of existing or pending compliance violations.

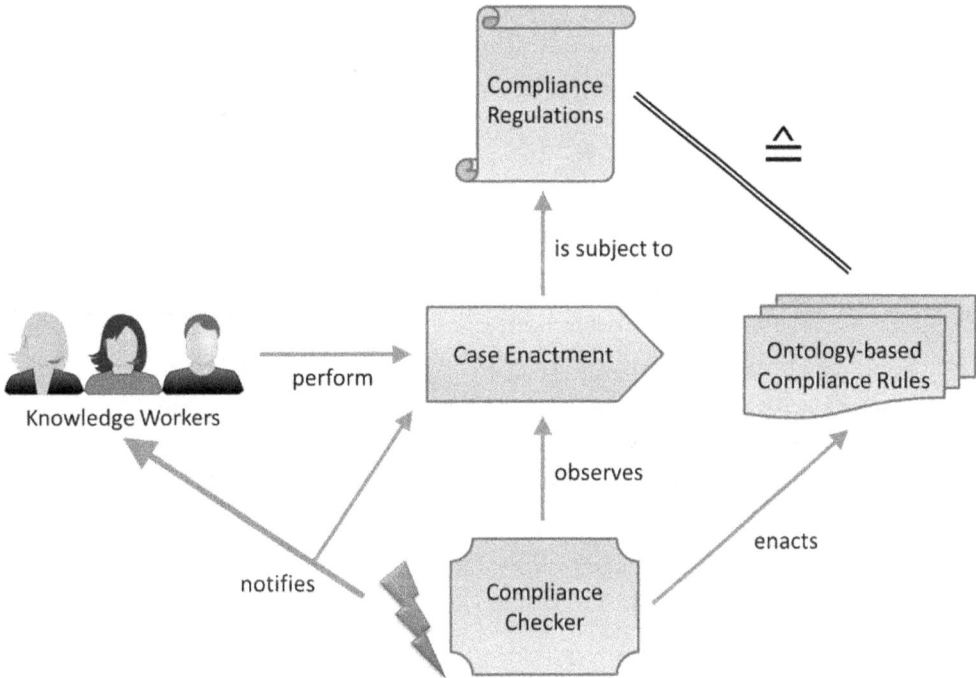

Figure 5: Automated compliance checking:
Detection of violations and notification

For the evaluation of the framework component that detects compliance violations, an automated compliance checker based on Complex Event Processing (CEP) (cf. Wu et al. 2006) can be used. CEP can handle a large quantity of events in near real-time, so it is well-suited for observing the large number of events occurring in business process management software. Please note that the framework does not prescribe any specific compliance-checking technique for its implementation. Compliance rule evaluation at runtime updates directly the user interface of the related case instance (cf. Figure 6) and transparently informs the knowledge worker about the current compliance state of that case.

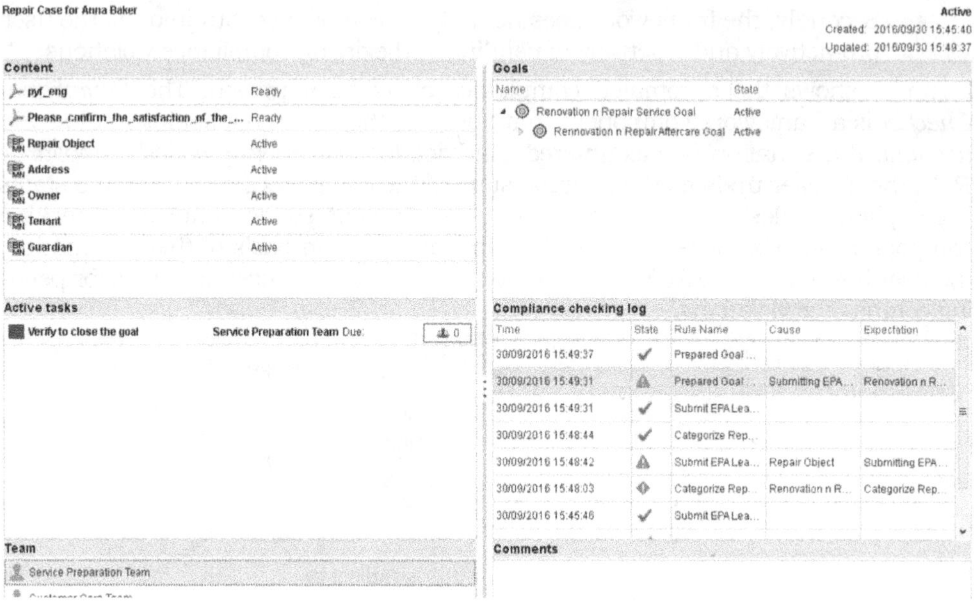

Figure 6: Compliance notifications in a repair service management case instance

DISTRIBUTING COMPLIANCE-AWARE KNOWLEDGE: RECOMMENDATION OF ACTIONS

To go beyond the detection and notification of compliance violations, the framework integrates a machine-learning recommendation component that suggests next actions that pro-actively avoid compliance violations and compensate existing ones.

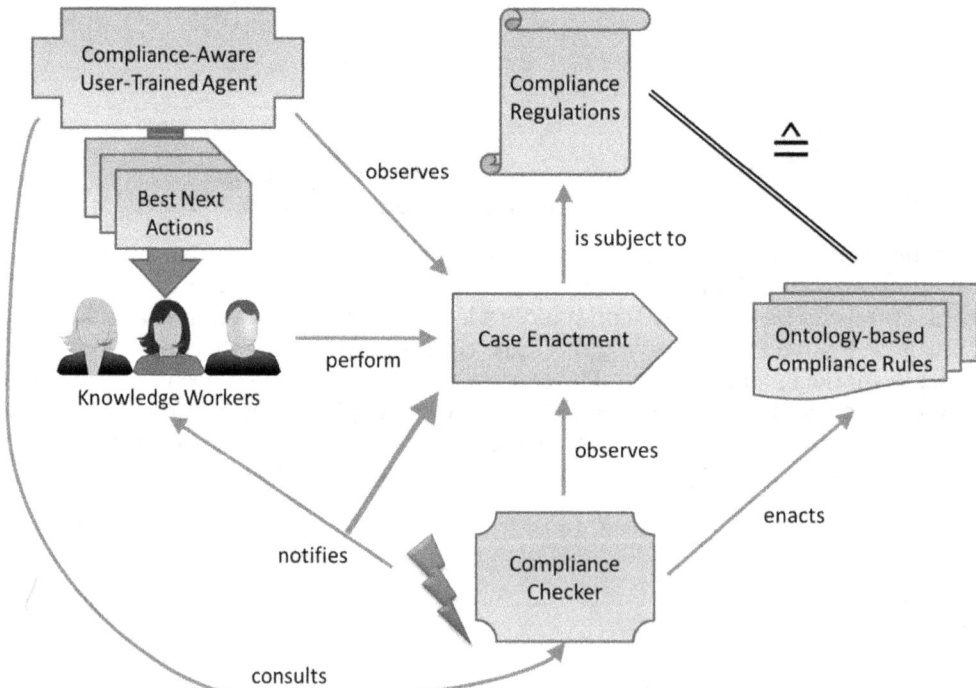

Figure 7: Compliance-aware recommendations

In Figure 7, the *Compliance-Aware User-Trained Agent* automatically learns from the actions of knowledge workers by observing the events in case instances. Those events also involve the compliance rule runtime state updates that are provided by the *Compliance Checker*. That is, the machine learning algorithm considers compliance rules, and it can suggest *Best Next Actions* based on the decisions made by knowledge workers that encountered similar situations. Before an action is proposed to the user, the *Compliance Checker* is consulted to check the potential impact of the action on the specific case instance. The *Compliance-Aware User-Trained Agent* learns from actions of knowledge workers and propagates the learned knowledge to other knowledge workers. This implicit knowledge-sharing capability of the framework can be realized by machine learning after having prepared the inputs for the learning process properly.

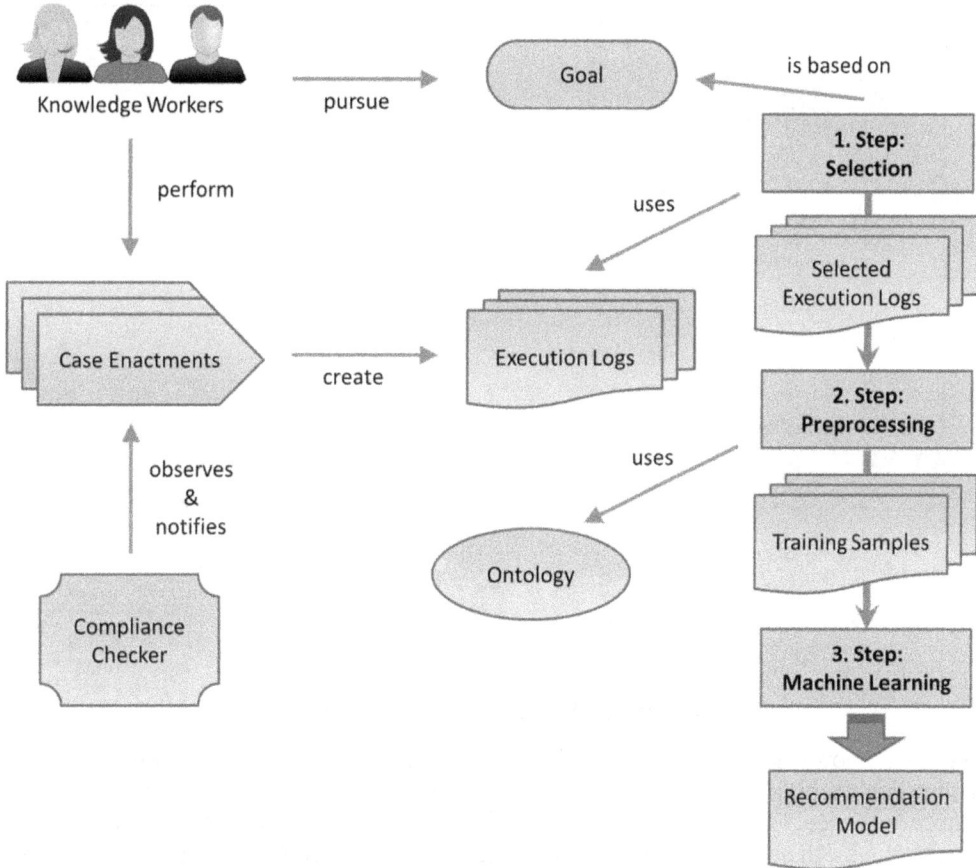

Figure 8: Learning from the decisions of knowledge workers

Figure 8 illustrates the learning process. The enactment of cases by knowledge workers is recorded as *Execution Logs*. *Selection* is a filtering process to consider only those execution logs that are needed to create a recommendation model for a specific *Goal*. By *Preprocessing*, the *Selected Execution Logs* are prepared for *Machine Learning* as *Training Samples*. Finally, a machine learning approach creates a *Recommendation Model* on basis of the provided training samples.

An important aspect of that preparation of the available data is the *Selection* of execution logs. For example, if a knowledge worker pursues the goal to compensate a compliance violation, only those execution logs might be included for learning decisions where this compliance violation was successfully resolved. If the current case execution is compliant, it could be harmful for achieving a specific goal to include execution logs into the learning process that could lead to non-compliance.

An execution log must contain all the information that might have an influence on the decisions of knowledge workers. That includes events related to activities or data adaption with meta-data such as the performer and timestamp of the action as well as information about compliance violations.

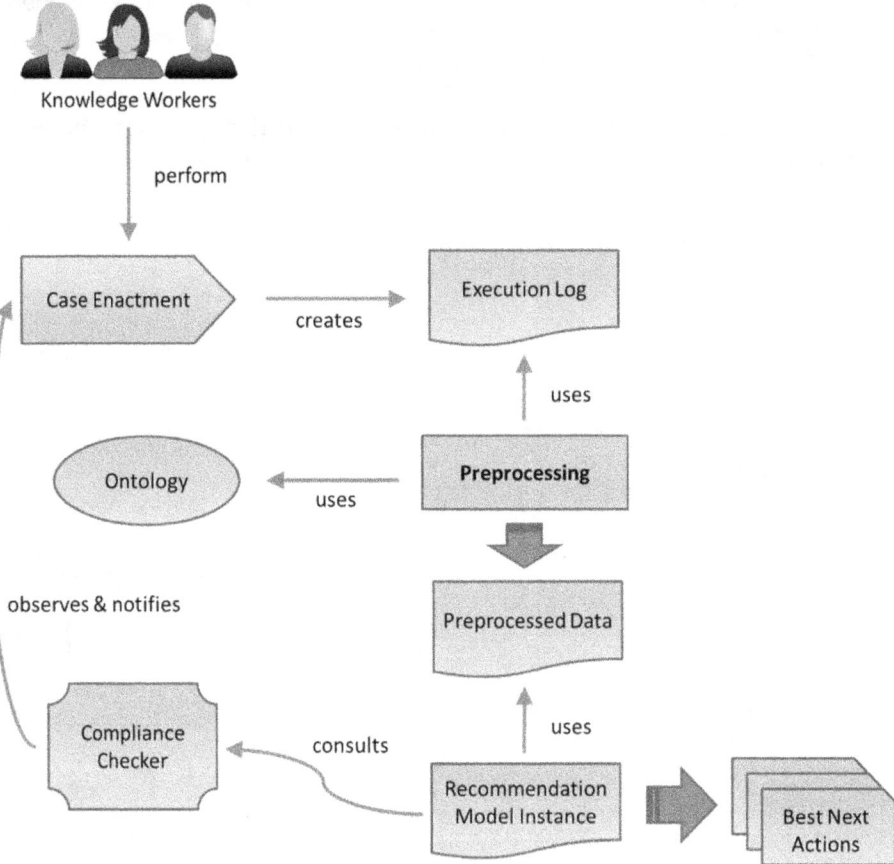

Figure 9: Suggesting next actions

Figure 9 shows how suggestions for best next actions are made. The *Preprocessing* component prepares the raw data from logs for the automated learning process. To improve the learning process, the framework suggests including temporal aspects of decision (cf. Shi et al. 2015) into the learning process. Moreover, it proposes the integration of domain knowledge given by the ontology and the states of compliance rules. This involves diverse ways to refine existing data for machine learning, such as:

- A relative or aggregated value is created from two or more data values for the same instant in time. For example, the account balance is computed from incoming and outgoing payments.
- The relative time between states of task, goals, events and compliance rules, such as the start or end time is calculated. For example, the time between the end of a medical examination and the start of a surgery is computed.

- The relative change of data values from one instant in time to another instant in time is computed. For example, the difference of temperature data is computed from its values at instant t-1 and instant t.
- Not only relative, but also a series of absolute values of the same data in different instants in time can be useful. For example: The temperature of a patient is above 39 degrees Celsius for a longer time which causes a special decision of a knowledge worker.

Each enacted case instance pertains information of all happenings in this instance (including the runtime states of compliance rules) in an *Execution Log*. Just as in the learning phase, *Preprocessing* prepares the data of the log as inputs for a *Recommendation Model Instance*, which is a concrete instance of the learned *Recommendation Model*. The *Recommendation Model Instance* contains probabilities for specific next actions that are used to propose best next actions to the knowledge worker. Before making a recommendation for specific next actions, the *Compliance Checker* is consulted to check against potential non-compliance of the proposal. Our implementation of the *Compliance-Aware User-Trained Agent* is based on decision tree learning (cf. Blockeel et al. 1998). Please note that the framework does not prescribe any specific machine learning approach for its implementation.

Figure 10 shows a screenshot of a possible implementation in the user interface for a healthcare case. In this implementation, the confidence of the best next action proposal is indicated by a 5-stars rating, and non-compliant proposals are dropped and never shown to the knowledge worker.

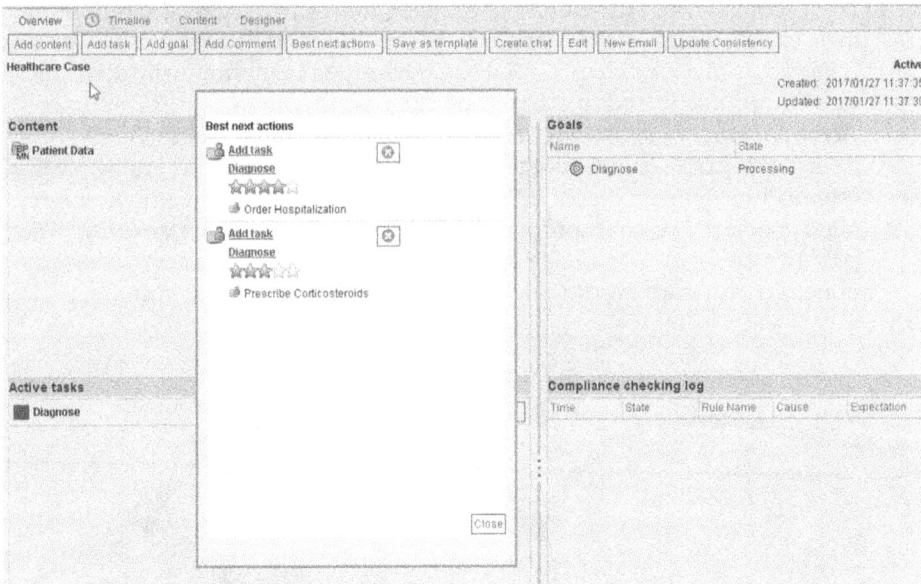

Figure 10: Recommendations in a healthcare case instance

CONCLUSION

Compliance is often perceived as an obstacle for knowledge work. As a result, the working experience of knowledge workers is impaired and so is the customer experience of affected customers. To counteract such potential negative effects of compliance regulations, the proposed framework focuses on supporting knowledge workers in being compliant to defined rules which are integrated into and enacted by the system rather than putting obstacles in their way. This way, business users are respected as knowledge workers and are always in full control of the compliance rules.

Changing compliance requirements can be covered promptly by the business user in the language of the business domain because of the ontology component of the framework that shifts the responsibility of compliance rule implementation from the technical to the business user. New business terms can be added to the domain specific ontology and related compliance rules are created. A role based access control system allows to define clear responsibilities for the maintenance of the ontology as well as compliance rules, e.g. a "business term administrator" and a "business compliance administrator". Moreover, knowledge workers are in full control of the enactment of compliance rules, so they can violate compliance rules if necessary. It is important that the ACM system does not prescribe or hinder actions since the ultimate decision is always the responsibility of the knowledge worker.

Nevertheless, knowledge workers are informed about happened and/or pending compliance violations, which is the main function of the compliance checking component of the framework. Even more importantly, the recommendation component of the framework (called *Compliance-Aware User-Trained Agent*) is capable of learning from the decisions of knowledge workers that are related to the fulfillment of compliance obligations. Consequently, both the compliance checking and the recommendation component enable an automated transfer of compliance-related knowledge among knowledge workers. Particularly, there are *two feedback loops* that enable the transfer of compliance-related knowledge between business users (cf. Figure 11):

- *Authoring & Enactment Feedback Loop:* Compliance-related knowledge is transferred to the ACM system by knowledge workers through the ontology-based compliance rule editor. These business-driven rules are automatically checked and knowledge workers are informed in case of any violation. As a result, the compliance-related knowledge is automatically disseminated and transferred to other knowledge workers.
- *Recommendation Feedback Loop:* Compliance-related decisions of knowledge workers are transferred to other knowledge workers by leveraging machine learning techniques. By specifying a specific compliance-related goal (e.g., staying compliant to all regulations or compensating a compliance violation), knowledge workers can force the recommendation component of the framework to deliver a specific learned behavior.

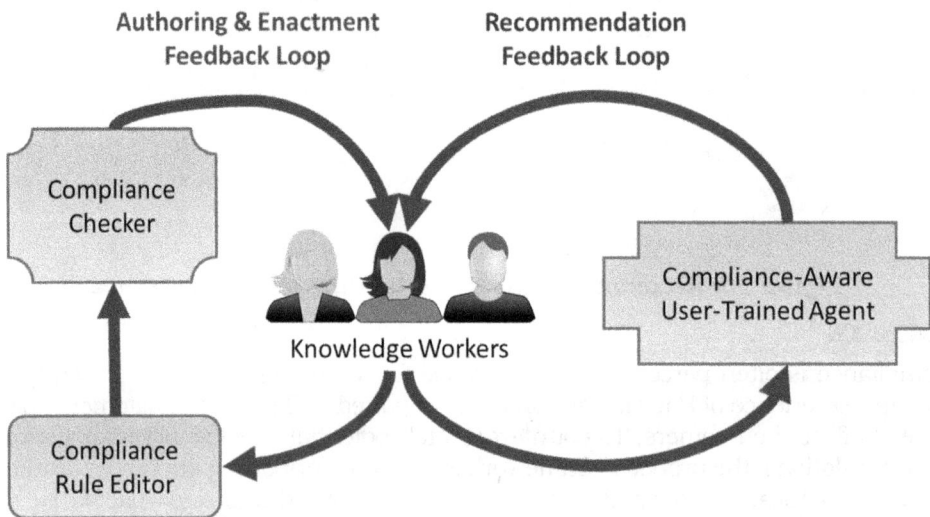

Authoring & Enactment Feedback Loop   **Recommendation Feedback Loop**

Compliance Checker

Compliance-Aware User-Trained Agent

Knowledge Workers

Compliance Rule Editor

Figure 11: Compliance-related knowledge transfer: Two feedback loops

The implicit knowledge sharing is of high value as there is no traditional business analysis by experts needed. Business users are just executing their work and the system learns from them and immediately proposes that knowledge to others in similar situations. As opposed to rigid compliance implementations, the proposed framework has six major advantages:

- *Autonomy:* Business users are in control of the compliance rules that are enacted by the ACM system. Deceiving the system (e.g., in case of an outdated compliance rule that is still in the system) is no longer necessary.
- *Adaptability:* Rules can be adapted as soon as the compliance requirements change. Long maintenance cycles caused by IT-driven compliance implementations become obsolete.
- *Flexibility:* Compliance rules are non-prescriptive, so the ACM leaves room for flexibility. Knowledge workers can violate compliance rules if necessary and compensate the violation at later time.
- *Receptiveness:* The system learns from compliance-related decisions of knowledge workers and includes them for future supportive measures.
- *Understandability:* Compliance rules are encoded in the language of the business domain and understandable for business users.
- *Transparency:* Rules are encoded in business language and one-to-one automatically transformed to technical representations for automated enactment. The error-prone manual transformation of compliance rules to executable rules in the IT system is no longer needed.

Obviously, the framework shifts the control over compliance rules where it belongs to, namely to the knowledge workers who are the experts in their business domain. Rigid compliance implementations are known for decreasing the user experience by putting obstacles in the way of knowledge work. By providing autonomy, adaptability, flexibility, receptiveness, understandability and transparency, the framework has a strong potential to improve the user experience of knowledge workers as opposed to rigid compliance implementations (or the general absence of automated support for compliance during case enactment). Moreover, ACM can also include process fragments for predefined automated flows which are invoked by the knowledge worker at runtime by adding them ad hoc to certain goals. Such process templates are defined by business administrators at design time with a BPMN type of graphical editor which can be also included into the compliance checking of the compliance framework. Compliance rules which would be violated during the design phase – e.g. defining wrong orders between certain tasks like "Shipping finished leads to Payment started" will be notified so that they can be corrected before the process template is released for production (Czepa et al. 2017).

While designing the framework, it has always been most important to us that the conceptual ideas are of practical value and thus, was implemented into the ACM solution of the Papyrus platform of ISIS Papyrus which utilizes the *User-Trained Agent* as a system-integrated business intelligence machine learning component. We must emphasize that the framework itself does not prescribe any specific technology or concrete implementation. It describes a generalized concept to influence the future of ACM software.

REFERENCES

(Blockeel et al. 1998) Blockeel, H., Raedt, L. D., and Ramon, J.: Top-down induction of clustering trees. ICML'98, pages 55–63. Morgan Kaufmann Publishers Inc., 1998.

(Czepa et al. 2016a) Czepa, C., Tran, H., Zdun, U., Tran, T., Weiss, E., and Ruhsam, C.: Plausibility checking of formal business process specifications in linear temporal logic. In 28th

International Conference on Advanced Information Systems Engineering (CAiSE'16), Forum Track, 2016.

(Czepa et al. 2016b) Czepa, C., Tran, H., Zdun, U., Tran, T., Weiss, E., and Ruhsam, C., Plausibility checking of formal business process specifications in linear temporal logic (extended abstract). In Mendling, J. and Rinderle-Ma, S., editors, 7th International Workshop on Enterprise Modeling and Information Systems Architectures (EMISA 2016), 2016.

(Czepa et al. 2017) Czepa, C., Tran, H., Zdun, U., Tran Thi Kim, T., Weiss, E. and Ruhsam, C.: Reduction Techniques for Efficient Behavioral Model Checking in Adaptive Case Management. The 32nd ACM Symposium on Applied Computing (SAC 2017), 3-6 Apr 2017, Marrakesh, Morocco, 2017

(Dwyer et al. 1999) Dwyer, M. B., Avrunin, G. S., and Corbett, J. C.: Patterns in property specifications for finite-state verification. In Proceedings of the 21st International Conference on Software Engineering, ICSE '99, pages 411–420, New York, NY, USA. ACM, 1999.

(Elgammal et al. 2016) Elgammal, A., Turetken, O., van den Heuvel, W.-J., and Papazoglou, M.: Formalizing and applying compliance patterns for business process compliance. Software & Systems Modeling, 15(1):119–146, 2016.

(EPA 2011) Small Entity Compliance Guide to Renovate Right. http://epa.gov/sites/production/files/documents/sbcomplianceguide.pdf. Last accessed: July 4, 2017.

(Haarst 2013) SBVR Made Easy, Business Vocabulary and Rules are a Critical Asset, Conceptual Heaven, 2013.

(Levenshtein 1966) Levenshtein, V. I.: Binary codes capable of correcting deletions, insertions, and reversals. In: Soviet Physics Doklady, volume 10, number 8, pages 707–710, 1966.

(Pucher 2011) Pucher, M. J.: Considerations for implementing adaptive case management. In Fischer, L., editor, Taming the Unpredictable Real World Adaptive Case Management: Case Studies and Practical Guidance. Future Strategies Inc., 2011.

(Ross 2013) Ross, Ronald G.: Business Rule Concepts. Fourth Edition Business Rule Solutions, LLC, 2013.

(Shi et al. 2015) Shi, Q., Zhao, Y., and Liu, M.: Towards learning segmented temporal sequences: A decision tree approach. In ICMLC'15, volume 1, pages 145–150, 2015.

(Swenson 2010) Swenson, K. D.: Mastering the unpredictable: how adaptive case management will revolutionize the way that knowledge workers get things done. Meghan-Kiffer Press, 2010.

(Tran Thi Kim et al. 2013) Tran Thi Kim, T., Pucher, M. J., Mendling, J., Ruhsam C.: Setup and Maintenance Factors of ACM Systems. In OTM Workshops 2013, pages 172-177, 2013.

(Tran Thi Kim et al. 2015) Tran Thi Kim, T. and Weiss, E., Ruhsam, C., Czepa, C., Tran, H. and Zdun, U.: Embracing Process Compliance and Flexibility through Behavioral Consistency Checking in ACM: A Repair Service Management Case. 4th International Workshop on Adaptive Case Management and other Non-workflow Approaches to BPM (AdaptiveCM 15), Innsbruck, Austria, 2015.

(van der Aalst and Pesic 2006) van der Aalst, W. M. P. and Pesic, M.: DecSerFlow: Towards a Truly Declarative Service Flow Language, pages 1–23. Springer Berlin Heidelberg, Berlin, Heidelberg, 2006.

(Wu et al. 2006) Wu, E., Diao, Y., and Rizvi, S.: High-performance complex event processing over streams. In SIGMOD '06, pages 407–418, ACM, 2006.

Section 2

Award-Winning Case Studies

Seven Trends Impacting the Case Management Landscape

Connie Moore, Digital Clarity Group, USA

THE WFMC EXCELLENCE AWARDS

The Workflow Management Coalition (WfMC), a standards organization for workflow and business process technologies, recently announced the 2017 winners of its **Excellence Awards in Adaptive Case Management**[1]. I always look forward to these announcements (and the related BPM Excellence Awards) and the follow-on book because the winners demonstrate the best of the best in workflow, business process management (BPM), digital process automation and case management.

During the awards ceremony, I introduced the seven big trends in case management and then Keith Swenson (president of the WfMC) and I announced this year's winners. For information about the case management and BPM books, see *WfMC Awards for Excellence in Case Management*[2]

The seven trends impacting the case management landscape in 2017 and 2018:

TREND #1: DIGITAL TRANSFORMATION IS SWEEPING THE BUSINESS LANDSCAPE.

Case management projects are not being done in a vacuum or because some manager decides to bring in new technology to replace older solutions. Instead, digital disruption, which is pervasive across all industries, is driving companies to strategically transform their end-to-end processes.

---

[1] http://adaptivecasemanagement.org

[2] https://bpm-books.com/collections/case-management

The organizational and technological fallout from digital disruption touches every single industry, organization, and business process. Companies can no longer operate in geographical and functional silos that may have been created over 100 years ago. As corporate directors, CEOs and the C-suite executives absorb this new reality and scramble like crazy to avoid being "amazoned" or "ubered," business leaders everywhere are taking a fresh look at their thoroughly outdated and outmoded business processes, which are usually too internally focused and don't leverage the power of recent advances. The digital disruption megatrend is driving virtually all business IT projects today, across a wide swath of technology.

TREND #2: DIGITAL TRANSFORMATION IS ALL ABOUT CUSTOMER EXPERIENCE.

In a world in which consumers, politicians, educators, students, and even kids thrive on new technologies (such as mobile apps, social media, virtual reality, games and gamification, analytics, ecommerce; the list goes on), consumer expectations have blown through the roof. People now have extremely high expectations for how the websites and mobile apps they use cater to their preferences and whims. And they have extremely low tolerance for delays and repeated questions about basic customer information while being passed mindlessly from one customer service rep to another, after calling a toll-free number for help. For digital transformation to be transformational, customer experience must be king.

TREND #3: CASE PROJECTS WILL BE DRIVEN BY DIGITAL TRANSFORMATION AND CX.

As an immediate response to digital disruption, companies are reconceiving their business processes and building new content- and data-centric, case management-driven processes that fully support new and engaging customer experiences.

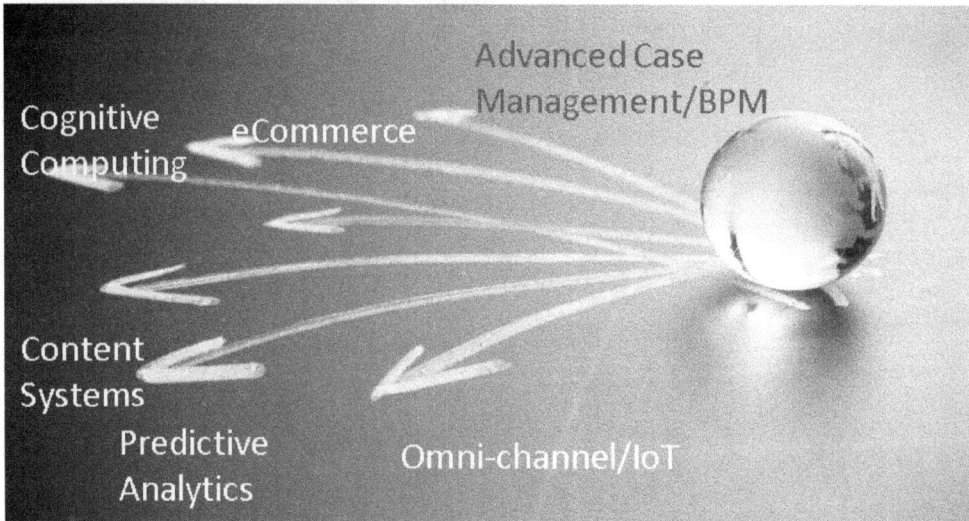

These customer experiences are designed to delight the customer and increase the customer life-time value by building repeat business and extreme customer loyalty. Going forward, these case management solutions will be increasingly combined with other emerging technologies such as omnichannel, predictive analytics for next best action, natural language processing and machine learning.

TREND #4: DIGITAL TRANSFORMATION WILL REQUIRE DIGITAL OUTSIDE/INSIDE.

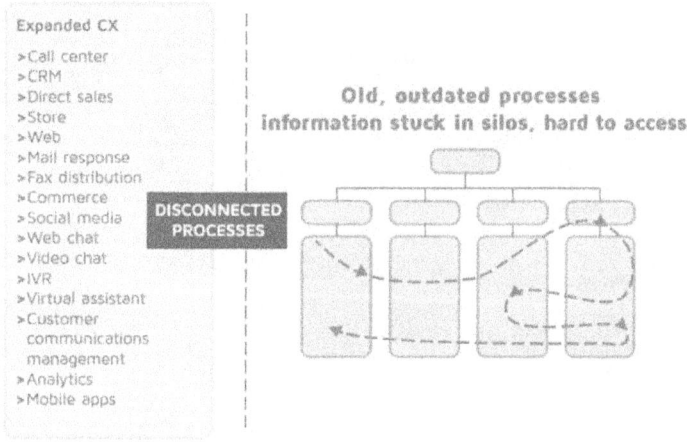

A great digital outside doesn't transform the inside

Expanded CX
- >Call center
- >CRM
- >Direct sales
- >Store
- >Web
- >Mail response
- >Fax distribution
- >Commerce
- >Social media
- >Web chat
- >Video chat
- >IVR
- >Virtual assistant
- >Customer communications management
- >Analytics
- >Mobile apps

DISCONNECTED PROCESSES

Old, outdated processes
information stuck in silos, hard to access

Most business leaders are well-aware of the vast disconnect between customer expectations and the experiences their organization actually delivers via telephone, websites, email, mobile, social, chat, kiosk, and even direct mail.

But often they don't know what to do about it, so marketing will start an omnichannel project and maybe a marketing automation effort, while internally-focused managers may launch a new processing center or deploy a new enterprise software suite. Unfortunately, tackling projects (even case management projects) in such a bifurcated way does not support digital transformation and will not deliver transformational results.

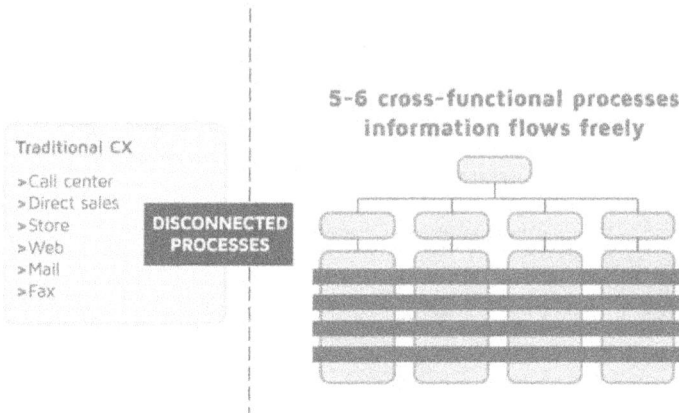

A great digital inside doesn't transform the CX

Traditional CX
- >Call center
- >Direct sales
- >Store
- >Web
- >Mail
- >Fax

DISCONNECTED PROCESSES

5-6 cross-functional processes
information flows freely

What happens with customers "outside" the organization (marketing's and sales' province) and "inside" business operations (dominated by service, support, finance and operations) simply cannot be cleaved into two separate worlds.

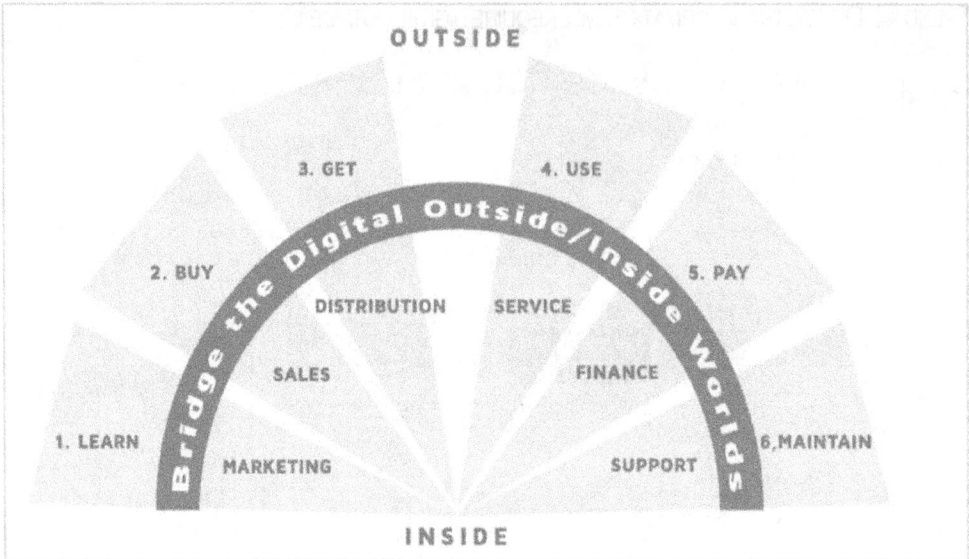

Source: Adapted from Earley Information Science

Today's thriving business is at risk unless it *seamlessly bridges* the customer experience with internal operations. (For more insights, see *Transform Customer Experience and Operational Excellence By Going Digital Outside and Inside*[3]·)

TREND #5: CASE MANAGEMENT AND BPM WILL CONVERGE.

Case management is both an approach and a type of software for automating complex, information-intensive work. Adaptive case management, as the WfMC calls it,

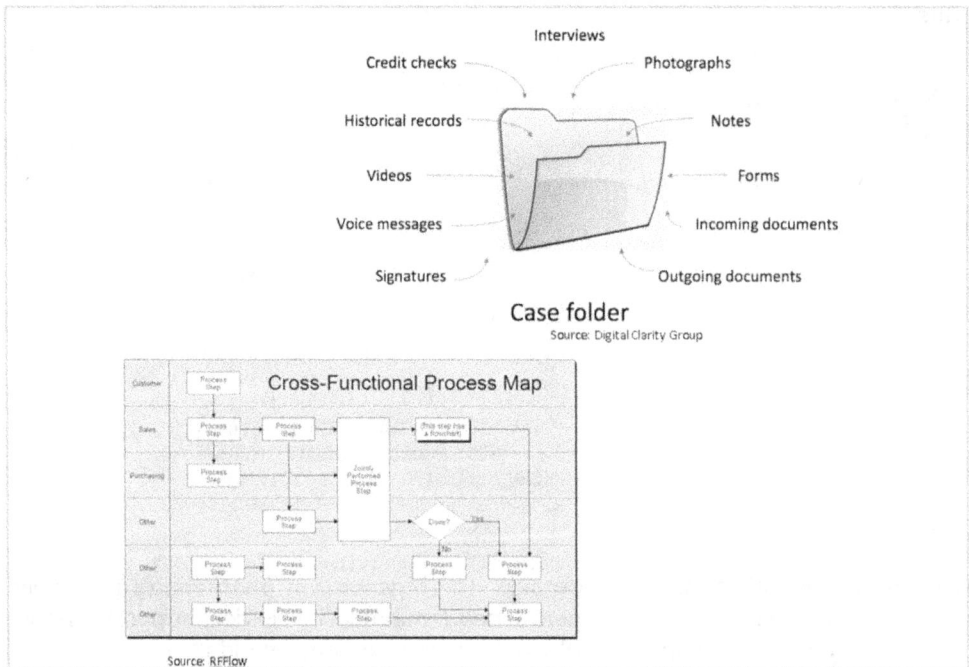

Case folder

Source: Digital Clarity Group

Cross-Functional Process Map

Source: RFFlow

---

[3] http://www.digitalclaritygroup.com/transform-customer-experience-and-operational-excellence-by-going-digital-outside-and-inside

differs from structured or orchestration BPM software; case focuses heavily on information, in addition to flow.

The vendor landscape is fuzzy, with some vendors offering traditional BPM and case management in the same product (e.g. Appian, BizAgi, OpenText, and Pegasystems) while others (most notably IBM) have separate products for automating different types of processes.

The WfMC treats the two as being different and gives separate awards for both types of BPM. But the markets are converging, and one could posit that they never diverged in the first place.

However, there is a big question over how to approach the "to be" business process–specifically, is it data/information centric or is it flow centric? —and this question is explored in more detail in *BPM: making the case for case management software*[4]. If you are considering BPM software, it's imperative to understand how case management works, how processes are automated using case, and how the products will converge.

TREND #6: WORK WILL GET SMARTER.

It's hard to have any technology discussion these days without mention of artificial intelligence, machine learning, deep learning and natural language processing. It's an indicator that we are truly on the cusp of moving to a new world of work, where work becomes "smarter." This is not a sudden development that blew in from nowhere; we've been progressing toward that elusive goal for decades. AI is used routinely for credit card validation, ecommerce, call centers, loan approval, news feeds, and virtual assistants. (For more, see *Artificial intelligence grabs center stage at AIIM's information management leadership council.*[5]) The world is now facing a huge shakeup in how we create, consume and process information. You may either dread this new world or look forward in anticipation (hey, I can't wait to spend more time on vacation while my AI software grinds away) . . . but work will undoubtedly be smarter. For example, robotic process automation (RPA), has already hit case management in a big way. RPA creates robots (or scripts) that automate routine, repetitive, mindless tasks. For example, RPA can be used to automate repetitive typing; log on to different business apps; copy information from one app to another; scan, read and compose e-mails; manipulate spreadsheets and move data; and automate aspects of on-boarding, customer service activities, compliance, and document capture. For more information, see *Robotic Process Automation (RPA): robots that automate routine and complex work.*[6]

TREND #7: PROCESS AUTOMATION PROJECTS WILL GET FASTER.

There's some good news on the case management and BPM front; it is taking less time than ever to deploy newly-transformed business processes that are based on case management software. In fact, the 2017 WfMC Case Management award winners exemplify how projects can be done more quickly than ever. There are several reasons, including: vendors and their solution partners are offering more out-of-the-box business processes, plus the vendor community is also providing more business

---

[4] http://www.digitalclaritygroup.com/bpm-making-case-case-management-software

[5] http://www.digitalclaritygroup.com/artificial-intelligence-grabs-center-stage-aiims-information-management-leadership-council

[6] http://www.digitalclaritygroup.com/robotic-process-automation-rpa-robots-automate-routine-complex-work

models, process models, accelerators, integrations, and process templates that help project teams speed up the entire project.

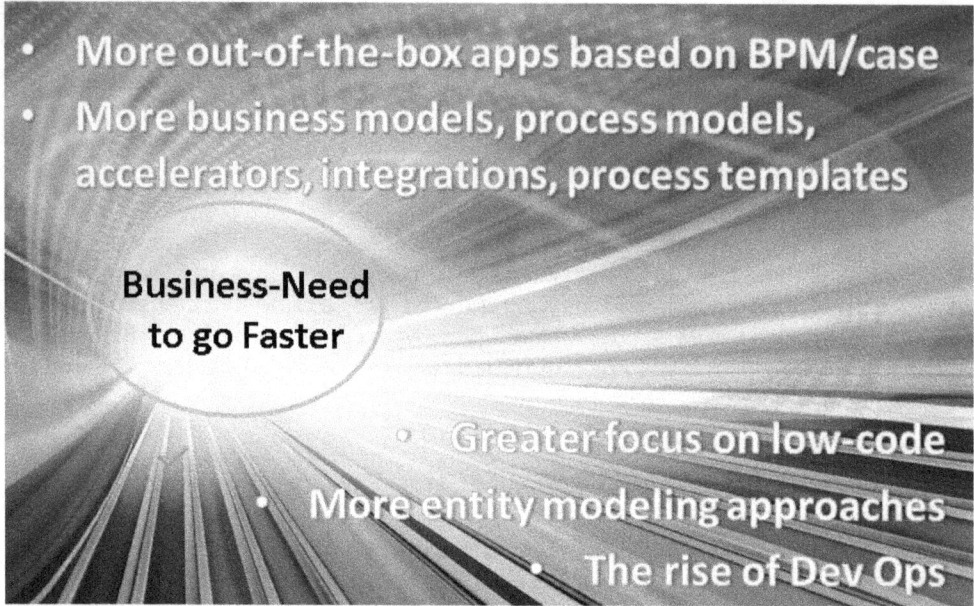

- More out-of-the-box apps based on BPM/case
- More business models, process models, accelerators, integrations, process templates

Business-Need to go Faster

- Greater focus on low-code
- More entity modeling approaches
- The rise of Dev Ops

The rise of DevOps and BPM/case management competency centers in many organizations has helped, as has the greater focus on low-code and entity modeling. (For more information, see *Use Entity Modeling to Streamline Business Process Design and Development.*[7])

These breakthroughs are important because BPM/case management projects can bog down into yet more application development projects if not careful. But the proof is in the pudding; take a look at the *case management winners*[8] for ideas on accelerating projects.

The case studies that follow describe the 2016 Award-winners. The current awards-winners will be published in a following publication.

---

[7] http://www.digitalclaritygroup.com/use-entity-modeling-streamline-business-process-design-development

[8] http://adaptivecasemanagement.org

Fein Such Kahn
and Shepard, P.C., USA

Nominated by Fujitsu America, USA

1. EXECUTIVE SUMMARY / ABSTRACT

Fein, Such, Kahn, & Shepard, P.C. is a general practice legal firm providing comprehensive service to clients in New Jersey for over 25 years. A good legal firm that performs consistently with the trust of their clients is virtually guaranteed repeat business, but Fein Such wanted more. In 2013, Fein Such embarked on a daring initiative to reform the way they run their business. One of the firm's principals with high-tech experience in Silicon Valley convinced the Fein Such Executive team that the same legal talent could do much more, if the tedious manual information activities were digitized and automated. He saw that handling individual documents, mostly on paper, was inefficient and that highly-trained people were wasting time searching for and manipulating documentation. Eliminate that, you eliminate a lot of waste, and you can preserve the knowledge workers' time for more important tasks than rearranging stacks of documents. It was this insight that brought Fein Such to take a step that reduced their processing time by around 50% over a period of two years.

2. OVERVIEW

Fein Such works in a highly-regulated field due to the legal nature of the business. Most guidelines are set by the Federal Government, meaning no mistakes can be made at all and documents have to be exact every time. There is no margin for error.

The firm's main function is to collect accurate and complete information from the customers, and then to perform the legal transaction. When mistakes are made they multiply the costs tremendously, so there is a large benefit to be gained from doing the process correctly the first time.

The biggest cost in any legal firm is the staff time that legal experts take doing a job. How much of that time is "legal work" and how much is mundane paper shuffling? It is hard to measure, but Fein Such had the sense that they were spending too much time shuffling papers.

Fujitsu built a robust and scalable business process management system for Fein Such to tackle this challenge, which drastically reduced the cost and greatly increased the efficiency and productivity. The system is capable of generating 174 different legal documents, which are being submitted to clients, courts and other customers. It supports over 300 legal experts doing their job using an estimated 350 different custom screens. During normal processing, as many as 70 different kinds of email messages can be sent to participants to support as many different kinds of interactions.

Around 45% of all Fein Such employees use this system on a daily basis to do their job. At any time during an average day, the system handles 150 end-users simultaneously. Almost all users of the system have legal training, so every hour saved adds significant value. The application was designed with these people in mind, which is why they found the solution comfortable from the start.

3. BUSINESS CONTEXT

- Through its Creditors' Rights department, Fein Such protects the interests of financial institutions and other creditors when loans they made become delinquent.
- In New Jersey and New York, while smaller (unsecured) debts may be recovered through non-judicial means (collections), Fein Such must navigate the lengthy and complex foreclosure and bankruptcy judicial processes in order to protect the interests of mortgagees.
- In the aftermath of the housing and financial crisis of 2007-2009, the average foreclosure timelines have increased by 200-300% due to a combination of ever more stringent court and client requirements.
- Fein Such greatly increased the amount of staff to process foreclosures; however, the increase in legal fees (revenue) has not kept pace with additional costs to justify incremental investments in labor.

Challenges

- Clients, investors, and jurisdictions introduce new requirements daily, altering workflow.
- Cases with audits and reporting come to a complete halt.
- Foreclosure production staff members must duplicate work in both the firm's internal case management system as well as myriad of different web-based client tracking systems.
- All systems require specialized training.
- Current Case Management system is outdated to the point that effective and efficient data transmission among the various systems is impossible.
- Anywhere from 33-50% of all paralegal work hours are devoted to manual, repetitive, and largely exception-handling processes.

Technical challenges

- Antiquated Systems
- High cost of support for Case Management system
- High cost of FTE to support existing applications
- Small IT organization
- Small IT Budget.

4.1 Business

Transparency was a key design consideration. Knowing what work is coming up and what work has been completed allows workers to coordinate their own activities more efficiently with each other.

Extreme customization was another key consideration. The application allows the users to create their own E-mail templates and respond to E-mail message directly. Who could imagine lawyers designing email templates? The fact is, though, these legal professionals know their own area better than anyone else. It would be a limitation to think that a single email template will work for all legal specializations. Fein Such found instead that such customization was necessary to handle business effectively and to delight clients.

4. THE KEY INNOVATIONS

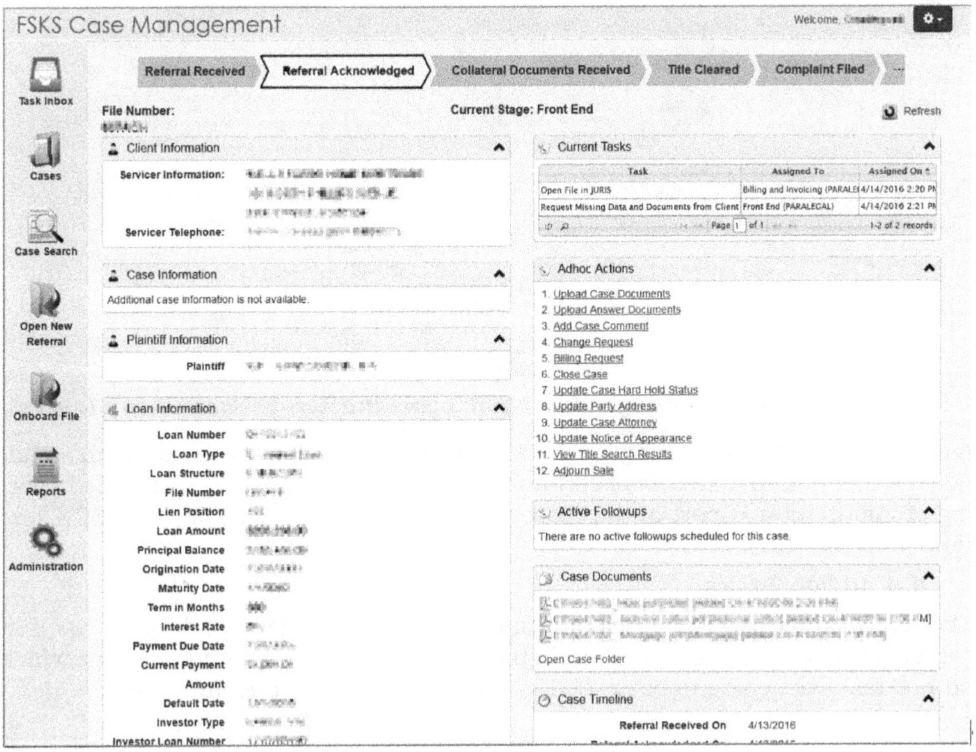

Figure 1. Main Case Dashboard

4.2 Case Handling in the Cloud

One of the biggest challenges was the idea of hosting in the cloud. Not only is the information being handled extremely sensitive, but Fein Such clients have made specific demands on exactly how information has to be protected, down to requiring locks on conference room doors in the Fein Such main facility. Even though encryption is well-known to be an effective guard for ensuring the privacy of data, the specific legal agreements, in many cases, required that all the data stay on the US soil at all times. At the same time, a disaster recovery center needed to be more than 100 miles away. The facility hosting the systems must comply with the strictest industry standards for security, with highly-controlled access to the physical environment and the strongest procedures in place to assure overall safety. Additionally, the firm cannot use any solution that cannot identify exactly where the data will be at any time.

4.3 Organization & Social

Given the sensitive nature of the work, the greatest consideration was given to strong access control of all the information. At the same time, there is a collaborative aspect to the system. Cases, documents and related information need to be forwarded to other colleagues for advice and referrals.

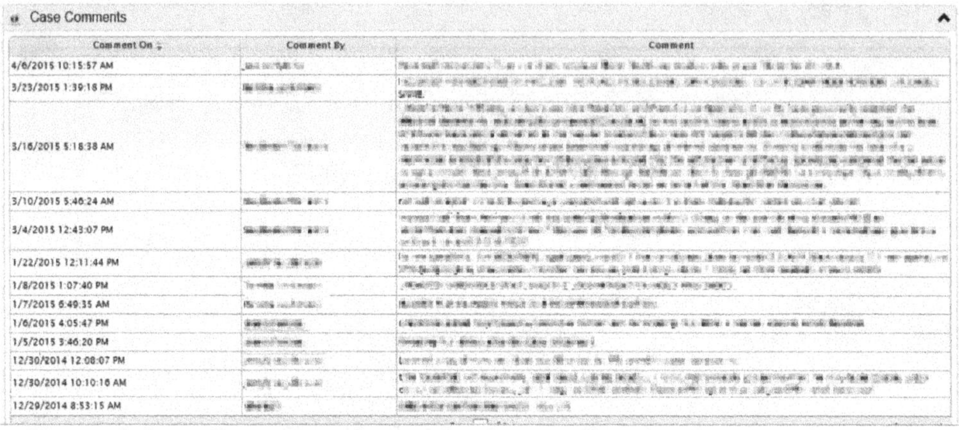

Figure 2 Case Comments form a basic coordination between key players

A basic commenting capability gives users the ability to inform each other in an ad-hoc manner and to take care of certain kinds of tasks. Careful and controlled sharing of information is part of the reason that case processing now takes 60% less time than before.

4.4 Ad-hoc Tasks

The real case managing capability comes from the selection of ad-hoc tasks that can be brought to bear at any point in time. You cannot predict ahead of time which ad-hoc tasks are going to be needed, nor how many times they must be repeated.

Figure 3: Ad-hoc Actions panel

4.5 Process Diagrams

Even though the system had case management diagrams available (reminiscent of more widely-known CMMN) these case management models were not required in the application. Instead, regular BPMN model were used when the process flow was predictable, and when the process was not predictable, users had permission to compose their processes using ad-hoc tasks. The ability to control which ad-hoc tasks were available at any given time to the lawyers was not considered to be necessary.

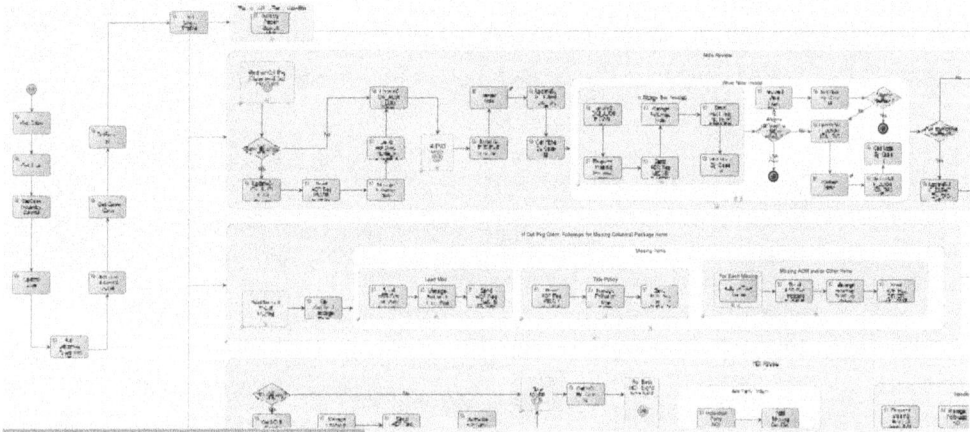

Figure 4: Sample BPMN diagram used in the application

5. HURDLES OVERCOME

Like any system that supports hundreds of full-time dedicated users performing business-critical tasks, it must be robust and scalable. Over the past 15 months, around 190,000 overall tasks have been submitted, and the system has processed just over 200,000 documents within the same timeframe. The total database size has grown to 760Gb in those 15 months.

The system is integrated with title vendors as well as legal document review companies. Any integration with outside firms is a challenge, but successfully managing that integration delivers tangible and lasting benefits. Documents are delivered instantly, reliably, and safely in both directions. The system is also integrated with Lexis Nexis's Juris for in-depth and up-to-date insight to the financial management marketplace. Users also use the Google Doc integration for real-time editing and submission of documents, which further assists collaboration.

5.1 Management

Key members of the Fein Such executive team were on board with the project from the beginning. It is reasonable to say that this is the key ingredient to embarking on a bold and substantial venture to reform the way people do work. Their involvement was necessary to ensure that the system had the support and backing to succeed. However, if the software system had not been responsive to the actual needs of the users, it would have faced difficult adoption and likely failure.

5.2 Business

External customers see no changes in the output, except that it is completed faster with fewer missteps.

5.3 Organization Adoption

We found that starting with a small core group was key to successful adoption. The application was not held back from users until it was totally ready. The first users of the application started using it with only a subset of the features. Over the next year, releases came out with new capabilities to handle more operations. At the same time, more users were enrolled onto the system once the confidence warranted it.

The users absolutely loved the solution. They came from the older system and switched to this solution which they found sleek, modern and very easy to use.

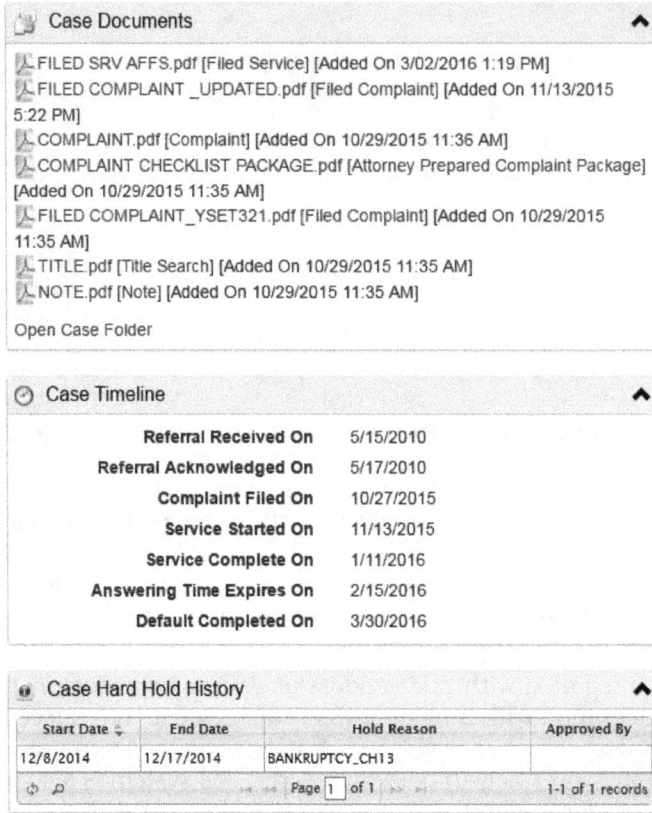

Case Documents

⬟ FILED SRV AFFS.pdf [Filed Service] [Added On 3/02/2016 1:19 PM]
⬟ FILED COMPLAINT _UPDATED.pdf [Filed Complaint] [Added On 11/13/2015 5:22 PM]
⬟ COMPLAINT.pdf [Complaint] [Added On 10/29/2015 11:36 AM]
⬟ COMPLAINT CHECKLIST PACKAGE.pdf [Attorney Prepared Complaint Package] [Added On 10/29/2015 11:35 AM]
⬟ FILED COMPLAINT_YSET321.pdf [Filed Complaint] [Added On 10/29/2015 11:35 AM]
⬟ TITLE.pdf [Title Search] [Added On 10/29/2015 11:35 AM]
⬟ NOTE.pdf [Note] [Added On 10/29/2015 11:35 AM]

Open Case Folder

Case Timeline

Referral Received On	5/15/2010
Referral Acknowledged On	5/17/2010
Complaint Filed On	10/27/2015
Service Started On	11/13/2015
Service Complete On	1/11/2016
Answering Time Expires On	2/15/2016
Default Completed On	3/30/2016

Case Hard Hold History

Start Date	End Date	Hold Reason	Approved By
12/8/2014	12/17/2014	BANKRUPTCY_CH13	

Page 1 of 1   1-1 of 1 records

Figure 5: Detail from main dashboard showing case timeline overview

6. BENEFITS

One of the most important aspects of any system to support legal work is the document management. The Fein Such system is no exception; however, we estimate that only about 20% of the capability can be considered to be document management.

Figure 6: Task List UI exposed to users to find their current tasks.

6.1 Cost Savings / Time Reductions

The overall processing time per case has been reduced by an estimated 50%, which is a dramatic improvement. This translates to a significant number of hours per case and therefore money saved across the board, as well as faster response to the customer.

All tasks are timeline-based, which means that they must be completed on time. The system provides the overall capability to manage and keep track of tasks. It is hard to estimate precisely the dollar value of being on time, but the benefit to Fein Such is significant. The other key benefit is the fact that the overall capability of the platform out-of-the-box is extensive, and this is vital for a company such as Fein Such, because they didn't have to make incremental investments in additional needed functionality.

6.2 Increased Revenues

The original justification of the system was that management wanted to grow the business, and they knew that there was more business to be acquired, but the limitation was the number of lawyers (around 300) in the company. Each legal professional can only handle a certain caseload and still keep the quality high. They were looking for a way to grow without necessarily hiring more people. Since the processing of each application takes 60% less time, Fein Such is now able to do more with the same talent pool, however, figures on the business growth are not currently available.

6.3 Quality Improvements

Staying on top of things that must be tracked is critical. An interface notifies the user of follow-ups and collects any update in status. If the issue has been resolved, the screen presents a form where the user can directly compose an email message. The email is sent, and then a PDF of the email is generated and stored as an official record of the communication in the document database.

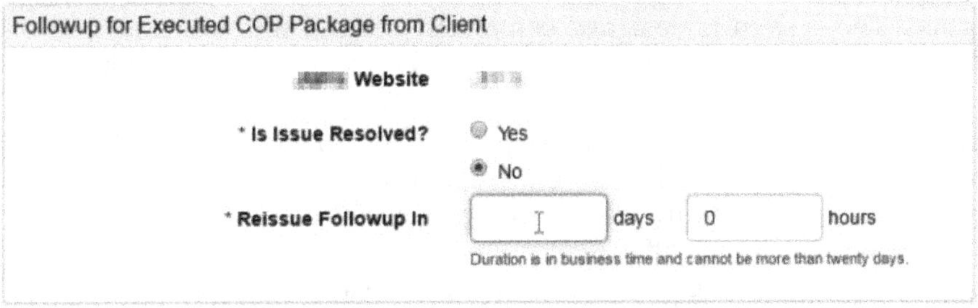

Followup for Executed COP Package from Client

Website

* Is Issue Resolved?   ○ Yes   ● No

* Reissue Followup In   [I] days   [0] hours

Duration is in business time and cannot be more than twenty days.

Figure 7: Follow Up prompt and ability to reschedule

If the issue is not resolved, the user simply notes a timeout to be reminded to try again.

7. BEST PRACTICES, LEARNING POINTS AND PITFALLS

7.1 Best Practices and Learning Points

✓ *It was difficult to determine the expected ROI before implementing the system. It was very important for management to understand up front what the benefit will be, but sometimes you have to move forward without the solid evidence.*

✓ *Build quality checks into the system to protect against the legal requirements and regulations, which have very strict guidelines.*

✓ *Build incrementally. Since the initial go-live (Jan. 2015), 9 major releases have been build and implemented, 4 Service Packs and 30+ patch releases have also been build, tested and implemented. There is no reason to wait until every capability is finished before getting the first users going.*

✓ *Work hard to keep the UI response time low. The system response time for end-users is consistently below 1 second, despite the massive amount of data processed, the number of tasks and documents handled.*

7.2 Pitfalls

✗ *Make sure that your user knowledge about the capabilities of the base plat-form is complete. With more knowledge, it may have been faster and easier to implement what is available today.*

✗ *The use of proprietary software was a calculated risk. Using an external com-pany to provide the solution in an industry which is very regulated and very precise means that steps have to be taken to assure that the solution works well. Fein Such overcame that, but it was still a risk.*

8. COMPETITIVE ADVANTAGES

The speed to respond to existing tasks is only the beginning. The basic capability to capture and perform knowledge work around documents can be expanded into many new domains. Because the processes are defined as a model, they are rela-tively easy to change. This allows Fein Such to be more agile, and to be able to entertain work in future emerging areas.

9. TECHNOLOGY

The system was built on Fujitsu's Interstage BOP middleware. This is a complete BPM and Case Management platform that can be offered as an on-premises offer-ing, or as a Software-as-a-Service cloud solution. Fein Such opted for cloud hosting from Fujitsu.

The process definitions were designed in BPMN and can be transported using XPDL file format. The system is designed completely around web services, and offers a modern and easy-to-use drag-and-drop interface for designing applications over standard generic web services.

The entire application is hosted at Fujitsu's Trusted Public S5 (TPS5) Cloud in Sunnyvale California, with backup infrastructure in Richardson Texas. TPS5 is a highly redundant and secure system designed to meet the demands for handling the most demanding application security needs.

The application was developed by Counterpoint Consulting Inc. based in Vienna, VA because of their extensive experience with the Interstage BOP platform.

10. THE TECHNOLOGY AND SERVICE PROVIDERS

Fujitsu America Incorporated is based in Sunnyvale California, and is a wholly owned subsidiary of Fujitsu Limited in Japan. With annual revenues around $50B, Fujitsu is the third largest IT equipment and services vendor in the world. Fujitsu America has long been known as synonymous with strong business process man-agement support, starting as far back as 1993 when it was still called workflow.

Grinnell Mutual, USA

Nominated by Hyland, creator of OnBase, USA

1. EXECUTIVE SUMMARY / ABSTRACT

Grinnell Mutual, in business since 1909, is the 114th-largest property casualty insurance company in the United States and the largest primary reinsurer of farm mutual companies in North America. The company provides reinsurance for farm mutual insurance companies as well as property and casualty insurance. Its products are available in 15 states.

To uphold service levels, improve collaboration among its Underwriting and Claims departments and support company growth, Grinnell Mutual needed a better way to manage information surrounding its policy underwriting and claims processes. At the time (pre-2010) these processes were manual and paper-centric. Employees in Claims and Underwriting had little to no visibility into one another's workloads or decision-making processes. They had no easy way to create, organize and track notes pertaining to a specific policy or claim. Information required to write policies and handle claims was scattered across paper files, network shares, email inboxes and the organization's AS400 processing system. As a result of this environment, auditing and reporting were both a challenge.

Grinnell Mutual, leveraging its longtime ECM vendor's case management capabilities, created a mission-critical application for managing the vital areas of policy underwriting and claims for all its clients. The case management application was built on an underlying content repository, leveraging native integration and workflow functionality. Rather than relying on traditional development or custom coding in IT, Grinnell Mutual's system administrator created the application via point-and-click configuration of the platform.

One of the main goals of the application was to better keep track of notes on the policy and claims files and improve collaboration between Grinnell Mutual's Underwriting and Claims departments. The solution equips the organization to roll up all policies by customer number and view all underwriting and claims information in one central place; improving departmental efficiency and ensuring more effective client service. More than 300 users within the Policy/Underwriting and Claims business units regularly use the case management solution, including claims adjusters and underwriters, as well as supervisors, directors and vice presidents for each area.

Over the past few years, the team has continued to expand and adapt the application to meet Grinnell Mutual's growing underwriting and claims management needs; responding effectively to end-user feedback. The case management solution brings Grinnell Mutual the tremendous visibility it needs to improve client service levels while mitigating compliance risks. Employees in both Underwriting and Claims have access to all the information they require to best manage their work, with a 360-degree view of all policy and claim information and the opportunity to make notes and collaborate on the case.

2. OVERVIEW

Challenges in visibility, collaboration and information management

Before implementing a case management solution for its Underwriting and Claims departments, Grinnell Mutual faced several challenges:

- Underwriting and Claims tracked and managed information supporting a policy or claim via paper scattered across desktops (with sticky notes for comments and questions) and disorganized Word files. Its legacy AS400 processing system did not provide sufficient note-taking capability. There was an overall lack of consistency in how policies and claims were handled.
- There was a lack of visibility between Underwriting and Claims in terms of information, actions taken and reasoning behind decisions on a policy.
- Employees had to manually search for claims information and any supporting documents across multiple locations, causing underwriting and claims-handling delays.
- Internal and external auditing and reporting were difficult without all policy and claim information being managed in one central place.
- Grinnell Mutual had no way to effectively tie accounts together and easily see all related accounts within an umbrella policy.

To mitigate these challenges, Grinnell leveraged its ECM vendor's case management and application configuration capabilities, creating a mission-critical application for managing policy underwriting and claims for all its clients.

A mission-critical application

The flexible case management application – built on an underlying content repository and leveraging native workflow functionality – was first created in 2010 by Grinnell Mutual's system administrator. While evaluating various solutions to improve policy, underwriting and claims processes, the administrator came across a video about the configurable case management capabilities of its ECM platform. After watching the video 10 times, she was inspired to use the tool to create an information-centric underwriting and claims case management application. The discovery, design and implementation work was completed internally by the system administrator (without professional services). She worked with two underwriting representatives and one claims representative, using their feedback, preferences and job requirements to design a tailored solution. The original design and implementation, done via point-and-click configuration, was accomplished in just 8-12 weeks.

The primary goal of the application was to better keep track of notes on a policy, providing underwriters with a place to document their thought processes in reviewing the policy for acceptance. Another objective was to thoroughly document the claims process, allowing adjusters to make and track notes on the claims file. Ultimately, Grinnell Mutual sought to improve key collaboration among the Underwriting and Claims departments.

More than 300 users within the Policy/Underwriting and Claims business units regularly use the case management solution, including claims adjusters and underwriters, as well as supervisors, directors and vice presidents for each area. Over the past few years, Grinnell has continued to expand and adapt the application to meet its growing underwriting and claims management needs.

Reaping benefits

The case management solution brings Grinnell Mutual the visibility it needs to improve client service levels while mitigating compliance risks. Employees in both the Underwriting and Claims departments have access to all the information they need in order to manage their work; displaying a 360-degree view of all policy and claim information in views tailored by role. Other benefits include:

- The case management application integrates with and complements the company's homegrown processing system. For example, data from open claims abstracts on the homegrown system screen are "scraped" directly into the case management application and automatically associated with the appropriate policy/file.

- Grinnell Mutual improves customer service levels with greater consistency across key processes. All underwriting applications are reliably collected and routed within OnBase. Underwriters receive only complete applications and must follow some established processing steps, ensuring that agents get consistent feedback to provide responses to customers sooner.

- The solution eliminates the need to switch among systems, applications, file shares and email inboxes to find the information needed to manage a case. Within the solution interface, a "Documents" tab is organized to show a dynamic, folder-like view of all the documents claims adjusters and supporting users need, such as Medical and Correspondence documents.

- Collaboration is greatly improved, with all underwriters and claims adjusters gaining access to the most up-to-date information at any given time. With the ability to add and review notes and link all supporting documents, employees benefit from a clear view of how and why decisions were made on a policy or claim.

- Internal auditors now have a way to see a complete picture of all actions take on policies or claims; including a decision trail, who handled the case, conversations that occurred and what actions were taken.

3. BUSINESS CONTEXT

Before consolidating and connecting all information surrounding underwriting, policies and claims within its case management application, Grinnell Mutual faced challenges with both visibility and collaboration.

Using an AS400 system for claim processing, Grinnell Mutual had no way to leverage that product to keep track of notes and effectively collaborate on the claim file. Notes pertaining to claims were scattered across desktops and electronic Word documents, and sticky notes were commonly used to keep track of relevant information. There were no historical tracking mechanisms or official record of decisions, conversations or actions taken on a claim or policy.

Additionally, policy information was disconnected from other critical supporting content like notes, conversations/correspondence and related documentation. Underwriters and claims adjusters had to manually search for information and supporting documentation to write a policy or handle a claim. They also couldn't easily roll up policies by customer number, which made it a challenge to handle multiple policies on an account.

Finally, there was little visibility between the Claims and Underwriting departments. The groups could not easily see the current status of a policy and had no awareness of why decisions had been made or what the other group was working on at any given time. A lack of all information in one central place also impacted both internal and external auditability.

4. THE KEY INNOVATIONS

4.1 Business

The case management project impacted Grinnell Mutual in several ways, improving value for both employees and the customers served. This includes the following:

- The solution equips Grinnell to underwrite more (and better) business faster. Standardizing underwriting processes across both its personal lines and commercial lines provided consistency across the department. Underwriters make quicker and more well-informed decisions on new policies and renewals, and they spend more time evaluating risk and less time searching for information.

- A self-documenting file for claims and policies (with some notes like status updates being automatically made on the case) allows underwriters to focus on making effective underwriting decisions and claims adjusters to focus on adjusting claims.

- Underwriters and claims adjusters have seamless access to all policy and claim-related documents in a dynamic folder structure, allowing them to more quickly handle inquiries from agents and customers. Alerts and exceptions are also flagged on the case (surfaced from the processing system), which helps ensure they are handled efficiently.

- Selected note types are exposed to external customers on an external Web portal, improving visibility and level of service.

4.2 Case Handling

Pre-Solution Case Handling

Before implementing its case management solution, Grinnell Mutual didn't have a formal, organized case handling process. While its policy- and claim-related documents were stored in its ECM system, notes pertaining to those policies and claims handling processes were scattered across the organization in a variety of formats (including paper documents, sticky notes and email correspondence). Underwriters didn't have a consistent or established way to document their thought processes and decisions, which would have been helpful for both internal audits and incoming claims. The Underwriting and Claims departments, while working with the same customers and with many of the same documents, didn't have a method of effectively sharing information about what was going on in the files. Grinnell was missing a complete view of all the claims for a given policy and all the policies for a given customer.

Post-Solution Case Handling

Grinnell Mutual's case management solution added great value to the underwriters, claims adjusters and other staff handling policies and claims. Because the solution was created on a platform that provides the ability to define relational data models, relationships and links are created among records for customers, policies and claims. Objects (data records) exist within the system for things like claims, policies and customers and, by leveraging common data elements such as policy number and customer number, users can easily access and view all connected information in one intuitive solution interface. This supports effective information management and case handling providing a 360-degree view of all related data, documents, tasks, notes and other information surrounding a "case" (i.e. policy or claim).

Additionally, every attribute defined in the data model is reportable and searchable; enabling users to execute queries and reports, such as reporting on all claims for a given customer or policy. With the solution, Grinnell Mutual has a comprehensive view of how many claims exist on a policy file, along with information like whether it's an at-fault claim or if there is a reserve on the claim.

These data relationships also enable unique views to be created for different roles; for example, while they might need to see some of the same data and documents, claims adjusters and underwriters have different needs overall. By creating linkages in the data models, Grinnell Mutual can expose individual views of all information, providing a tailored view for each knowledge worker with the same system, rather than trying to custom-integrate separate applications.

In addition to linking records, the administrator links document types/document keywords corresponding to content in the underlying content repository to specific data elements on the records. Documents are dynamically surfaced based on these connections within the record itself, within an organized folder structure. And because they are surfaced in virtual folders rather than part of a static attachment, the same document can appear in various views for different knowledge workers, ensuring that any updates or modifications are surfaced simultaneously and that work isn't siloed on desktops or email inboxes.

Case Handling Example – First Notice of Loss & Medical Bills

When a First Notice of Loss (FNOL) is received, it is routed via workflow automation to the Claims setup area. Staff use an established task to assign a claims adjuster and the object (data record) is then initially created for the claim. Accordingly, when the adjuster receives the FNOL in their queue, the claim object has already been created and linked to the policy object and is now ready for the adjuster to quickly review the policy information, note the assigned underwriter and review any necessary policy documents.

As the adjuster begins to work the claim, the processing system sends information to the case management application, auto-creating notes for the claim and keeping a chronological order of what is happening on the case. If an adjuster or manager is changed, the case is updated; if a reserve is set or changed, that is logged in the notes on the case itself.

Next, while processing a claim, an adjuster can handle many medical bills for a number of claimants. When a medical bill is received and processed via workflow automation, the system creates a Medical Log object (data record), if one doesn't currently exist for the claimant. The system then creates a Medical Bill object, which includes date of service, date of review and amount, along with some other data attributes. When the medical bill is sent to a third-party vendor for review, the date is updated within the object (data record). When Grinnell Mutual receives a response back from the third-party, another date is updated, automatically keeping all medical bill information up-to-date for the adjuster managing the case. When the adjuster or their manager reviews the medical bills, they can open the case for the claim and select the Medical Log for the claimant, easily drilling down into each bill for review. The medical bill document itself is also attached to the claim object for quick and easy access.

Additionally, by linking claim objects to policy objects, Grinnell Mutual provides a comprehensive view for the underwriter. At renewal time, the underwriter reviews the policy case for notes, alerts or exceptions that may have occurred over the course of the year and also has a view into all the claims that have been made on the policy.

Roles and Role-Based Security

More than 300 users within the Policy/Underwriting and Claims business units use the solution, including:

- VP and AVP of Underwriting
- Underwriting Supervisors and Directors
- Underwriters
- Underwriting Associates and Assistants
- VP and AVPs of Claims
- Claims Adjusters
- Claims Supervisors, Directors and Managers
- Claims Associates and Assistants

The administrator controls who can see which information via user security leveraging Active Directory (AD). For example, underwriting assistants don't have access to claim information, so when they go into the application to view a particular policy, they don't see that context.

4.3 Organization & Social

- The solution improved collaboration between Underwriting and Claims, with a complete, central view of all information, content and ability to track, view and modify notes on policy decisions, claims handling tasks, etc.
- Rather than spending time searching for information on desktops, email inboxes and other applications, employees writing policies and managing claims can now focus on valuable analysis and decision-making.

5. HURDLES OVERCOME

Management

Grinnell Mutual's system administrator got buy-in from management before implementing the solution with the expectation that the solution would bring great value to the Claims and Underwritings processes.

Organization Adoption

The system administrator who designed and implemented the solution worked very closely with liaisons from the Underwriting and Claims business units. By having the right conversations and conducting the appropriate discovery, she was able to design personalized user experiences fit for each role. This greatly improved user adoption from the start. Claims adjusters specifically embraced the solution almost immediately, realizing right away that the system could automate many of their previously manual notes and tasks, and allow them to focus on more valuable work.

Over time, as needs changed and users had a chance to use the solution and provide feedback, the administrator could easily add data elements and adapt views via point-and-click configuration of the platform (without the need for time-consuming custom coding). For example, she recently added a feature to the solution that displays alerts and exceptions for a policy – such as a restricted driver – within the main view by pulling in information from the processing system.

Grinnell Mutual also has an internal training department, and every new employee receives some training on the solution and the underlying platform upon hire. This is complemented by solution-specific documentation to ease the transition and provide a better user experience.

6. BENEFITS

6.1 Cost Savings / Time Reductions

Several features of the solution save Grinnell Mutual's business units valuable time that was previously spent on tedious tasks.

For example, an area within the application enables certain notes taken by the claims adjusters and underwriters to be displayed for agents on their secured site. This provides agents with access to claims updates in real time as required by the adjusters or the legal team. This has made agents extremely happy because they no longer have to call the adjuster for updates. It also saves Grinnell Mutual time by minimizing the need to field phone calls and emails to answer questions about claims.

A template-based document composition component is also a time-saver. Claims adjusters can auto-generate more than 10,000 documents per month, with approximately 789 templates to choose from. An extensive workflow process makes the creation of these as easy, fast and straightforward for users as possible.

An integration between the application and Grinnell's AS400 processing system eliminates dual entry for items such as whom claims are assigned to. This expedites the claims process, getting claims to the adjuster faster.

The ease of solution configuration has been extremely valuable. The system administrator can easily add data elements and adapt the solution to changing needs and user feedback. Because the platform allows for point-and-click configuration, changes can be made very rapidly and surfaced to all users simultaneously.

6.2 Quality Improvements

By implementing a case management solution and moving from paper to electronic processes, Grinnell Mutual has transformed its Underwriting and Claims business units.

- Underwriters can write better business faster with a complete view of all information and the ability to consolidate all required data and documentation. The underwriting process is now consistent across Grinnell Mutual.
- Internal and external auditors have a one-stop-shop for all information on claims and policies; improving the audit process and mitigating risk. In the past, during an underwriting audit, auditors never had a full picture.
- Transparency between Underwriting and Claims has improved tremendously with the ability to see all notes surrounding a policy or claim, as well as a decision trail.
- When claims adjusters or underwriters transition or transfer, the employee taking over their book of business has a complete snapshot of everything that has happened thus far, including a trail of all decisions, notes and collaboration about the case. Before the case management solution, all of this information might have been in the underwriter's personal email inbox or somewhere else' making the move a challenge.

7. BEST PRACTICES, LEARNING POINTS AND PITFALLS

7.1 Best Practices and Learning Points

✓ When it comes to defining a data model and relationships within the solution, it's helpful to have it all written out. More planning up front – including documenting relationships and having the business units review and approve the potential case "views" – makes a big impact in the long run.

✓ Work with the business units early in the process to truly understand their needs and requirements. This is helpful when designing tailored, personalized interfaces that will be most valuable in their day-to-day work.

7.2 Pitfalls

✗ Think carefully about which information should be defined in the case management solution and in what order to best create relationships among records. For example, it would have been beneficial to first identify and define the customer information record before defining the related policy and claim records (this was done the other way around in the initial solution).

8. COMPETITIVE ADVANTAGES

By streamlining policy underwriting and claims processes, the case management solution equips Grinnell Mutual to deliver the high-quality, personalized customer service that it strives to provide.

9. TECHNOLOGY

Grinnell Mutual used the OnBase enterprise information platform's case management capabilities to point-and-click configure its claims and policy underwriting application, which is referred to internally as Global Notes. This solution was created by Grinnell's system administrator without outside services and was designed to serve as the centralized hub for all claims- and policy-related information and related collaboration. Using the existing OnBase SQL server backend, the solution also acts as a central point of documentation for any communication that occurs between policy holders and Grinnell Mutual, replacing a previously all-paper process.

Grinnell Mutual seamlessly designed the application to connect to key content in the underlying ECM repository and benefit from natively integrated workflow routing and automation capabilities. Workflow capabilities currently help automate the creation of the policy and claims objects (data records) and seamlessly build the cases, adding and tracking related information and collaboration along the way. This enhances the overall process, enabling the adjusters and underwriters to focus on valuable case handling. To further improve the process, Grinnell Mutual leverages specific preconfigured folders (removing the need for coding) so that as documents are ingested into the system, they are automatically associated to a claim/policy (via Claim # or Policy #) and segregated automatically so that users can find the necessary document quickly when needed.

Additionally, Grinnell Mutual's solution also includes an integration with Microsoft Word 2010/2013 and a document composition capability to generate pre-defined letters and documents that are sent to customers. By using the pre-defined structures, fields are automatically populated by metadata residing in OnBase, reducing the chance of possible clerical errors and streamlining the process. Along with these functions, Grinnell Mutual also takes advantage of a full range of native platform capabilities within the solution, including electronic forms, data transfer between line-of-business system and OnBase, and document security.

10. THE TECHNOLOGY AND SERVICE PROVIDERS

About OnBase by Hyland

OnBase is a single enterprise information platform for managing content, processes and cases. OnBase has transformed thousands of organizations worldwide by empowering them to become more agile, efficient and effective.

OnBase provides enterprise content management (ECM), case management, business process management (BPM), and capture all on a single database, code base and content repository. Enterprise file sync and share (EFSS) for the OnBase platform is available with our complementary offering, ShareBase.

For more information, please visit OnBase.com.

About Hyland, creator of OnBase

Hyland is the creator of OnBase, a single enterprise information platform for managing content, processes and cases. For 25 years, Hyland has enabled more than 14,900 organizations to digitalize their workplaces and fundamentally transform their operations. Named one of Fortune's 2016 Best Companies to Work For®, Hyland is widely known as both a great company to work for and a great company to do business with.

For more information, please visit OnBase.com.

Leading European Bank Banking Correspondence Management System

Nominated by ISIS Papyrus Europe AG, Austria

1. EXECUTIVE SUMMARY / ABSTRACT

This case study describes the implementation of an Adaptive Case Management system—Banking Correspondence Management System (BCMS)—in a leading European Bank (in the following named 'the Bank').

The Bank is one of the largest players in the world with roots anchored in Europe's economic history. With presence in more than 70 countries and over 180,000 employees, the Bank is a leader in the Eurozone and a prominent international banking institution. For the Bank, the existing solution to create mass business communication as online requested business documents had become slightly outdated and called for a complete remake to use more efficiently the human resources of the output management department dealing with document design, development as well as production.

The newly-defined Banking Correspondence Management System (BCMS) aims to facilitate flexibility in the document management processes that are daily executed, enabling ad hoc changes directly by the business departments in order to react on short notice to new document requirements and become less dependent on IT development resources. The solution supports design, sign-off, deployment and production of customized individual online correspondence as well as mass batch document production. On average, 20-25 new document template definitions are released every month producing typically 15,000 online documents per hour and more than 20 million batch documents for central printing each month.

Moreover, BCMS links independent working environments of different departments to facilitate cooperation and teamwork among all knowledge workers. The goal is to establish a flawless communication among involved people and departments controlling the whole document lifecycle across all departments of the Bank.

Built upon an Adaptive Case Management (ACM) framework, BCMS provides the flexibility, spontaneity and transparency for case management, handling the document lifecycle from design over development including deployment into production as well as production management.

BCMS empowers knowledge workers to create and maintain a huge amount of document templates in a flexible manner with consistency by design and compliance of contents. Further, the system facilitates the collaboration between business and IT to increase the efficiency and timeliness of production processes enabling also multichannel output based on client's preferences.

2. OVERVIEW

Document design is an important factor in the business communication of the Bank. Documents sent to their customers not only transfer information but also represent the image of the bank. Producing high-quality documents that have consistent design in every case and follow all regulations is critical and thus document templates are strategic elements of their customer communication. Using document templates can facilitate writing in the same style; publishing in single or batch documents with automatic data input; and maintenance for thousands of designs. Moreover, document templates classified in different language versions can reduce the complexity of multi-language documents adhering to the same standards.

BCMS aims to facilitate the document design and development process by providing a common working environment for a productive collaboration between business users and IT developers. The acknowledged benefits gained from the project are improved document content quality and reduction of time and effort along with the increasing number of documents generated every month. Besides the good results, the project also encounters some challenges from user perspective and from the techniques applied for the system.

In BCMS, business users are responsible for the document design and act as knowledge workers in the ACM-based BCMS. They fully participate in the document development process and design the documents directly in the change managed production system. The system brings an intuitive interface to business users for creating document layouts and defining business logic on document building blocks. An important goal is to empower business users in the creation of business logic with no, or only minimal, support from IT. The document logic including data interfaces that are out of the scope of business users is described for IT people in the document specification as comments using natural language. This way, the communication gap between business users and IT developers is closed with the middle to long-term expectation that after some learning period business users can care for all the business logic themselves. All teams are working in a common system using the same document objects under the control of a change management system.

The change management is part of the ACM framework and enables multiple versions and project stages of business entities in BCMS. Users have private projects where they freely develop their ideas independently from others and publish to public projects when ready. The release handling process of BCMS ensures that different types of projects are managed for individuals as well as whole teams. Further, the change management ensures a harmonious working environment where independency and cooperation can go hand in hand.

BCMS produces high-quality documents by using professional document design functions. Various regulatory and industry standards are aligned in every single document template. To achieve these results, business users needed to adapt to the new technology for document design and get used to the new system. After overcoming the obstacles that usually occur during the introduction of new complex systems, the system has been launched into production and an increased number of users is added gradually for daily release and production work.

3. BUSINESS CONTEXT – THE INITIAL STATE OF THE BANK

Communication with millions of customers is a key focus in the Bank where retail banking is a large business unit of the organization. Documents for customers in diverse business domains require different layouts. Therefore, document design needs to be flexible and quickly adapted to meet various requirements.

Collaboration between business users and IT developers

The output management department has a size of about 20 persons with responsibility for more than 2,500 document layouts, with a growth of around 250 new templates per year. Business users draft document layouts with MS Word and describe the specification for the document development process. Based on the drafts along with specifications, IT developers build document layouts in an application specific for document development with business data integration. This kind of application requires IT skills from users that are not suitable for business users. In order for the document development to fully meet the business specifications, IT developers need to have a good communication with business users to understand the expected products.

In the initial system, the document design and development processes were quite isolated in terms of working environments and people involved. Business users provided document specifications and document layouts as material for the document development process. They could not really participate in the process where IT developers were working on their desired document applications. The communication between IT and business users used mainly emails with attachments of document specifications. Due to the lack of a seamless communication system, which allowed all involved people to access all necessary information, misunderstandings caused time-consuming communication loops that affected the productivity of the process.

Document design in MS Word-based systems

The maintenance of a document template library is managed by the output management team. Thousands of document templates in different languages were handled through standard file management systems that were not designed to support the linkage between document templates and its language variants and versions. Moreover, the creation of a new document had to be started from scratch without inheriting useful definitions from the existing documents. With up to 25 new document layouts per month, maintenance of the document template library became a challenge for the team.

4. THE KEY INNOVATIONS OF THE NEW SYSTEM

Business

Improve the response capability on customer requests

Reworking of documents can be minimized in BCMS as business users are able to create new versions of document templates, which were defined by business in cooperation with IT developers. In case of a simple document without new data structures, the document template can be fully handled by the business user and quickly released into the production stage. Moreover, business users have flexibility to reopen a closed document design case without involving a complex process of authorization.

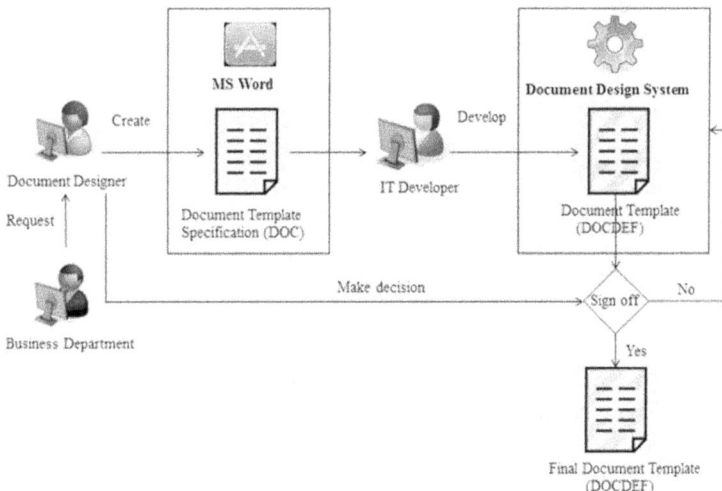

The system not only reduces the efforts in document design but also increases the quality of document templates. According to an internal statistic, in average 20-25 new document template definitions are released every month producing 15,000 online documents per hour and more than 20 million batch documents for central printing each month.

Figure 1: Change Management in the MS Word based system

Case Handling

The initial system with isolated working tools

In the initial system, business designers create document layouts with MS Word based on the requirements from business departments (see Figure 1)

Every new document is created from scratch or by duplication from existing similar documents. The details of the document layout and its business logic are described by the business department requesting a specification for IT development from document designers. The document draft attached to the specification is sent to IT developers for implementation in the document design system. The document designer signs off the document development for entering the test phase. The business department signs off the document template specification its content and layout as well as the IT development part for production during the test phase.

The overall system architecture of the new BCMS

Built on ACM, BCMS is a solution for correspondence design and management. The system provides GUIs for different types of users with different roles. Document designers construct document templates following the document template specification received from business departments. The business logic that needs the implementa-

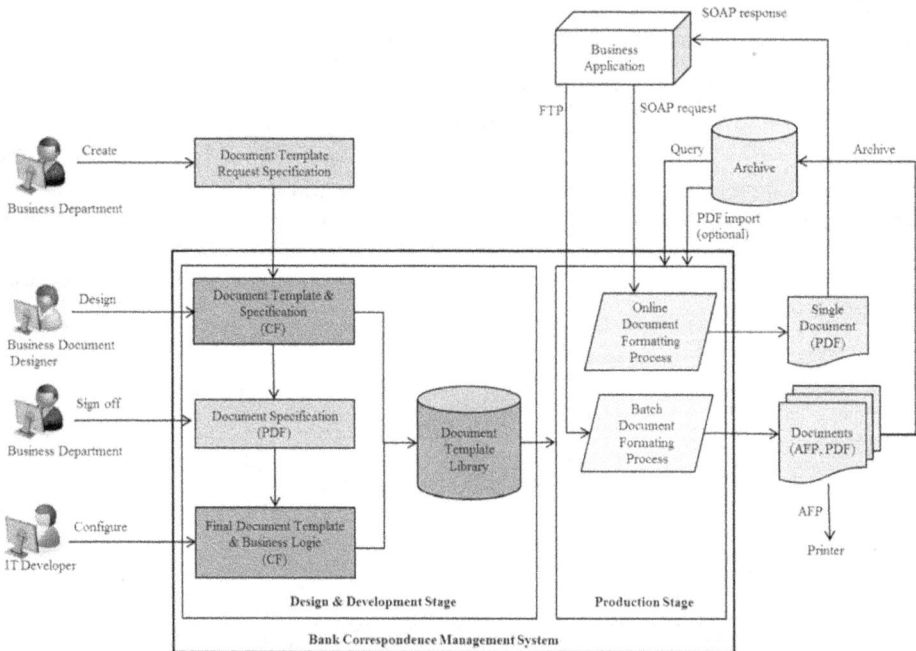

tion from IT developers is specified as annotation comments attached to the document template. Business departments evaluate the document designs before IT developers implement the technical parts. The document templates are located in a central document template library as common storage providing access to every authorized user.

Figure 2: Overview of BCMS

After completion in the design and development stage (see Figure 2), document templates are delivered to the production stage for online as well as batch production. Printing and archiving are consecutive steps outside BCMS. In the production stage, an external business application sends a Webservice SOAP request to trigger formatting of a single online document or trigger via FTP a batch file for a mass document formatting run. Single documents are sent back to the business application via SOAP responses as PDF documents. Mass documents are handed over to external print services in AFP format and are archived in PDF format. During document formatting, pages from archived PDF documents can be directly imbedded into the newly-formatted documents.

In BCMS, business users, aka knowledge workers, have autonomy to design and operate ad hoc actions based on their current business situation. Those ad hoc actions are managed and harmonized by change management and compliance-checking techniques implemented in BCMS with ACM, as discussed in the following sections.

Change management and role assignment of the new BCMS

The change management principle applied in BCMS is a fully customizable ACM-based process and aims to involve the right people for the right work at the right time. Figure 3 represents the change management process through all stages of a project where users with assigned roles have responsibility for changing of transitions.

In the *private development stage*, document designers, i.e. business users, and IT developers create document entities, such as document building blocks, document templates, building block language variants, etc. based on the requirements from

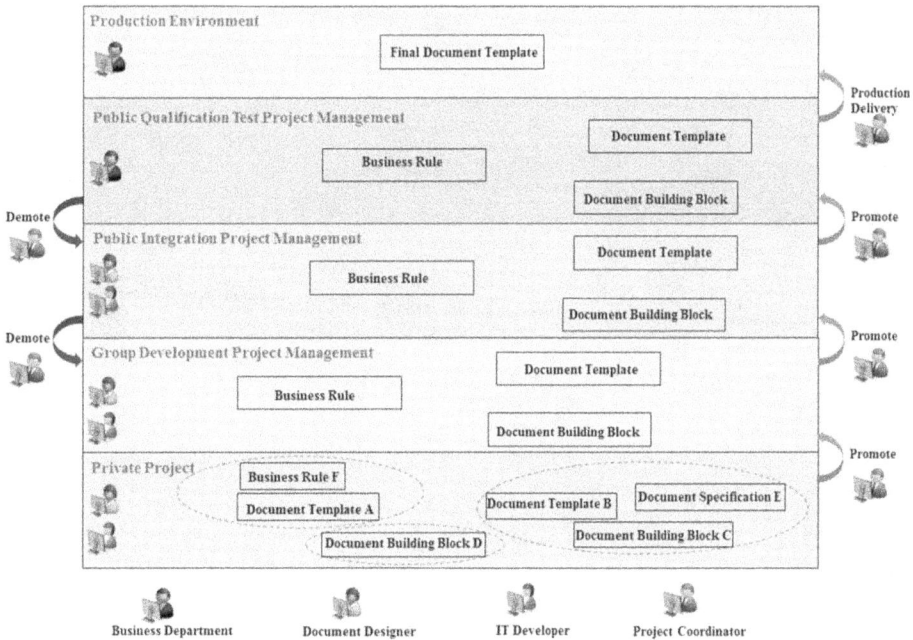

business departments. The private projects belong to each person and cannot be seen by the others until they are published. When completing the private development, users notify project coordinators for promoting their document entities to the group development projects for teamwork.

Figure 3: Change management in BCMS

In the *group development project management stage*, users, who are either document designers or IT developers, can access commonly accessible document entities for their working assignment and do initial development integration tests. Business departments validate the document design and specification before handing over to IT developers. Supervisors of the development team assign the tasks to available IT developers. Business coordinators validate the documents before promoting them to the next stage, which is the public integration stage.

In the *public integration project management stage*, the new development is tested for integration with existing components. Before the document items are released to the *production environment*, they are tested in the *public qualification test project management*. Project coordinators have the responsibility to promote or demote document entities between the stages of the change management system. The details of document design and change management are represented by use cases as follows. Document template design in the new BCMS

Figure 4 shows an ACM case view where users have all functions to deal flexibly with a case. A document design is managed within a case, aka a project in the business perspective of business users, including a set of predefined steps and related data. Besides the predefined tasks, business users are allowed to add goals or ad hoc tasks under a particular regulation that ensures the consistency of the case.

Access control and configuration

The system authorizes each user with access rights specified by roles and privileges. The user information is shown along with their username, role and organization they belong to. Business users can easily customize basic application settings, such as the UI language.

Various workplaces

The system provides GUIs for different types of users with different roles. As seen on the left side of Figure 4, the user can select among different workplaces like the workplace shown for case management. The second workplace is for document design and the last one is for document reporting, e.g. querying statistics about document templates that meet particular conditions.

Goal orientation

The case management workplace provides all functions for case management. A new case is instantiated by the function "New Case" executed by business users, independent from IT developers. A case is driven by a single goal or several structured goals which can be defined by the user. The goal represents a completion criterion for closing a case successfully.

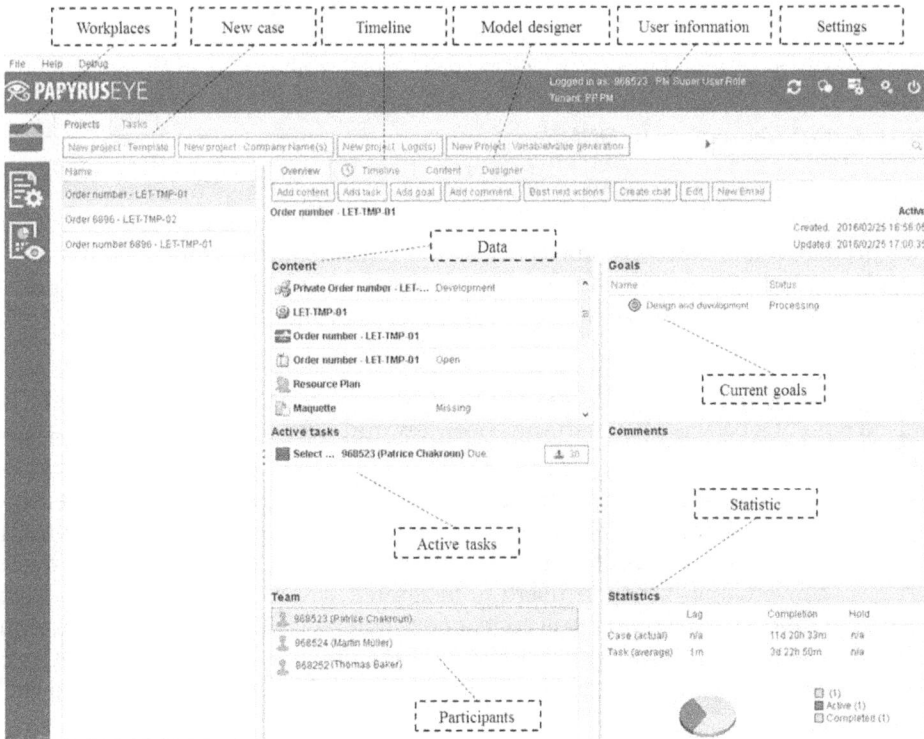

Figure 4: A case management view

Visualization

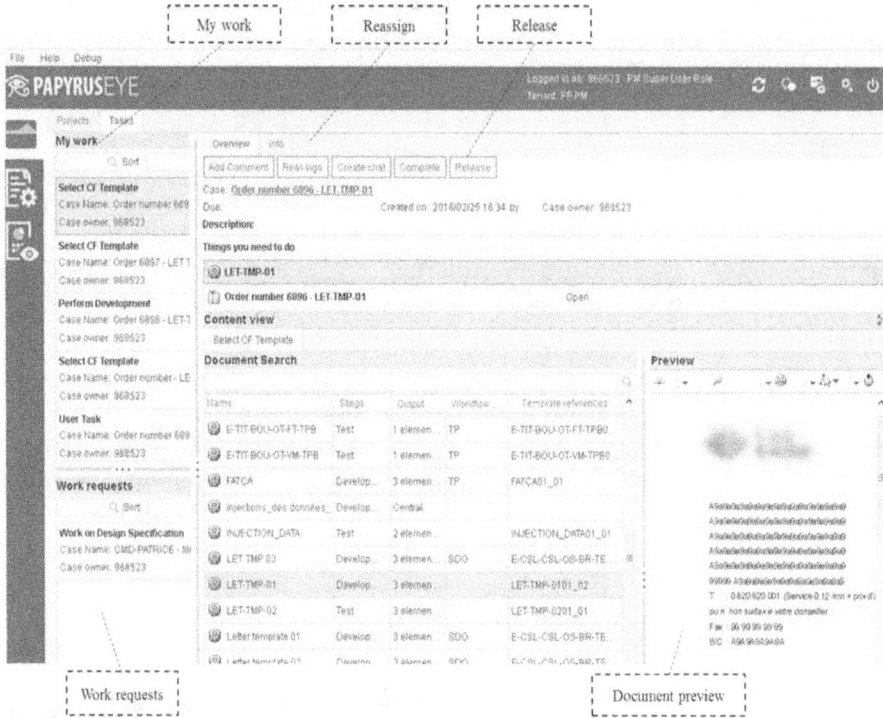

Figure 5: Collaboration in BCMS

To facilitate full case management, the system provides access to a case model designer, statistics and a task timeline. The model designer shows a visualization of the so far prepared and executed processes. In the timeline, the executed list of tasks is chronologically presented for the temporal view on a case. The statistics information shows the state of the current work in graphical diagrams.

Collaboration

The list of participants shows who is able to work on a case or a certain task. The involved data of a case is shown in the case view and used for previewing the associated task.

Figure 5 shows the task view where business users have the overview of their own currently active tasks and tasks assigned to them. They must accept a task from the work requests, reassign a task to another user or release a task back to a case owner. Moreover, conversation between users is facilitated within the system by an integrated chat function. The data involved in a case can be visualized in a preview panel on the right side of the figure, with full control of the document and its layout. During template definition where no business data are available placeholders are shown.

Access to the document template library

Users can access the document template library to select a suitable template for the current document design (see Figure 6). The library is categorized based on building block types, which can be text language variants, image language variants, business data variables or complete document templates. Users can create a new item, edit or delete the existing one, or create a document from multiple parts if the desired template is not existing yet. Moreover, users can simulate the business logic in the template by importing test data to have a complete overview of the document in all data constellations that will be delivered to customers.

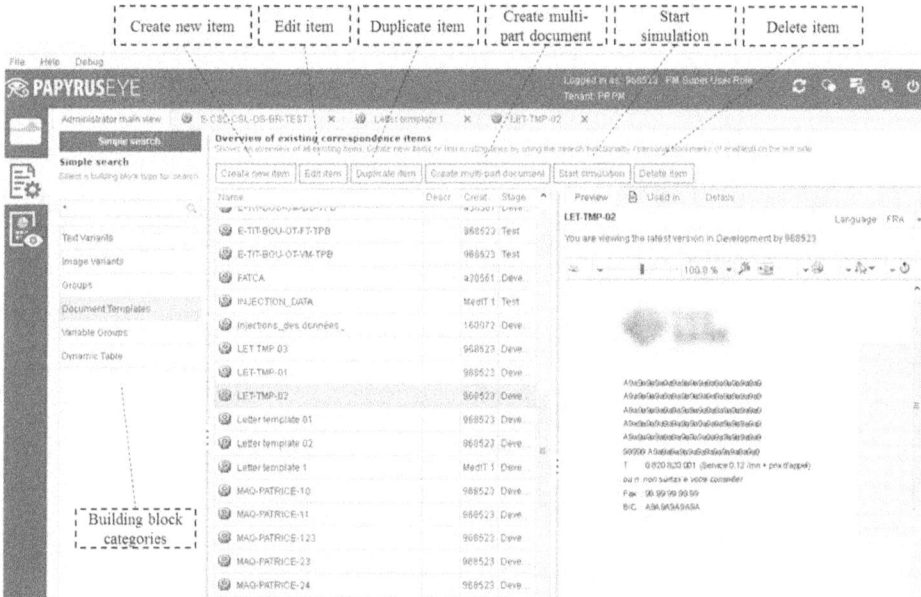

Figure 6: Document template library

Document building blocks

Document building blocks are the constructing components of a document template. Figure 7 shows how a document template is built from several building blocks. It is important that business users can independently select a user interface language (English in Figure7) and the correspondence language (French in Figure7) which supports a predefined set of company defined languages with spellchecking and hyphenation.

Each building block has multiple versions in different languages that can be specified on the interface by the language setting. The left frame displays the whole document template while the frame on the right bottom corner previews a single building block which can be added to the document template at a certain position.

To add such a building block from the library to the document template, users simply drag a block from the building block library and drop it onto the right position of the document tree structure. Properties of each building block contain attributes which define exact position and format on the document canvas.

Each building block can have rules defined in natural language to make its invocation dependent on certain input data variables.

Change management

Business departments verify the document template designed by document designers, as shown in Figure 8. If the "Validate" function is selected, the document is sent further to developer supervisors. With "Reject" it is sent back to document designers with attached comments including requirements for improvement.

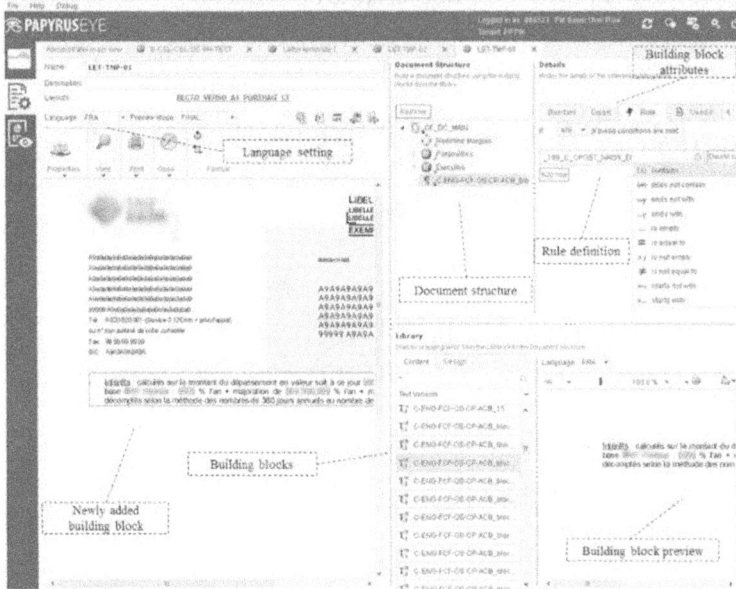

Figure 7: Document building blocks

Figure 8: Document design validation

Figure 9 shows the workplace of developer supervisors where they assign available IT developers to a certain case. The selected IT developers will receive the document

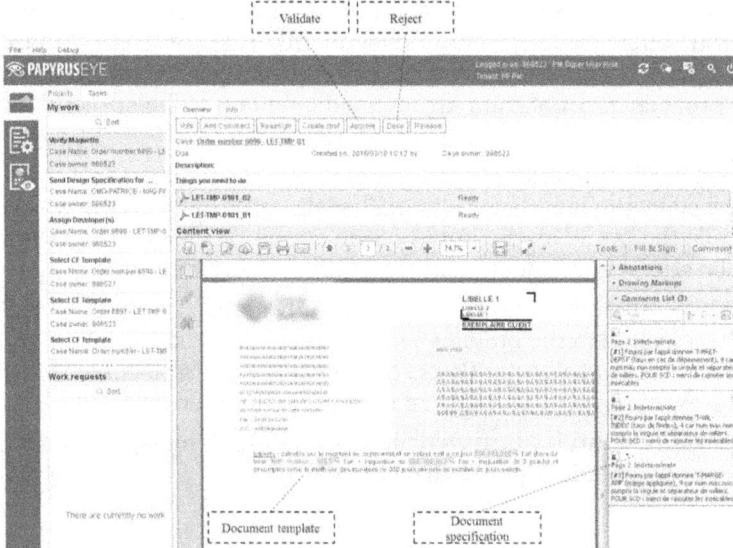

template to finish the document development which is mainly about technical configurations related to more sophisticated document elements, such as data interfaces for input of business data, complex business rules or dynamic tables. When the document is finished, it is sent to project coordinators who verify the development, as seen in Figure 10. A "compare view" shows two versions of a document template to facilitate the verification. If the document is rejected, it is returned to IT developers. If it is validated, business department will test the document and decide whether it is released in production

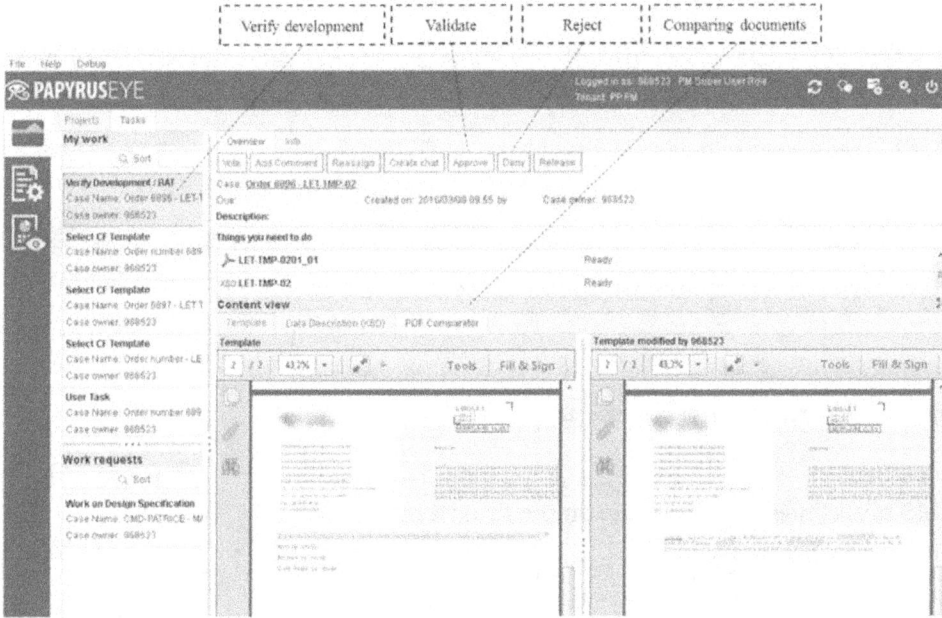

Figure 9: Assign developers

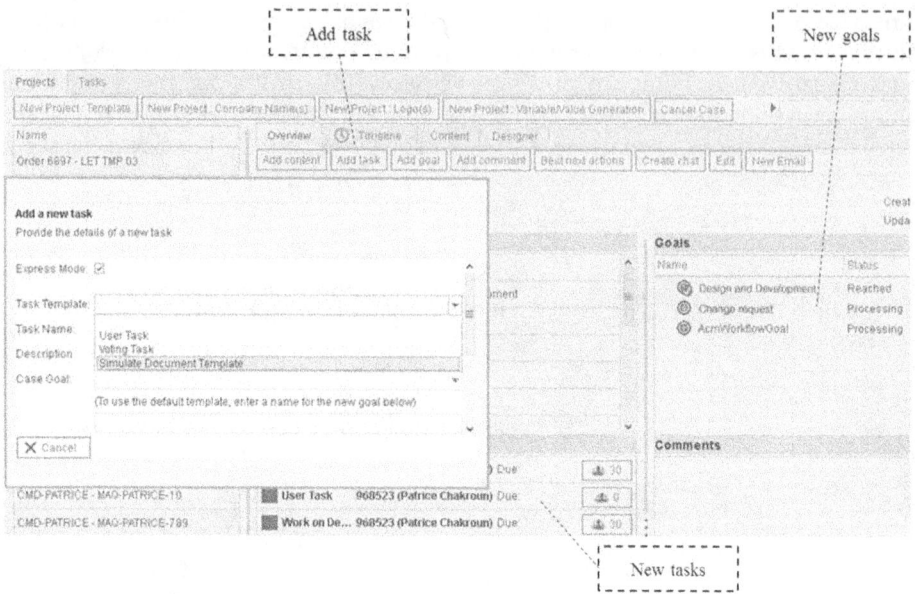

Figure 10: Validate development

Ad hoc actions

BCMS allows users to add tasks on the fly or reopen a case.

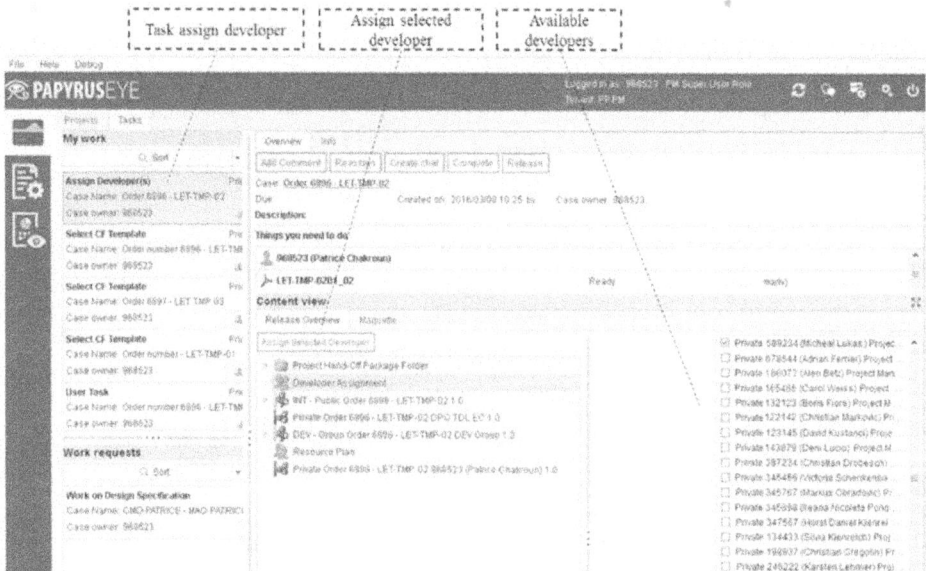

Figure 11: Ad hoc actions in BCMS

As seen in Figure 11, a case is closed when the main goal is reached. However, the user interface allows users to simply reopen the case and continue editing a document when, for example, the need for a late change was recognized. A new goal is added on the goal structure and a new task also appears in the task list. Moreover, users can add an ad hoc task that was not planned for the case by clicking the "Add task" button. A selection of task templates is offered in a browse window which contains beside generic task templates also specific templates for ad hoc situations that were not expected. For example, the task "Simulate document template" can be added in the middle of a document design process to preview the document with a set of test input data. The selected ad hoc task is added to the case via a generic goal, as the AcmWorkflowGoal seen in Figure 11.

5. ORGANIZATION & SOCIAL

Seamless communication and productive collaboration between business users and IT developers

Communication between business users and IT developers is a key factor leading to an efficient system where IT developers can satisfy effectively the business requirement specified by business users. Because of the big difference between their knowledge-intensive domains, the communication is a challenge especially when users are in different locations and use different terminologies. Instead of using emails to exchange work packages, business users and IT developers share their work in a unified system. The workflows between people are seamlessly operated without media breaks as seen in the former system. BCMS facilitates harmonious collaboration between private projects and teamwork and thus bring seamless workflows between individuals and groups. Therefore, BCMS enables an efficient communication between business users and IT developers.

Business teams are satisfied that they can design document templates more quickly and independently

BCMS provides business teams with business user GUIs with full capabilities to design document layouts. After some training for the change management processes, business users are able to work independently on document design tasks. If some parts of the document demand for business logic definitions, business users specify the requirement for IT developers who develop the technical components. However, the document design by business users is released into the central document library ready for the next steps of the document design process. IT developers complete the definition of documents based on the specifications imbedded in the document templates.

IT developers enforce corporate identity consistently through predefined layout templates.

BCMS manages the production of thousands of customer communication documents to meet corporate, regulatory and industry standards for the global financial organization of the Bank. It ensures the consistency and compliance of the document layouts by providing predefined templates for business users. The corporate identity is enforced in thousands of document templates and thus, it ensures well-designed and high-quality documents representing the Bank to their customers.

6. HURDLES OVERCOME

The changing of working environments is a challenge to the users and requires a transition period for full acceptance of the new way of working. Thus, BCMS was initially deployed but continuously adapted based on daily feedback of the Bank's employees. Trainings were provided to all business users in order to promote the usage of the system. Besides communicating the benefits for daily work, the management of the Bank encouraged employees to accept BCMS also by highlighting the commercial benefits that the Bank gains through the system, as discussed in Section 6.

BCMS allows business users to directly participate in the document development process. Although the user interfaces are designed especially considering the needs of business users, some background knowledge about document design with reusable building blocks and change management helps to understand the new approach. Moreover, the system provides professional document design functions, such as building block composition, content formatting including spellchecking in the related document language and sign-off which requires additional skills from the business users. Therefore, the document design process needed in the early stage of BCMS uses less time than in the old system.

7. BENEFITS

Cost Savings / Time Reductions

- The development time is reduced by 50% in the development phase and up to 90% in the release phase of document templates.
- The total effort for the whole process is cut down on average by 50%.

1.1 Increased Revenues

- In the first phase of the project, the revenues cannot be estimated.

Quality Improvements

- Consistency in document layouts and content
- Well-designed format
- Corporate identity enforced in every document

8. BEST PRACTICES, LEARNING POINTS AND PITFALLS

Best Practices and Learning Points

✓ *The work of document designers can be reused and continued by IT developers.*

✓ *As a key factor for a successful system implementation, the collaboration among involved teams must be in focus in every phase of the project.*

✓ *A solid but adaptable change management process is essential for an expanding collection of document templates with different versions.*

✓ *Data visualization facilitates users in capturing the overview as well as details of a document design case.*

Pitfalls

✗ *The background knowledge required for the new system should be imparted to users as early as possible.*

✗ *Business users should be involved in the user interface discussion early, so that they get familiar with the new system and contribute from their experiences to increase user acceptance.*

✗ *Professional trainings for business users are important to seamlessly introduce a new system for correspondence management.*

9. COMPETITIVE ADVANTAGES

Allowing business users to develop documents themselves is the most competitive advantage of BCMS. The gaps among business users and document developers were eliminated as they can collaborate and seamlessly share work. As a long-term plan, this collaboration will increase the benefits as the business can get into full control of the process producing their desired documents. Moreover, the system ensures the consistency of corporate identity and high quality in every document design.

Built on ACM, BCMS inherently supports flexibility in the document design process. Business users can create or edit a document template at any time independently from document developers. Moreover, the change management in BCMS with a flexible release process handles different versions of document templates efficiently and gives the control of the release process to the business departments.

10. TECHNOLOGY

ACM is used as a framework to combine ad hoc flexibility with predefined processes for a document design and release management system. The unique benefit of ACM for BCMS is that a document design case can be handled flexibly along the design process. The system provides a full set of functions for document design prepared with predefined templates. However, business users can independently edit a document case to flexibly deal with the challenges of daily work.

Change management is applied in BCMS to support the collaboration of business users and IT people. The release process allows business users to promote or demote business entities to another release stage depending on the assessment of the current development situation.

Correspondence management provides business users with a design tool for document templates. BCMS models documents from separate building blocks including business logic. The building blocks are treated as independent document entities and can be reused in different document templates to benefit from shared resources. A tradeoff between reduced development efforts vs. increased testing efforts when shared resources are being changed must be found. With this technique, BCMS empowers the Bank's document designers as well as IT developers to apply their expertise to daily development work.

11. THE TECHNOLOGY AND SERVICE PROVIDERS

ISIS Papyrus Europe AG delivers BCMS for correspondence design and management based on the standard software Papyrus platform. ISIS Papyrus offers a consolidated, end-to-end solution for inbound and outbound business communication and process management, using standard software components and solution frameworks:

- Papyrus WebRepository with ACM Solution Framework
- Papyrus Correspondence Solution
- Papyrus DocExec document formatter
- Papyrus DocExec/PDF
- Papyrus Designer for IT document development

ISIS Papyrus Communication and Process Platform:

https://www.isis-papyrus.com

Molina Healthcare Inc., USA

Nominated by Datum Solutions, United States

1. EXECUTIVE SUMMARY / ABSTRACT

Molina Healthcare, Inc. (Molina), offers health plans, clinical care and health information management to families and individuals covered by Medicaid, Medicare and other government-funded programs. With data held in complex medical charts, Molina found it challenging to meet deadlines for evaluations and audits by the Centers for Medicare and Medicaid Services (CMS), risking millions of dollars in potential lost revenue and audit penalties. By centralizing medical records in a single repository with integrated case management, the organization can retrieve chart data 50% faster—helping it meet regulatory requirements, avoid penalties and potentially qualify for millions in bonus payments.

2. OVERVIEW

Molina established a centralized repository for medical charts and other unstructured medical information, and introduced integrated case management and automatic coding for medical charts.

One of Molina's first steps was to create an enterprise taxonomy for properly categorizing content across the organization. This taxonomy was then leveraged by the enterprise content management (ECM) system to define the various document, folder, case, and tasks ensuring a consistent metadata model to be followed throughout Molina.

In order to facilitate better searching, retrieval, viewing, and management of documents, Molina established a single, centralized repository for medical charts and other unstructured medical information sources. Authorized users can request files through a chart target list, making it quick and easy for staff to access the information they need.

With these improvements in place, Molina introduced Central Medical Charts Management (CMCM); a new case management platform for handling CMS audits and evaluations.

When Molina receives a new CMS audit request, the ECM system automatically imports the file and creates a case in CMCM. Each case typically comprises hundreds of quality measures, which are represented as tasks. To complete a task, Molina employees search the content repository for pertinent data and use it to code charts with various scoring measures, using an electronic form for data entry. Once all tasks are completed, the case files are compiled into an aggregate report and automatically bundled with the requested medical charts and associated HEDIS measures sheets for delivery to CMS.

3. BUSINESS CONTEXT

As a Medicare plan provider, Molina is subject to rigorous evaluations and audits from CMS. Every year, CMS rates health plans using a five-star system. Ratings are based on a number of measures, such as the ability to effectively coordinate care, manage chronic illnesses and improve member retention.

Star ratings play a crucial role in helping Molina to maintain its Medicare contract with CMS and determine the level of payment incentives it receives from federal programs.

A significant portion of the quality measures contributing to the star ratings report is calculated using data from the Healthcare Effectiveness Data and Information Set (HEDIS) – a tool used to measure performance on important dimensions of care and service.

Each year, Molina has a strict timeline to submit HEDIS rates and source validations for a selected sample of members to CMS. Molina must collect medical records for as many of its selected members as possible within a five-month period.

A CMS request for HEDIS measures will involve approximately 300,000 medical charts on an annual basis. This means that each medical chart must be examined and coded with various scoring measures. The results for each medical chart are the collected and put into a comprehensive report provided to CMS for review and evaluation.

Due to the volume and complexity of the organization's medical charts, as well as the time required to manually search for pertinent performance data, Molina estimated that it completed fewer than half of its targeted pursuits in a given year. This meant that the organization was potentially missing opportunities to boost its star rating and to qualify for greater bonus payments.

To add to the challenge, Molina is required to respond to annual CMS audits. If the organization cannot provide the requested information to CMS within specified deadlines, it can be subjected to penalties ranging up to $20 million.

4.   THE KEY INNOVATIONS

The solution accelerates chart data retrieval by 50% and has greatly reduced errors—helping Molina respond to audit requests in a timely, accurate manner, avoiding penalties and potentially qualifying for millions of dollars in bonus payments.

4.1 Business

Molina is now able to meet all CMS requests for HEDIS quality measures, which are used in large part to determine the organization's CMS star rating. Not only has Molina shortened the time taken to respond to audit requests, it has significantly improved the level of data accuracy in its reports.

4.2 Case Handling

Prior to the case management solution implementation, teams at Molina spent many hours going through its archives to find and score each medical chart. Due to the lack of an enterprise catalogue, it often would take a great deal of time to locate a single chart. Once the chart was located, staff had to manually track a HEDIS measure score sheet and file it, along with the associated chart, into a secured shared drive for final assembly. Finally, a separate team aggregated all of the information into a single report, ready to be delivered to CMS. Due to the time involved with each step of the process, Molina was only able to respond to approximately 50% of charts requested each year by CMS.

With the new CMCM platform in place, Molina has automated the ingestion of charts sent by CMS, and streamlined many aspects of the chart coding process. The result was an increase to over 75% in the response rate for charts requested by CMS and able to meet compliance and audit requests within the deadlines mandated.

Molina developed its case management system using IBM ECM products in a shared services deployment. The shared services approach has enabled Molina to scale both horizontally and vertically while minimizing the amount of infrastructure required resulting in significant savings on those costs. The organization leverages the following IBM solutions and services:

- IBM Enterprise Document Services – Web Services layer providing a standard set of library services calls into the IBM Case Foundation libraries for actions such as document creation and retrieval.
- IBM Case Manager – case management platform which forms the foundation of the CMCM solution and other case-based systems at Molina.
- IBM Content Collector for File Systems – a tool used to ingest CMS evaluation requests for the medical charts.
- IBM Forms Server – an electronic forms tool leveraged as the data input user interface (UI) at each step of the medical chart coding process.

Molina has a HEDIS team responsible for the management of all information requested by CMS. As part of the CMCM solution, a Coding User is responsible for reviewing the medical chart and coding for the CMS report.

- The main business activities served by the CMCM solution are:
  - CMS Request – a request for gathering, scoring, and delivery along with a summary as a CMS Request Submission report.
  - Medical Chart – an individual medical chart requested that must be gathered, scored according to HEDIS measures, and submitted as part of the CMS Request Submission report.
  - CMS Request Submission – a report that has an aggregate summary of all HEDIS measures across all medical charts requested along with each individual medical chart and its associated scoring sheet.
- The CMCM Template was leveraged to provide the basis for a separate Risk Assessment and Management Program (RAMP) case-based solution at Molina. The ability to leverage the case type, meta-model, and security models greatly enhanced time-to-market for the Risk Adjustment business group.

4.3 Organization & Social

The overall HEDIS process has improved Molina's operational efficiency and accuracy. Coding Users no longer have to search through various locations to find a requested medical chart, as all information is now held in a single, easily searchable repository. Additionally, use of electronic forms has enhanced data quality while reducing error rates by leveraging data field validation.

5. HURDLES OVERCOME

Management

Molina's management teams across both HEDIS and RAMP had to agree on the centralization of medical charts and technologies required for addressing this and the processing tasks. It took a coordinated effort in order to handle both parties' concerns, as well as leverage the IBM technology, which had been purchased by Molina but was not yet in wide use prior to implementation of the solution.

Business

As with any process changes, whether system based or not, business end users are often resistant because they are not yet able to visualize the end results. However, changing from managing the requests by tracking them in spreadsheets and finding medical charts in various locations prior to coding and final submission, any form of automation was welcomed as an improvement.

Organization Adoption

Molina has expanded primarily through organic growth over the past 25 years. This growth brought in talent from a wide range of industries, who were used to leveraging vendor-provided platforms upon which to build solutions. This influx enabled Molina to further mature its IT-based solution approach to solving business needs and industry demands. Molina also infused its teams with various industry consultants, bringing with them overall best practices in process and technology.

6. BENEFITS

6.1 Cost Savings / Time Reductions

Prior to implementing the new solutions, Molina managed over 500,000 medical charts as part of the HEDIS programs. The manual retrieval of records from various systems or locations would take the following times:

- 94% - Charts found in less than 10 days.
- 4% - Charts found in full 10 days allotted.
- 1% - Charts never found in allotted time.

Following implementation, the following efficiency was achieved:

- 100% - Charts found in less than six days; most instances under one day.

That was an elimination of charts not found in allotted time and overall time reduction of 50%.

6.2 Increased Revenues

The overall bonus payment incentives received from this quality improvement and time reduction have enabled Molina to recoup millions of dollars each year while simultaneously mitigating penalties of up to $20 million from missing deadlines or delivering poor quality data.

6.3 Quality Improvements

Molina was able to improve quality in several areas by replacing manual data entry with automatic medical chart coding, and introducing more rigorous review processes. In fact, the organization has reduced the number of chart coding errors by 25 percent, ensuring that the information it submits to CMS is highly accurate.

6.4 Efficiency gains

Molina can use the automated medical chart workflow to track vendor performance and measure the productivity of internal coders in meeting audit and compliance timelines—allowing it to make targeted improvements to boost productivity. The organization has realized savings equal to 4 FTEs by automating chart-coding for a specific initiative.

7. BEST PRACTICES, LEARNING POINTS AND PITFALLS

7.1 Best Practices and Learning Points

- ✓ *Define an enterprise catalogue or single ECM system to manage all unstructured content in your organization.*
- ✓ *Leverage best-of-breed technologies/platforms wherever possible for your solution.*
- ✓ *Take advantage of a service provider/partner with a proven track record in your industry to gain valuable insight/knowledge.*

7.2 Pitfalls

- ✗ *Do not start the endeavor without first defining your organization's taxonomy.*
- ✗ *Trying to migrate all unstructured content to a single system as a prerequisite to embarking on any solution.*
- ✗ *Trying to deliver the solution in one fell swoop.*
- ✗ *Trying to implement a solution without expert help from definition to production.*

8. COMPETITIVE ADVANTAGES

Molina has increased its HEDIS measures positively as reported to CMS. This has enabled Molina to benefit from potentially higher bonus payments. The solution also has enabled Molina to further automate other facets of operations while adhering to regulatory requirements.

The CMCM solution has further areas for improvement such as automating of the coding information extraction by leveraging document capture technology to ICR/OCR/MCR information contained within each medical chart as related to ICD-10 coding standards.

9. TECHNOLOGY

Molina has standardized on a suite of IBM Enterprise Content Management solutions. Specific products were used for specific purposes and benefits as described below.

- IBM Case Manager – used as the basis for the CMCM solution, streamlining the process of coding each medical chart request as part of a CMS audit.
- IBM Case Foundation – the centralized, enterprise catalogue securely managing all medical charts as part of the HEDIS programs.
- IBM Content Collector for File Systems – leveraged to automate the ingestion of files delivered by CMS listing what medical charts are being audited.
- IBM Forms Server – the electronic forms generator which is leveraged as part of the data input user interface (UI) by the coding users. This UI is accessed as part of the IBM Case Manager UI called the Case Client.

10. THE TECHNOLOGY AND SERVICE PROVIDERS

Molina worked with Datum Consulting Group, LLC, DBA Datum Solutions (Datum) (www.datumsolutions.net), who acted as the solution implementer. Datum is a pioneer in the delivery of customized enterprise content management solutions offering high-quality, results-orientated software development and consulting services.

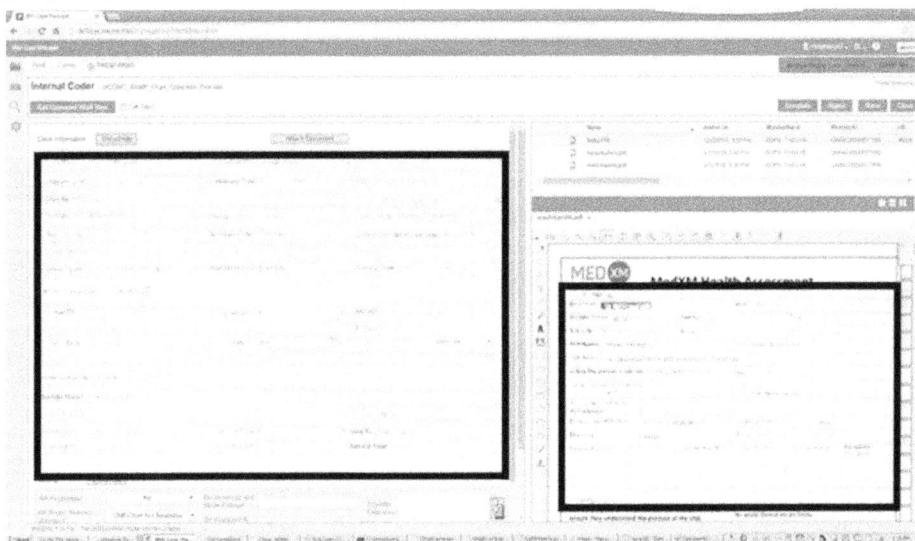

IBM Forms user interface as part of a Medical Charts Case used for data entry for ICD-10 coding input within the IBM Case Manager-based solution.

UniCredit Leasing Croatia

Nominated by EMC, USA

1. EXECUTIVE SUMMARY / ABSTRACT

UniCredit Leasing Croatia is part of UniCredit Group, which offers corporate and investment banking, small and midsize enterprise banking, retail banking, and other financial services. It is among Europe's leading commercial banks, with 155,000 employees serving 40 million customers in 20 European countries.

To address market-based and operational challenges, UniCredit Leasing Croatia needed improve efficiency, protect shrinking margins, and deliver high-touch service to more demanding customers. But inefficient and disjointed document-related processes made these goals difficult to reach. In response, UniCredit sought a technology solution.

2. OVERVIEW

UniCredit Leasing Croatia is the leading provider of automotive, equipment, and real estate leasing services in the Croatian market. With Zagrebačka Banka, the company is part of UniCredit Group, which offers corporate and investment banking, small and midsize enterprise banking, retail banking, and other financial services. UniCredit Group is among Europe's leading commercial banks, with 155,000 employees serving 40 million customers in 20 European countries.

Croatia is an emerging market, with strong tourism, industrial, and agricultural sectors. Nevertheless, the country's economy struggled following the 2008 economic downturn. The financial services sector was particularly hard-hit, with many businesses and individuals reluctant to invest in the face of tepid economic growth. These challenges added pressure to an already fiercely competitive environment, with major international banks vying for a piece of the market.

To address these challenges, UniCredit Leasing Croatia needed to achieve greater efficiencies, protect shrinking margins, and deliver high-touch service to more demanding customers. But inefficient and disjointed document-related processes made these goals difficult to reach. Incoming and outgoing mail, procurement and invoicing, complaints, underwriting, and other processes lacked clearly defined workflows, end-to-end consistency and connectivity, and real-time visibility. In response, UniCredit sought a technology solution.

3. BUSINESS CONTEXT

"We had inefficient processes in which almost all documents as well as pieces of information were handled multiple times," explains Eugen Paić-Karega, CEO of UniCredit Leasing Croatia. "We had no real-time ability to understand where a document was at any point in the process. Making process improvements to achieve greater efficiency and effectiveness was of utmost importance to maintaining competitive advantage."

UniCredit Leasing Croatia's needed to transform its document processes to simultaneously lower costs and improve responsiveness to customers and partners. Its goal was to retain its position as the No. 1 leasing provider while driving greater profitability. The organization also wanted to position itself to respond quickly as the Croatian economy rebounded.

Increasing regulatory agency and intra group reporting requests, as well as the volume of information required, put added pressure on employees. So UniCredit needed to heighten efficiency and security while finding smarter, more integrated ways to handle increasingly complex caseloads.

Facing significant business growth and expanding market potential, UniCredit Leasing Croatia sought capture-increased demand with same number of employees and at the same time retain its best-in-class customer satisfaction index, which was significantly higher than it market peers.

4. THE KEY INNOVATIONS

4.1 Business

To reach its goals, UniCredit Leasing began integrating its core technologies with the business processes that delivered key services. The company deployed a capture and content management solution that enabled the organization to intelligently capture documents, apply advanced recognition technology, transform information into usable business data, and connect that information to core systems and processes. The solution also empowered employees and management to automate complex, information-intensive processes, apply real-time monitoring and analytics, drive better business decisions, and deliver higher levels of service to customers and partners.

UniCredit Leasing started by digitizing and automating its incoming mail, which includes customer and partner correspondence, leasing documents, proof of insurance, invoices, and other financial records. As mail arrives, documents are captured and identified with a unique barcode. Scanned documents from any location enter a centralized repository. Optical character recognition supports keyword search on document content. Staff can also use the system to capture data such as invoice numbers directly from a document to act as meta-data that supports advanced search.

With the same technology foundation, UniCredit implemented an automated process for managing accounts payable tasks such as budgeting, procurement, incoming invoices, and payments. The system captures invoices and assigns them to the right employee and cost center-based on document type. The solution also automatically captures and enters approved invoices into the company's ERP system. This cuts out manual data input and minimizes the number of times documents are handled—saving time and reducing errors.

The last phase of solution implementation will automate the underwriting process, which will:

1. Accelerate decision making through a reduction in manual activities
2. Produce higher quality decisions via improved information throughput
3. Reduce response time to client or partner claims
4. Increase sales and protect net margins

The solution features a high-level integration with UniCredit Leasing systems such as ERP, systems used by other members of the UniCredit Group, and third-party systems such as credit bureaus. It also enables sales personnel and other specialists to collaborate while preparing client financing.

The solution monitors and manages business processes through embedded business rules that include security protocols. It automatically collects required data and performs necessary calculations. This maximizes the time sales personnel can spend serving clients while enabling the organization to respond quickly with comprehensive, accurate information.

4.2 Case Handling

- **Overall System Architecture**

Before implementing its document management solution, UniCredit's incoming and outgoing mail, procurement and invoicing, complaints, underwriting, and other processes lacked clearly-defined workflows, end-to-end consistency and connectivity, and real-time visibility. Moreover, all processes required substantial time-consuming manual effort in gathering information and system monitoring.

The first phase of the project involved case handling modules for:
- Mailroom (incoming and outgoing documents)
- Procurement
- Incoming invoices
- Complaints
- Anti-money laundering (AML)
- The solution's technology architecture included:
- User requirements and functional specifications assessment application
- Digitization platform
- Case management and document management platform

The second phase deployed UniCredit's underwriting solution, which included the implementation of a decision support system (DSS).

Assignment and Management of Key Roles

An application module describes and defines UniCredit's organizational structure, which determines case workflow and specific operating procedures. Roles are assigned and managed through Documentum groups. Individuals performing a specific role, such as leasing specialist or risk specialist, join the corresponding group. As case processing continues, group members receive tasks according to steps in the predefined process.

Each step must satisfy a number of prerequisites before moving to the next step. Some early steps, such as data gathering, may be completed with partial documentation, but the case cannot be closed until all the proper documentation lives in the case folder.

Embedded checklists and reports provide immediate status information to the user, including new cases and status changes to existing cases. Multiple cases can be handled simultaneously and management has insight across the entire case load, with automatic alerts eliminating assuring that no case "falls through the cracks." It is also simple to change roles when processes change.

Main business entities

Process reengineering was divided into phases. The first phase focused on back office processes— the digitization and automation of incoming mail. Next UniCredit Leasing implemented automated accounts payable management. The final component of the end-to-end solution involved implementing automated sales support and underwriting, which significantly improved service quality and allowed front office staff to dedicate more time to active sales and support.

Case template design and use

The case templates accommodate a client request or a specific document as the trigger for opening a case. It links seamlessly with all organizational electronic and hard copy entry points including email, fax, and scanned documents. The template puts key information at the fingertips of account specialists via a modern, intuitive interface.

For example, in the underwriting module the template captures the initial client request and all relevant documents. Its workflow routes the case through offering and underwriting to contracting and disbursement. The template can integrate with other internal systems such as sales, and third-party applications such as risk evaluation. The flexibility enables fluent collaboration across the company, delivering a 360-degree view of the customer.

Supporting the system and case template are integrated product and documentation catalogs and a rules database. These entities can be modified by the system administrator, enabling changes to made quickly across the system.

As a result, the case template:

- Decreases operational and credit risk
- Ensures compliance with business rules and legal requirements
- Eliminates significant manual effort
- Streamlines information gathering from diverse sources
- Speeds calculations

4.3 Organization & Social

Unlike it previous system, which relied heavily on manual workflows and paper documents, the new system enables employees quickly and easily in secure digital environment.

To accelerate deployment and time to value, UniCredit Leasing invested substantial time and effort in training and gaining staff buy-in. Employees attended their first training workshop during the testing phase. They were encouraged to offer feedback on ways to fine-tune the implementation and optimize its effectiveness.

As a result, the solution has completely transformed UniCredit Leasing processes. "We're aiming to have automated end-to-end processes and digitalize for every piece of paper that comes into the organization," comments Paić-Karega. "And everything will be linked to our underlying core applications. This will be a significant leap forward in terms of process efficiency and effectiveness."

Managers benefit from dashboards that provide easy-to-use graphical views of document types, volume, and trends over time. Analytics let them track number of documents/cases per employee, identify workload peaks and valleys, and fine-tune staff assignments to improve throughput.

Business analysts can link monitoring and reports to key performance indicators and the organization's performance-appraisal system. That way, document processing contributes to performance goals for individual employees and departments. In turn, that integration drives faster turnaround and better service to customers and partners.

5. HURDLES OVERCOME

Management

UniCredit Leasing Croatia identified four success factors for solution development and implementation

Thorough project preparation

Before starting the project with the solution vendor, UniCredit Leasing prepared a comprehensive business requirement document (BRD). As-is processes were described, but the document was based on what was considered, "a new way of thinking" about how technology is used to integrate with services that the organization provides. In the BRD process, document, and data flows were described, as well as business rules and calculations.

Competent team members and value-added partners

The solution team represented all parts of the organization. Great attention was paid to selection of competent team members—specialists with the ability to think "outside the box" and the willingness to adopt innovations. Implementation partner needed to be reliable with a proven ability to execute.

Experienced project management

UniCredit Leasing believed that the project manager should have significant project management experience in the implementation of complex IT solutions. In addition to these credentials, the project manager also required expertise in the field of process optimization for the finance industry. UniCredit Leasing engaged an external consultant for this role.

Strong executive oversight

A Steering Committee made up of UniCredit Leasing Management Board members provided strategic and supervisory control of the project. The Chairman of the Management Board was the project sponsor.

Business

During the preparation phase, middle management was involved in project planning and preparation as well as the verification of prepared documents. A range of functional specialists were involved in the analysis phase to ensure a comprehensiveness business scope for the solution.

Organizational Adoption

UniCredit Leasing announced the project with a thorough overview of scope, goals, and implementation phases. Project evangelists marketed the solution internally, stressing benefits and providing regular status reports to all levels of the organization.

As described earlier, all employees received suitable training and user manuals. The company also set up a help desk to provide support for employees as the solution rolled out.

6. BENEFITS

"Our employees have really seen how this solution helps them do a better job more easily," notes Paić-Karega. "It enables them to spend more time responding to customer demand, which has been reflected in more complex transactions and more customers."

6.1 Cost Savings / Time Reductions

UniCredit Leasing achieved significant time and cost reductions in handling cases and documents. By the end of 2015, UniCredit leasing had reduced FTE per new leasing contract by 42.6 percent.

6.2 Increased Revenues

UniCredit Leasing increased sales by 80 percent and its market share of new sales by 25 percent without increasing staff. Through improved efficiency, the organization can react faster to customer or partner claims than its competition, protecting net margin.

6.3 Quality Improvements

With faster response time and improved decision making, UniCredit Leasing raised its customer satisfaction index to 100 (compared with the industry average of 77) even with an increase in sales and market share.

7. BEST PRACTICES, LEARNING POINTS AND PITFALLS

7.1 Best Practices and Learning Points

✓ *Involve the user population in the development process early and often*
✓ *Engage subject matter experts throughout design and development;*
✓ *Prepare a comprehensive business requirements document (BRD) based on optimized and redefined processes;*
✓ *Engage experienced and strong project management with deep subject matter expertise*
✓ *Provide a substantial tangible benefit to users to incent adoption*
✓ *Include auditing to encourage good decision-making*
✓ *Pilot the system with a cross section of users.*

7.2 Pitfalls

✗ *Don't over-complicate automated workflows—keep it simple and let case managers think;*
✗ *Expect to make updates and tweaks to the system post go-live.*

8. COMPETITIVE ADVANTAGES

As noted earlier, UniCredit competes in a market crowded with 25 other leasing companies. Nevertheless, few of its competitors compete across all leasing sectors. So UniCredit often competes with specialists in individual sectors such as automobiles, real estate, and equipment. The faster and more accurate its processes, the greater its ability to deliver the kind of high-touch customer service that builds customer loyalty.

Competition has driven many leasing market participants to sacrifice profitability for volume. On the other hand, UniCredit's focus remains on profitability. It is willing to pass on potential contracts if they don't meet the company's profitability measures.

"We really look to return on equity as an important KPI," continues Paić-Karega. "Also our cost-to-income ratio, which is a good right now at 40 percent. Our net spread is 300 basis points. And we continue to lead the market in terms of assets and new sales. We're constantly optimizing volume and profitability."

Over the next several months, the company plans to extend its document and case management system throughout the enterprise. All managers and staff will have access to the same capture, workflow automation, core system integration, and process monitoring for processes such as underwriting, leasing, and resolving customer complaints. For example, employees will no longer need to directly access the ERP system to handle the underwriting process. That will simplify training, improve control mechanisms, and better protect customer data.

9. TECHNOLOGY

EMC Documentum xCP delivers an integrated development environment with all the necessary tools in one place. xCP is the foundation for the UniCredit Leasing Croatia application, which uses the following components:

- MOLA MOLA Business Visualizer for User Requirements and analysis
- EMC Documentum xCP for case management including workflow

- EMC Documentum content management repository for storing structured and unstructured data
- EMC Captiva for document capture
- SCHUFA Decision Support System for complex rules settings
- Modern intuitive interface

10. THE TECHNOLOGY AND SERVICE PROVIDERS

Mola Mola is a company with a mission to support digital transformation in the financial sector, using a process-focused approach. It achieves value delivery through careful, end-to-end business process design that integrates agile, value-driven requirements management and IT delivery. The outcome: faster time to market and improved quality, while reducing lifecycle costs and risks for custom, highly tailored enterprise solutions with a great user experience. This is achieved by blending the best of enterprise solutions, custom software development, and business rules/decision automation services.

http://www.mola-mola.hr

WPS Health Solutions

Nominated by Naviant, Inc. & Hyland, USA

1. EXECUTIVE SUMMARY / ABSTRACT

WPS Health Solutions is a Medicare Administrative Contractor (MAC). As a MAC, one of the services WPS provides is to credential and enroll more than 100,000 physicians and medical facilities that would like to offer services to Medicare patients.

The credentialing process for provider enrollment is a labor-intensive process of research and validation of the 300+ pieces of information that are submitted in a standard application – all in an effort to ensure providers follow industry standards, and to detect and minimize potential fraud and waste in the Medicare system.

Before WPS deployed a Case Management solution, it took the organization approximately 60 days on average to complete the enrollment process, and they had a backlog of thousands of providers waiting to be credentialed or recertified. Tasks included completing web searches, phone calls, and validation of addresses and other data against multiple fraud and terrorist databases. Work was manual and tracked in spreadsheets, in email, and on paper – literally millions of pages of paper, making it difficult for managers and caseworkers to locate the information they needed to complete their work in a timely fashion. WPS' contract allowed for the completion of provider enrollment within 60 days.

Within six months of the deployment of its Case Management solution, WPS reduced the average time to complete a provider enrollment review to 19 days, among the best MAC results in the nation. The solution – which incorporates Case Management and Workflow capabilities – completes the mundane system tasks and allows knowledge workers to more effectively and efficiently make the more difficult decisions, adapting to the scenario that is presented to them. Space that was previously used to house paper files was reclaimed as WPS reduced printing of millions of pages annually. And gone are the days when WPS had to make herculean efforts to try to complete work within the 60-day standard; the organization is now a model of efficiency and will capture over several million dollars in savings over the next five years as part of its Case Management deployment.

2. OVERVIEW

Prior to the deployment of a Case Management solution for the Provider Enrollment department of its GHA Division, WPS experienced a number of challenges:

- For several years, WPS was missing the deadline outlined in its Service Level Agreement (SLA) of processing enrollments in under 60 days. This lag was leading to revenue reduction and lower profitability.
  - o Some enrollment applications were easier to work than others, which led to "cherry picking" by some of the provider enrollment staff. Some staff would first choose to pursue the easier work, while the most important work that needed more attention was left to languish and miss SLA requirements.
  - o Before the implementation of a Case Management and Workflow solution, WPS needed to run multiple reports from its systems to understand where work resided. This was a tedious, manual process with the potential for many errors and delays.

- Numerous attempts were made to add staffing and revise work processes, but the problem persisted.
- Each staff member had over 600 active cases to manage simultaneously, which required significant overtime, increased employee stress, and lowered morale as staff tried to manage six different piles of paperwork and priorities for each day.
- Storage rooms were overflowing with paperwork as WPS printed several million pages annually to manage the submission process and store all mail that was received.
- Often there were lines at the printer stations to retrieve electronic submissions and to complete the associated research required as part of the credentialing process.

WPS management knew they needed to get a better handle on improving their controls around reducing paper, document handling and defining requirements for process improvement.

They ultimately decided to deploy a Case Management solution that provided a 360-degree view of all the information that knowledge workers needed to better make decisions on the cases that required human intervention, while allowing process automation technology to complete the mundane system tasks.

The 17-week WPS Case Management deployment included the ability to ingest documents and information from multiple sources, including scanning paper into images and electronically ingesting emailed and faxed submissions. In an effort to minimize the need for human intervention to classify the types of submissions received, Optical Character Recognition (OCR) technology was used to identify document types and apply a set of business rules to extract information about the submission automatically.

Once a submission is ingested into the Case Management solution, automatic timers are set to prioritize the different types of documents received to ensure that the WPS staff are working on the next most important cases, rather than the easiest cases.

Eliminating the need to physically search across multiple locations to access paper and additional reporting information was critical to the success of the deployment. Case Management allows WPS staff to conduct their research from one comprehensive application that is tied to the multiple information sources workers need to validate data received on the submission. By instantly accessing postal databases, federal watch lists, and a plethora of other data sources all from one application, WPS can quickly and easily manage all of the more than 300 discrete data elements that are part of each case.

When a submission is missing information, the system alerts the knowledge workers and helps them handle the collection. The Case Management solution includes an automated letter-writing (document composition) component that comes complete with multiple template choices enabling staff to easily create requests for information. All other mailing content is automatically pulled from a database that includes all of the submitter's pertinent information, eliminating the duplication of data entry and streamlining the process to request additional information from the submitter.

In addition, because all submissions are scanned immediately on receipt, rather than waiting for the paper application to be processed (as was done in the past), gone are the days when staff need to guess where their work might reside. Also, WPS no longer needs to run multiple manual reports, which were frequently too late to be useful in identifying when work was going to be late. Now, the solution includes automated workflow timers that enable WPS staff to understand weeks ahead of time before they are in jeopardy of missing a deadline. Throughout the process, a reporting dashboard is automatically generated and shared with line managers so they can quickly identify bottlenecks and reassign staff as needed.

Post-deployment results include:

- Because of significant performance improvements, WPS has been able to reduce necessary departmental headcount by 35%. This, along with a reduction in printing and lower solution support costs, will allow them to capture more than several million in savings over the next five years.
- All contract requirement standards for Timeliness & Quality have been met since deployment, with inventories that are the best in the nation among all MACs.
- Staff stress levels have improved dramatically as they no longer have to manage 600+ cases at a time. Now they manage only the next most important piece of work, leading to overall improvement in morale.
- WPS is no longer printing millions of pages of paper annually, and printers are no longer being used. This reduced printing costs by $140,000 and perhaps even more importantly, freed up staff time waiting in lines. The storage rooms that were previously used to house paper have been converted to additional conference rooms.

Case Management has been such a success at WPS that leadership has since decided to deploy this solution across the entire Government Health Administrators (GHA) division, allowing for better communication among departments and even faster turnaround of work. This expanded deployment is currently ongoing, so ROI results have yet to be determined.

In addition, in December 2015, WPS made a strategic decision to implement Case Management and Workflow capabilities across the entire organization, including its Military and Veterans Health division, Health Insurance division and back-office operations such as Accounts Payable, Human Resources, etc.

3. BUSINESS CONTEXT

WPS has a strong legacy of serving the people of Wisconsin for more than 70 years. Founded in 1946, WPS is a leading Wisconsin not-for-profit health insurer, offering affordable health plans and benefits administration.

The expertise that WPS developed over the years has enabled the company to be a successful provider of administrative services for the U.S. government. The WPS GHA Division administers Part A and B benefits for millions of seniors in multiple states, and the WPS Military and Veterans Health Division serves millions of members of the U.S. military and their families.

WPS rounds out its product offerings through two wholly-owned subsidiaries:

- Arise Health Plan, based in Green Bay, offers HMO and point-of-service plans to group and individual markets.
- The EPIC Life Insurance Company offers term life, disability, dental, vision, and voluntary benefits.

WPS decision-makers recognized they needed to make a dramatic change to their provider enrollment processes to deliver on the timeliness and quality standards dictated as part of it contract, and the deployment of the Case Management solution could not have had a more dramatic effect.

Within a short window – just 17-weeks to deploy the solution – WPS could turn around its delivery time to become one of the most efficient Medicare Administrative Contractors for provider enrollment. Within the first month after deploying its solution, WPS was meeting all 30 performance standards that it was measured against. In fact, WPS had the lowest inventories of all providers. The efficiency of its Case Management deployment allowed WPS to reduce provider enrollment staffing by 35%.

After seeing the initial solution results, WPS leadership recognized the power of Case Management. In December 2015, leaders made the decision to deploy a Case Management solution across the entire organization, touching approximately 3,000 workers in multiple divisions. The effort will take several months, but will ultimately position WPS to be more competitive when bidding on new contracts and business. Case Management is truly transforming WPS.

4. THE KEY INNOVATIONS

4.1 Business

Prior to the deployment of its solution, the time it took for WPS to provide its customer with the performance measures on assigned work was measured in days. Today, reporting information is available in real time and takes seconds to access and share with the customer.

WPS now has the lowest provider enrollment inventory (amount of work to be completed) of all Medicare Administrative Contractors. Because of this increased position of strength, WPS is well-positioned to accept additional work and increase bottom-line revenue generation.

4.2 Case Handling

For more than 20 years, WPS received paper applications for provider enrollment to provide services to be paid by Medicare. There are multiple types of applications that had to be sorted and distributed in paper form to be worked.

Most WPS staff in the Provider Enrollment department managed, on average, 600+ cases at any given time. Finding a specific case on the desk of each of the caseworkers mirrored finding a needle in a haystack and could take several minutes. Cases were tracked in spreadsheets, which were managed by different managers. These spreadsheets were printed and posted along with other reports to manage the distribution of work.

Caseworkers validated application information by searching websites and manually evaluating other various data sources. Validating some 300 pieces of information on each application included printing screenshots and generating a hard copy of the content to be included in the case file. If additional information was needed, a letter would be manually generated and mailed to the applicant. The case would be held in a "pending" status file until the information requested was returned and manually matched to the file. Upon the successful completion of application validation, all contents of the file were delivered to a central scanning operation, where the entire case would be scanned into a document management system.

Now, after the deployment of the Case Management solution, staff no longer house 600+ case files on their desks or in storage rooms. Applications are scanned as soon as they are received, and OCR technology captures as much information as possible. The captured information is pre-populated into an electronic form, which is segmented based upon the specific section of the application. The data is presented in a tabular format (follows the same format as the paper application) on one computer screen and the image of the application is presented on another computer screen. Staff can quickly validate data by searching various websites and sources, taking notes within the solution, and then attach all content to the file electronically.

Work is distributed and managed based upon user knowledge and is presented one case at a time based upon the next most important application that needs to be worked. Managers have instant access to the inventory worked and can track individual performance metrics (key performance indicators) to identify average processing times, as well as the strongest and weakest performing workers. Lower-performing workers receive additional attention to identify a corrective course of action to align performance with standard averages, or conversely, are reassigned to another area of the organization where their skills will bring more value.

Because the Case Management solution that WPS chose can be easily adapted (point-and-click configuration instead of development by software coders), feedback and changes can be made to take advantage of best practices and new learning in near real time. While the solution provided immediate performance improvements, additional incremental increases were gained as caseworkers better understood the technology and its additional capabilities. Improvements were iterative.

4.3 Organization & Social

The deployment of its Case Management solution has had a significant impact on the employees of WPS. Previously, knowledge workers had stacks and stacks of paper dominating their workspaces. A typical worker had a small cubicle to complete their work that was filled with stacks of paper. The elimination of the paper case files from this space had an immediate positive influence on employee morale.

Because the new solution had such a dramatic impact on delivery timeframes, WPS had an opportunity to capture significant cost savings through headcount reduction. The new Case Management technology provided better tracking mechanisms to identify individual performance against the entire group, making it easier to identify the individuals that were underperforming. When the underperforming staff were released, morale for the remaining staff again improved as the rest of the team knew everyone was pulling their weight.

5. Hurdles Overcome

Management

WPS leaders recognized that significant changes would need to be made. Operational staff performing the work were empowered to identify changes to the workflow using OnBase and/or automation to streamline the application process. This empowerment produced a streamlined approach to prioritize and complete work more efficiently.

Business

The business unit was aligned with management and knew something had to be done. Custom training on the Case Management solution had been developed by WPS' in-house training staff. After the initial production go-live of the solution, WPS was still not meeting all its anticipated performance results, and the organization identified that additional training was needed in conjunction with staffing changes. Very quickly after these changes were made, WPS began to recognize the results it had been hoping for.

Organizational Adoption

To foster support for an entirely new software investment (OnBase), WPS had custom building blocks made, with each block signifying a different concept around the divisional core beliefs: Foundation, Integration and Innovation.

Sample Building Blocks

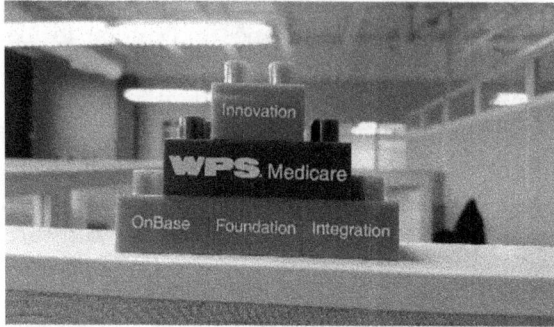

WPS encouraged staff teams to create building-block projects that captured the spirit of the change within the division. Here are a few pictures of the more than 30 team submissions:

"Taking the Right Steps to the Top"

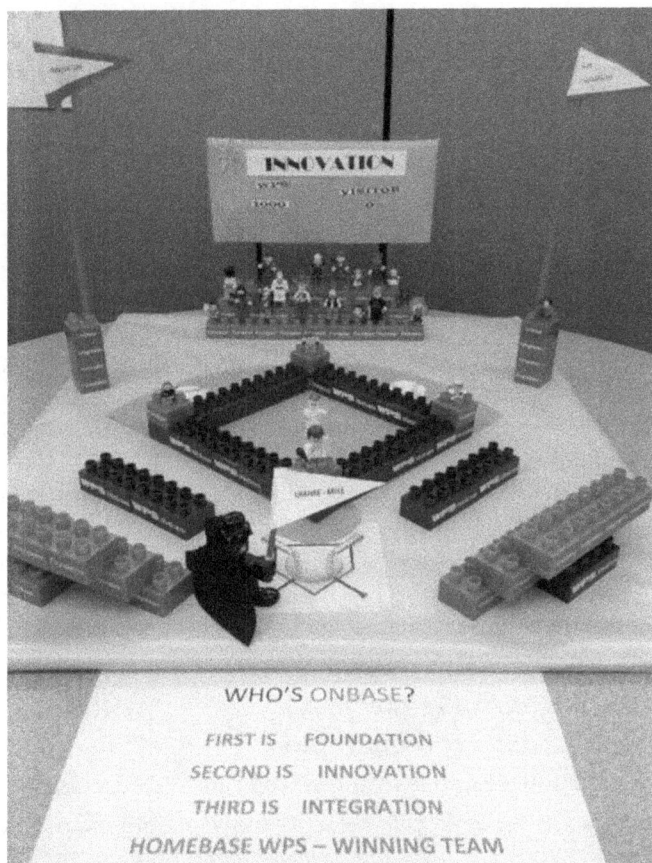

Who's OnBase? HOMEBASE WPS – Winning Team

In addition, WPS provided each member of the team affected by the new technology and processes with a "Survival Kit." Each kit included a thermal tumbler, cap and straw. Inside of each tumbler were items to help users cope with the change: a small package of tissues, lip balm, hard candy, breath mints, and a candy bar.

6. BENEFITS

6.1 Cost Savings / Time Reductions

Prior to its Case Management deployment, WPS took approximately 60 days to complete the review and certification of provider enrollment applications. Because of the delay in delivery, WPS was being financially penalized, decreasing profitability for the work completed. Now, WPS only takes 19 days to deliver the same work, an improvement of 69%. WPS is now meeting all 30 performance standards that it's measured against, and in fact the organization has the lowest inventories of all Medicare Administrative Contractors providers.

This dramatic performance improvement has allowed WPS to reduce overall headcount of the Provider Enrollment department by 35%. WPS no longer prints millions of pages of paper annually (i.e., screen prints and supporting validation information).

The headcount reduction, reduction in printing and lower cost for the support of the solution equates to a savings of several million dollars over the next five years for WPS – a true game-changer.

6.2 Increased Revenues

As WPS deploys Case Management across all divisions, it is better positioned to acquire new contracts with the federal government. Because costs are lowered, WPS can be more aggressive when bidding work.

6.3 Quality Improvements

During the process review and solution deployment with Naviant (OnBase Solutions Integrator), WPS uncovered more than one process where staff were completing work that was not necessary to deliver the contract. These processes were eliminated immediately. Work activities are defined by the solution automatically and managers receive real-time updates, allowing them to identify bottlenecks and make proactive (rather than reactive) decisions on work and resource allocation. The Case Management solution was configured to deliver the next most important piece of work that staff need to complete, rather than letting the individual caseworkers pick and choose easier tasks. By breaking the process down into much easier, more manageable steps, caseworkers don't feel as overwhelmed and can focus on the specific task at hand. Each step has a defined due date to ensure that metrics are met.

WPS leveraged workflow technology to complete menial tasks that don't require a human brain to make the decision, while equipping its knowledge workers with better tools to make the most important decisions. Case Management has raised the bar on the quality and timeliness of work generated by WPS.

7. BEST PRACTICES, LEARNING POINTS AND PITFALLS

7.1 Best Practices and Learning Points

Here are some best practices and learning points that WPS has identified:

- ✓ *Don't simply use technology to replicate the same processes that were taking place; you will replicate the same problems in a new environment. Use the opportunity to look closely at ways to improve and streamline the overall business process first, then use technology to execute the process improvements.*
- ✓ *Increase communication across the management team to better manage the transition to new technology and minimize staff concerns over the change.*
- ✓ *Develop a long-term strategy for the review of processes, as they can change rapidly. WPS must adapt to an ever-evolving landscape to retain its leadership position.*
- ✓ *Develop a Project Charter that includes executive sponsorship, business sponsorship, and a steering committee to review major decisions. Coordinate regularly scheduled meetings to make decisions more quickly and keep the project advancing.*
- ✓ *Training, training and more training! When working with a staff of a few hundred, some employees will learn at different paces than others, and some will refuse to adapt and embrace the change. Be willing to accept that training will be an ongoing activity and create synergies among employees to assist in the development and assistance of others.*

7.2 Pitfalls

Here is a pitfall that WPS has identified:

- ✗ *When dealing with significant changes, it is better to over-communicate the strategy and reasoning behind the changes taking place; user adoption can improve with additional communication.*

8. COMPETITIVE ADVANTAGES

The Case Management technology WPS implemented supports a low-code, point-and-click configuration approach rather than one that requires significant custom development of software. This deployment model allowed for a faster implementation (17 weeks) and the opportunity to capture process improvements and cost savings. WPS can also more easily modify the solution on the fly to gain additional efficiencies identified after the project was initially deployed. Continual process review and improvements are part of the long-term planning strategies defined by WPS.

WPS developed an overall strategy for its Case Management implementation by looking at all departments within the GHA division to complete an analysis of the timing for deployment. The analysis included prioritization based upon a number of criteria, including: need, readiness, value, risk, dependency.

The deployment of Case Management across all departments within the GHA division allows WPS to use continual process improvement as a competitive advantage. This allows the costs associated with managing content and data to be significantly less than what the competition is spending on those same issues. The agility and adaptability of the Case Management solution also allows WPS to be better prepared to take on more work without necessarily adding headcount.

9. TECHNOLOGY

An OnBase case management application was deployed by Naviant for WPS in their own environment. The brand-new implementation – which leverages OnBase WorkView | Case Manager and Workflow components – includes an on-premises based deployment in a virtualized environment for the users in the Provider Enrollment department.

An application server is deployed in conjunction with a SQL database, and client access is delivered through a one-touch deployment to the desktops of users in Madison, WI; Wausau, WI; Marion, IL; and Omaha, NE.

The case management user interface (provided by WorkView | Case Manager) was configured with multiple tabs to match the format of the provider enrollment applications that are received – enabling knowledge workers to easily access and work with all information. Without the need for technical development or custom coding, these tabs can be easily adjusted and configured to account for changes in the format of the application from time-to-time.

The solution also includes integration with Outlook to provide seamless interaction between OnBase and the email application in a common user interface. In addition, the solution includes a customized letter-writing template capability called Document Composition to automate the request of additional information from submitters, thus minimizing manual typing of the request by pulling information from the Case Management system.

Next, reporting dashboards were also deployed to provide real-time metrics around the performance and health of the processes. These dashboards provide early notification to management that there may be a bottleneck or issue with an employee's performance, equipping them to proactively adjust staffing as needed to maintain their SLA.

In addition to case management functionality and the components above, WPS leverages the full range of native built-in capabilities within its solution, including data and document management, electronic forms, workflow automation and process logic, and security controls.

Hear directly from WPS about solution benefits and ROI by watching the following videos: *WPS Insurance Automates Processes with OnBase Case Management*[1] and *50% More Productive with OnBase Case Management*[2].

10. THE TECHNOLOGY AND SERVICE PROVIDERS

About Naviant

Naviant, Inc. provides sophisticated enterprise content management (ECM) and business process management (BPM) solutions that drive efficiencies and insights into business data and processes.

As a top OnBase solutions integrator and workflow automation consultant, Naviant has achieved the highest level of recognition as a Platinum and Diamond Support Partner. The Diamond Support level is awarded to select Hyland partners that provide excellent support and service and maintain outstanding customer retention levels. Within the insurance industry, Naviant helps insurers create competitive advantages through streamlined processes, reduced costs, increased internal controls, audit assistance, and improved customer service.

For more information about Naviant's ECM solutions, please visit https://naviant.com

About OnBase by Hyland

OnBase is a single enterprise information platform for managing content, processes and cases. OnBase has transformed thousands of organizations worldwide by empowering them to become more agile, efficient and effective.

OnBase provides enterprise content management (ECM), case management, business process management (BPM), and capture all on a single database, code base and content repository. Enterprise file sync and share (EFSS) for the OnBase platform is available with our complementary offering, ShareBase.

For more information, please visit https://www.onbase.com

About Hyland

Hyland is the creator of OnBase, a single enterprise information platform for managing content, processes and cases. For 25 years, Hyland has enabled more than 14,900 organizations to digitalize their workplaces and fundamentally transform their operations. Named one of Fortune's 2016 Best Companies to Work For®, Hyland is widely known as both a great company to work for and a great company to do business with.

For more information, please visit https://www.onbase.com

---

[1] https://naviant.com/resource/case-management-roi-insurance/

[2] https://naviant.com/resource/onbase-case-management-insurance/

Section 3
Appendices

WfMC Structure and Membership Information

WHAT IS THE WORKFLOW MANAGEMENT COALITION?

The Workflow Management Coalition (WfMC), founded in August 1993, is a non-profit, international organization of BPM and workflow vendors, users, analysts and university/research groups. The Coalition's mission is to promote and develop the use of collaborative technologies such as workflow, BPM and case management through the establishment of standards for software terminology, interoperability and connectivity among products and to publicize successful use cases.

WORKFLOW STANDARDS FRAMEWORK

The Coalition has developed a framework for the establishment of workflow standards. This framework includes five categories of interoperability and communication standards that will allow multiple collaboration products to coexist and interoperate within a user's environment. Technical details are included in the white paper entitled, "The Work of the Coalition," available at www.wfmc.org.

ACHIEVEMENTS

The initial work of the Coalition focused on publishing the Reference Model and Glossary, defining a common architecture and terminology for the industry. A major milestone was achieved with the publication of the first versions of the Workflow API (WAPI) specification, covering the Workflow Client Application Interface, and the Workflow Interoperability specification.

In addition to a series of successful tutorials industry wide, the WfMC invested many person-years over the past 20 years helping to drive awareness, understanding and adoption of XPDL, now the standard means for business process definition in over 80 BPM products. As a result, it has been cited as the most deployed BPM standard by a number of industry analysts, and continues to receive a growing amount of media attention.

Workflow Reference Model

The Workflow Reference Model was published first in 1995 and still forms the basis of most BPM and workflow software systems in use today. It was developed from the generic workflow application structure by identifying the interfaces which enable products to interoperate at a variety of levels. All workflow systems contain a number of generic components which interact in a defined set of ways; different products will typically exhibit different levels of capability within each of these generic components. To achieve interoperability between workflow products a standardized set of interfaces and data interchange formats between such components is necessary. A number of distinct interoperability scenarios can then be constructed by reference to such interfaces, identifying different levels of functional conformance as appropriate to the range of products in the market.

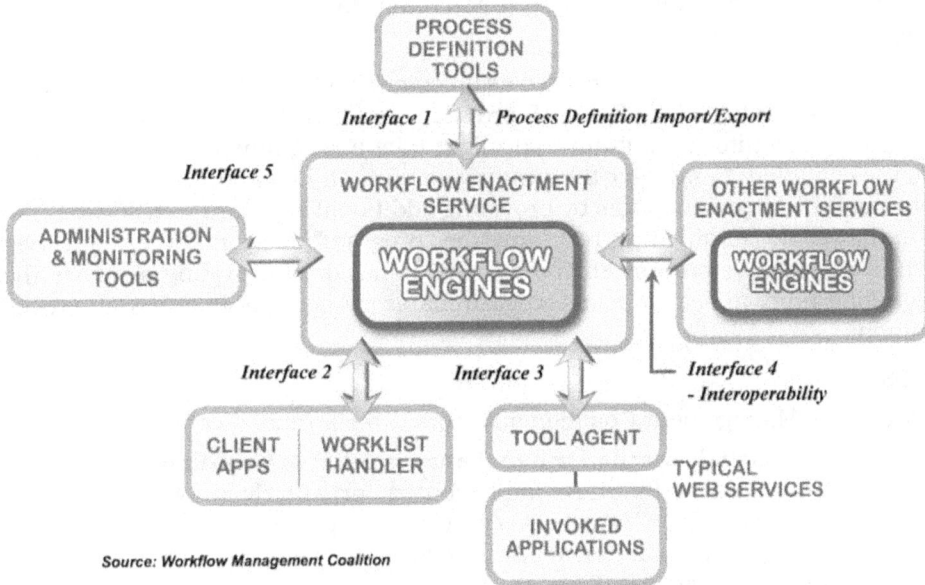

WORKFLOW REFERENCE MODEL DIAGRAM

XPDL (XML Process Definition Language)

An XML based language for describing a process definition, developed by the WfMC. Version 1.0 was released in 2002. Version 2.0 was released in Oct 2005. The goal of XPDL is to store and exchange the process diagram, to allow one tool to model a process diagram, and another to read the diagram and edit, another to "run" the process model on an XPDL-compliant BPM engine, and so on. For this reason, XPDL is not an executable programming language like BPEL, but specifically a process design format that literally represents the "drawing" of the process definition. Thus it has 'XY' or vector coordinates, including lines and points that define process flows. This allows an XPDL to store a one-to-one representation of a BPMN process diagram. For this reason, XPDL is effectively the file format or "serialization" of BPMN, as well as any non-BPMN design method or process model which use in their underlying definition the XPDL meta-model (there are presently about 60 tools which use XPDL for storing process models.)

In spring 2012, the WfMC completed XPDL 2.2 as the *fifth* revision of this specification. XPDL 2.2 builds on version 2.1 by introducing support for the process modeling extensions added to BPMN 2.0.

BPSim

The Business Process Simulation (BPSim) framework is a standardized specification that allows business process models captured in either BPMN or XPDL to be augmented with information in support of rigorous methods of analysis. It defines the parameterization and interchange of process analysis data allowing structural and capacity analysis of process models. BPSim is meant to support both pre-execution and post-execution optimization of said process models. The BPSim specification consists of an underlying computer-interpretable representation (meta-model) and an accompanying electronic file format to ease the safeguard and transfer of this data between different tools (interchange format).

Wf-XML

Wf-XML is designed and implemented as an extension to the OASIS Asynchronous Service Access Protocol (ASAP). ASAP provides a standardized way that a program can start and monitor a program that might take a long time to complete. It provides the capability to monitor the running service, and be informed of changes in its status. Wf-XML extends this by providing additional standard web service operations that allow sending and retrieving the "program" or definition of the service which is provided. A process engine has this behavior of providing a service that lasts a long time, and also being programmable by being able to install process definitions.

AWARDS

The Workflow Management Coalition sponsors three annual award programs.

1. The **Global Awards for Excellence in BPM & Workflow**[1] recognizes organizations that have implemented particularly innovative workflow solutions. Every year between 10 and 15 process solutions are recognized in this manner. WfMC publishes the case studies in the annual Excellence in Practice series.

2. **WfMC Global Awards for Excellence in Case Management**[2] recognizes successful use cases for coordinating unpredictable work patterns. Case Management represents an adaptive approach to supporting knowledge workers in today's leading-edge organizations. ACM provides secure, social collaboration to create and adapt goal-oriented activities that enable informed decision-making using federated business data and content.

3. The **Marvin L. Manheim Award For Significant Contributions**[3] recognizes an individual or a group for their influence, contribution or distinguished use of workflow systems. The award is named in honor of the late Professor Marvin L. Manheim, co-founder of the Black Forest Group* and co-founder of the WfMC. Professor Manheim was the William A. Patterson Distinguished Professor of Transportation at the Kellogg Graduate School of Management at Northwestern University from 1983 until his death in August 2000.

The Workflow Management Coalition offers members the unique opportunity to participate in the creation of standards for the workflow industry as they are developing. Your contributions to our community ensure that progress continues in the adoption of royalty-free workflow and process standards.

THE SECRETARIAT

Workflow Management Coalition (WfMC.org)

Nathaniel Palmer, Executive Director

---

[1] www.BPM-Awards.org

[2] www.adaptivecasemanagement.org

[3] http://bpmf.org/MarvinLManheimAward.html

Author Appendix

CHRISTOPH CZEPA

University of Vienna, Austria, Austria

Christoph Czepa is a researcher at the Faculty of Computer Science, University of Vienna, Austria. His research areas include Business Process Management (BPM), Adaptive Case Management (ACM), Domain-Specific Languages (DSLs), software architecture, software engineering, compliance/consistency and the application of machine learning and formal verification methods in the aforementioned domains. He has received a master degree in computer science in December 2013 (with distinction). Currently, he is pursuing a PhD in computer science. Christoph is the (co-)author of more than 15 peer-reviewed scientific articles and papers, and he participated in two research projects, namely the CACMTV (Content-Aware Coding for Mobile TV) project and CACAO (Consistency Checking, Recommendations, And Visual Modeling For Ad Hoc Changes By Knowledge Workers In Adaptive Case Management) project.

LAYNA FISCHER

Publisher, Future Strategies Inc., USA

Ms Fischer is Editor-in-Chief and Publisher at Future Strategies Inc., the official publishers to WfMC.org. She was also Executive Director of WfMC and BPMI (now merged with OMG) and continues to work closely with these organizations to promote industry awareness of BPM and Workflow.

Since 1994, Future Strategies Inc. (FutStrat.com and bpm-books.com) has published imperative business reading for executives, managers, business analysts, and IT professionals to understand theory, guidance and execution of Business Process Management, Adaptive Case Management, Business Architecture and BPMN.

Content comprises peer-curated papers from thought-leaders in these segments across all industries, together with real-world award-winning case studies.

Future Strategies also manages the prestigious annual *WfMC Awards for Excellence Business Process Management and Adaptive Case Management.*

SANDY KEMSLEY

BPM architect and industry analyst, Kemsley Design Ltd, Canada, Canada

Ms Kemsley is an independent analyst and application architect specializing in business process management and the social enterprise. She has a 25-year history of software design and systems architecture in several technology areas, combined with a deep understanding of business environments and how technology impacts them. She has founded and run three companies – a systems integration services company, a software product company, and her current consulting company – and held the position of BPM evangelist for a major BPM vendor.

Currently, Ms Kemsley practices as a BPM industry analyst and process architect, performing engagements for end-user organizations and BPM vendors. She writes the popular "Column 2" BPM blog at www.column2.com and is a featured conference speaker on BPM and digital transformation. She is the 2016 recipient of the Marvin L. Manheim Award For Significant Contributions in the Field of Workflow. Ms Kemsley holds a BASc in Systems Design Engineering from the University of Waterloo.

SETRAG KHOSHAFIAN

Chief Evangelist and VP of BPM Technology, Pegasystems Inc., USA

Dr. Setrag Khoshafian is one of the industry´s pioneers and recognized experts in Digital Enterprises, especially Digital Transformation through intelligent BPM, Internet of Things (IoT), and CRM. He has been a senior executive in the software industry for the past 25 years, where he has invented, architected, and steered the production of several enterprise software products and solutions. Currently, he is Pega's Chief Evangelist and strategic IoT & BPM technology thought leader involved in numerous technology, thought leadership, marketing, alliance, and customer initiatives. The majority of his time is spent with Fortune 500 companies, specifically on their transformational journeys leveraging digital technologies (especially process digitization The majority of his time is spent with Fortune 500 companies, specifically on their transformational journeys leveraging digital technologies (especially digital transformation, IoT, agility & process improvement through Pega). Previously he was the Senior VP of Technology at Savvion where he invented and led the development of the world's first web centric BPM platform. He was a senior architect at Ashton-Tate where he invented Intelligent SQL, and previously an OODBMS researcher at MCC, where he invented several object databases technologies. Dr. Khoshafian is a frequent speaker and presenter at international workshops and conferences. He is the lead author of more than 10 books and more than 50 publications in various industry and academic journals.

Dr. Khoshafian holds a PhD in Computer Science from the University of Wisconsin-Madison. He also holds an MSc in Mathematics.

SUSHIL KUMAR

Senior Director, Cloud Services and Engineering, Pegasystems Inc., USA

Sushil Kumar is a technically accomplished, senior software executive at Pegasystems. He plays a key strategic role in the engineering and service aspects, of the Pega cloud offerings. His 25+ years of experience in the software industry, encompasses digital transformation initiatives, leveraging globally dispersed engineering teams, hybrid cloud solutions, predictive analytics and the build out of highly scalable enterprise products and solutions.

Previously, he has worked both in startups and fortune 100 companies, leading business, technical and architecture teams that were heavily focused on agile development, rapid delivery and exceptional customer experience. Sushil has a graduate degree in Computer Science from the Indian Institute of Science, Bangalore and a Post-graduate certificate in Systems Engineering, from MIT-SDM-Sloan school. Sushil is a frequent speaker at industry events and has published numerous articles and research studies in various technical journals and magazines.

CONNIE MOORE

Senior Vice President, Research, Digital Clarity Group, USA

As Senior Vice President of Research at Digital Clarity Group, Connie has unparalleled experience working with senior executives in business technology, marketing, and government throughout the globe. She has managed international teams in developing ground-breaking thought leadership in topics such as customer experience management challenges and trends, the changing world of business process transformation, the evolving role of digital content and omnichannel, and the ubiquity of business analytics. Her leading-edge research topics encompass the future of work in an IoT world; best practices in organizational change management; the emerging relationship of cybersecurity to customer experience management; and the impact of location marketing on trust, privacy and marketing. Connie is highly sought-after as a keynote speaker and conference chair on five continents.

In 2014, she was honored by her peer group for thought leadership in adaptive case management and BPM software when she received the highly-coveted Marvin L. Manheim Award For Significant Contributions in the Field of Workflow, an industry recognition created by the Workflow Management Coalition (WfMC.org).

Prior to DCG, Connie was a Vice President, Research Director and Principal Analyst at Forrester Research for more than 20 years. She came to Forrester through the acquisition of Giga Information Group and BIS Strategic Decisions. Prior to that, she was Vice President, Product Marketing at BancTec (formerly TDC), a manufacturer of document capture systems. Connie started her career at Accenture (formerly Arthur Andersen) as a manager in the consulting division, and at Wang Labs. Connie holds an MBA in Information Systems from George Washington and a BA from East Carolina University. She is a former director of AIIM International, the leading professional association for information management.

NATHANIEL PALMER

Executive Director, WfMC, USA

Rated as the #1 Most Influential Thought Leader in Business Process Management (BPM) by independent research, Nathaniel is recognized as one of the early originators of BPM, and has the led the design for some of the industry's largest-scale and most complex projects involving investments of $200 Million or more. Today he is the Editor-in-Chief of BPM.com, as well as the Executive Director of the Workflow Management Coalition, as well as VP and CTO of BPM, Inc.

Previously he had been the BPM Practice Director of SRA International, and prior to that Director, Business Consulting for Perot Systems Corp, as well as spent over a decade with Delphi Group serving as VP and CTO. He frequently tops the lists of the most recognized names in his field, and was the first individual named as Laureate in Workflow. Nathaniel has authored or co-authored a dozen books on process innovation and business transformation, including "Intelligent BPM" (2013), "How Knowledge Workers Get Things Done" (2012), "Social BPM" (2011), "Mastering the Unpredictable" (2008) which reached #2 on the Amazon.com Best Seller's List, "Excellence in Practice" (2007), "Encyclopedia of Database Systems" (2007) and "The X-Economy" (2001).

He has been featured in numerous media ranging from Fortune to The New York Times to National Public Radio. Nathaniel holds a DISCO Secret Clearance as well as a Position of Trust with in the U.S. federal government.

PEDRO ROBLEDO

Director, BPMteca, Spain

BPM Trusted Advisor and Industry Analyst, BPMteca, Spain

Pedro Robledo is one of the most influential Spanish thought leaders in Process Management using BPM. He has been dedicated to promoting industry awareness of Business Process Management in Spain and Latin America for over 16 years. Mr. Robledo is Director of BPM for Digital Transformation Master in Universidad Internacional de la Rioja (UNIR). As BPM Interim Manager, he helps organizations with their BPM and Digital Transformation initiatives. He is a frequent speaker and presenter at international BPM workshops and conferences. Since 2013, he has participated as a judge on the WfMC Awards for Excellence in BPM and Workflow. He writes his own blog about BPM and Digital Transformation (http://pedrorobledobpm.blogspot.com.es). Mr.Robledo is currently an active participant in the Artifical Intelligence and Robotics Research Group in UNIR. He holds a Bachelor of Computer Science from the Polytechnic University of Madrid.

CHRISTOPH RUHSAM

ISIS Papyrus Academy Manager, ISIS Papyrus Europe AG, Austria

Dr. Christoph Ruhsam is Senior Manager at ISIS Papyrus. He is head of the ISIS Papyrus Academy focusing on applied application research for the Papyrus platform and coordinates scientific projects with external partners. The Academy team works also on user interface and usability concepts and produces all Papyrus software related documentation, education programs and executes the Papyrus certification program. He received his doctoral degree in 1994 at the Vienna University of Technology for digital signal processing of biomedical signals. Since 1995 he has been working at ISIS Papyrus in a variety of management positions and he established a dedicated project supervision team in 2003, caring for ISIS Papyrus' large scale installation projects. In 2012 he established the ISIS Papyrus Academy to stimulate scientific research projects in the context of ACM.

DAVID RR WEBBER

Global Public Safety Expert, Huawei Enterprise Business Group, USA

With Huawei David is focused on providing customers with solutions for Public Safety systems. Guiding government customers in adopting attainable public safety strategies. The Huawei Public Safety platform is the most comprehensive and proven on the market today. Providing the C-C4ISR collaborative suite of technologies for all aspects of public safety including policing, emergency response, intelligence, command center and communications. Technically working on key delivery areas with OpenStack, PaaS, Cloud, GIS, Smart Video, Big Data analytics, Deep Knowledge, Mobile, Cyber and G2G and G2C solutions. Understanding and harnessing all this is what our team brings to customer engagements.

David Webber is an industry recognized practitioner and author on BPM and Information Integration. David manages an open source project for information exchange automation and works on a variety of open standards initiatives. For OASIS he participated in the original BPEL and BPSS standards work. He developed one of the first BPMN visual editors for SmartDraw. David holds two US Software Patents for XML and EDI processing that are cited by over 35 industry patents from IBM, Dell, Oracle et al. David is a Senior Member of the ACM since 2007, and is the DHS appointed industry representative to the NIEM Technical Architect Committee (NTAC). In 2014 PESC gave him a Distinguished Service Award for work on aligning information standards in Education. David holds a degree in Physics with Computing from the University of Kent at Canterbury. David works tirelessly on simplifying solution delivery tools to minimize the gap between business requirements and logical representations that are directly machine processable. Profile: http://en.wikipedia.org/wiki/David_Webber

KAY WINKLER

Director and Partner at NSI Soluciones; Founder & President of the ABPMP Panama Chapter, NSI Soluciones, Panama

Kay Winkler earned his PhD in economics and business administration at the Universidad Latina de Panama. His investigation focused on establishing measurement frameworks for BPM benefit determination with "time" as a main variable. At NSI he is responsible for the distribution and implementation of BPM and ECM solutions in Latin America. Having been responsible for the automation and optimization of mission-critical processes for hundreds of international companies, he had the opportunity of accumulating proven and applied practices related to BPM and IT business solutions. He is sharing this knowledge together with insights from other recognized experts in his role of president at the local ABPMP chapter.

He can be reached through LinkedIn at: https://pa.linkedin.com/in/kaywinkler

UWE ZDUN

Head of Research Group, University of Vienna, Austria, Austria

Prof. Dr. Uwe Zdun is a full professor for software architecture at the Faculty of Computer Science, University of Vienna. Before that, he worked as assistant professor at the Vienna University of Technology and the Vienna University of Economics respectively. He received his doctoral degree from the University of Essen in 2002. His research focuses on software design and architecture, empirical software engineering, distributed systems engineering (service-based, cloud, mobile, and process-driven systems), software patterns, domain-specific languages, and model-driven development. Uwe has published more than 210 articles in peer-reviewed journals, conferences, book chapters, and workshops, and is co-author of the books "Remoting Patterns – Foundations of Enterprise, Internet, and Realtime Distributed Object Middleware", "Process-Driven SOA – Proven Patterns for Business-IT Alignment", and "Software-Architektur." He has participated in 26 R&D projects. Uwe is editor of the journal Transactions on Pattern Languages of Programming (TPLoP) published by Springer, Associate Editor of the Computing journal published by Springer, and Associate Editor-in-Chief for design and architecture for the IEEE Software magazine.

Index

Reading and Resources

Get special 40% Discount on ALL these Books (see below)

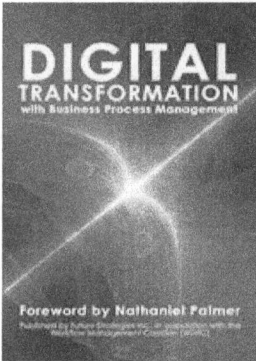

DIGITAL TRANSFORMATION WITH BPM

https://bpm-books.com/products/digital-transformation-with-bpm

"Today's BPM platforms deliver the ability to manage work while dynamically adapting the steps of a process according to an awareness and understanding of content, data, and business events that unfold," says Nathaniel Palmer. "This is the basis of intelligent automation, making BPM the ideal platform for digital transformation."

Retail $39.95

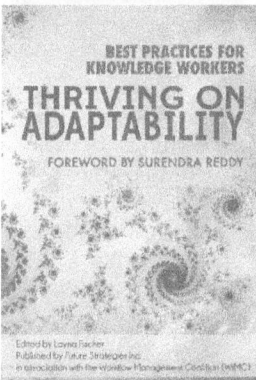

THRIVING ON ADAPTABILITY: BEST PRACTICES FOR KNOWLEDGE WORKERS

https://bpm-books.com/products/thriving-on-adaptability-digital

ACM helps organizations focus on improving or optimizing the line of interaction where our people and systems come into direct contact with customers. It's a whole different thing; a new way of doing business that enables organizations to literally become one living-breathing entity via collaboration and adaptive data-driven biological-like operating systems. --*Surendra Reddy*. **Retail $39.95**

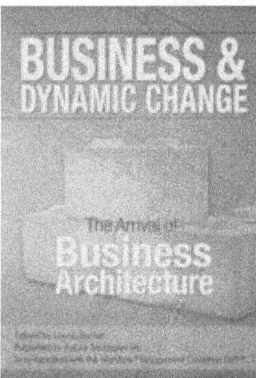

BUSINESS AND DYNAMIC CHANGE

The Arrival of Business Architecture

http://bpm-books.com/products/business-and-dynamic-change

These visionaries see the need for *business* leaders to define their organizations to be agile and robust in the face of external changes.

This book will stimulate thinking about a more complete approach to *business* architecture. As such, it is imperative reading for executives, managers, business analysts, and IT professionals that require an understanding of the structural relationships of the components of an enterprise. **Retail $49.95**

BPM EVERYWHERE

Internet of Things, Process of Everything
http://bpm-books.com/products/bpm-everywhere-print

Critical issues currently face BPM adopters and practitioners, such as the key roles played by process mining uncovering engagement patterns and the need for process management platforms to coordinate interaction and control of smart devices.

BPME represents the strategy for leveraging, not simply surviving but fully exploiting the wave of disruption facing every business over the next 5 years and beyond.

Retail $59.95

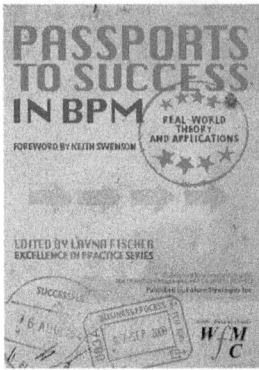

PASSPORTS TO SUCCESS IN BPM:
Real-World Theory and Applications

https://bpm-books.com/products/passports-to-success-in-bpm

Is your BPM project set up for success or failure?

Knowing what BPM success will look like before you even begin will help you achieve it. So will knowing what are the most common causes of failure.

BPM projects fail more often as a result of missed expectations than inadequate technology.

Retail $39.95

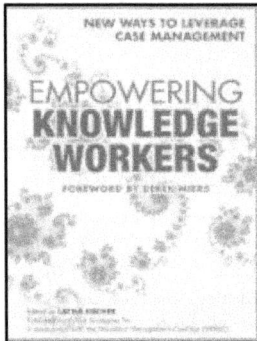

EMPOWERING KNOWLEDGE WORKERS: NEW WAYS TO LEVERAGE CASE MANAGEMENT

https://bpm-books.com/products/empowering-knowledge-workers-print-edition

ACM allows work to follow the worker, providing cohesiveness of a single point of access. Case Management provides the long-term record of how work is done, as well as the guidance, rules, visibility and input that allow knowledge workers to be more productive. ACM is ultimately about allowing knowledge workers to work the way that they want to work and to provide them with the tools and information they need to do so effectively.

Retail $49.95 (see discount online)

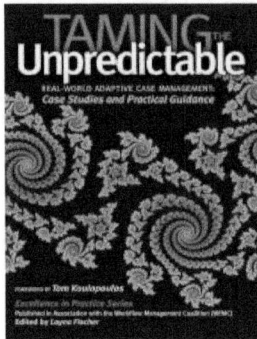

TAMING THE UNPREDICTABLE

https://bpm-books.com/products/taming-the-unpredictable-print-edition

The core element of Adaptive Case Management (ACM) is the support for real-time decision-making by knowledge workers.

Taming the Unpredictable presents the logical starting point for understanding how to take advantage of ACM. This book goes beyond talking about concepts, and delivers actionable advice for embarking on your own journey of ACM-driven transformation.

Retail $49.95 (see discount on website)

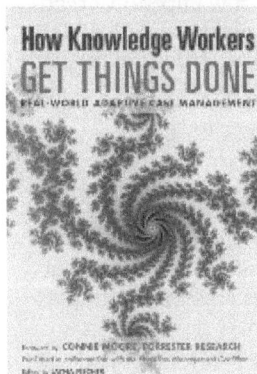

HOW KNOWLEDGE WORKERS GET THINGS DONE

https://bpm-books.com/products/how-knowledge-workers-get-things-done-print

How Knowledge Workers Get Things Done describes the work of managers, decision makers, executives, doctors, lawyers, campaign managers, emergency responders, strategist, and many others who have to think for a living.

These are people who figure out what needs to be done, at the same time that they do it, and there is a new approach to support this presents the logical starting point for understanding how to take advantage of ACM.

Retail $49.95 (see discount offer on website)

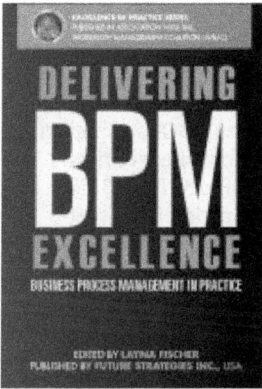

DELIVERING BPM EXCELLENCE

https://bpm-books.com/products/delivering-bpm-excellence-print-edition
Business Process Management in Practice

The companies whose case studies are featured in this book have proven excellence in their creative and successful deployment of advanced BPM concepts. These companies focused on excelling in *innovation, implementation* and *impact* when installing BPM and workflow technologies. The positive impact includes increased revenues, more productive and satisfied employees, product enhancements, better customer service and quality improvements.
$39.95 (see discount on website)

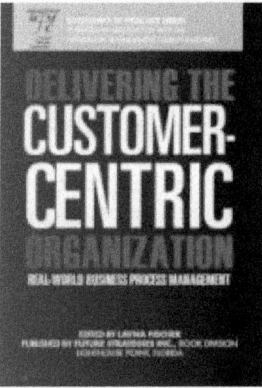

DELIVERING THE CUSTOMER-CENTRIC ORGANIZATION

https://bpm-books.com/products/delivering-the-customer-centric-organization-print
The ability to successfully manage the customer value chain across the life cycle of a customer is the key to the survival of any company today. Business processes must react to changing and diverse customer needs and interactions to ensure efficient and effective outcomes.

This important book looks at the shifting nature of consumers and the workplace, and how BPM and associated emergent technologies will play a part in shaping the companies of the future. **Retail $39.95**

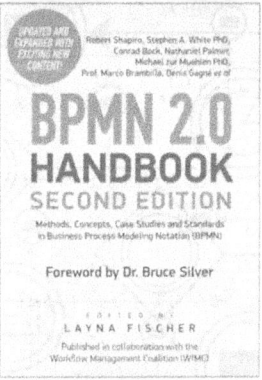

BPMN 2.0 Handbook SECOND EDITION

(see two-BPM book bundle offer on website: get BPMN Reference Guide Free)
http://futstrat.com/books/bpmnhandbook2.php

Updated and expanded with exciting new content!

Authored by members of WfMC, OMG and other key participants in the development of BPMN 2.0, the BPMN 2.0 Handbook brings together worldwide thought-leaders and experts in this space. Exclusive and unique contributions examine a variety of aspects that start with an introduction of what's new in BPMN 2.0, and look closely at interchange, analytics, conformance, optimization, simulation and more. **Retail $75.00 (see discount online)**

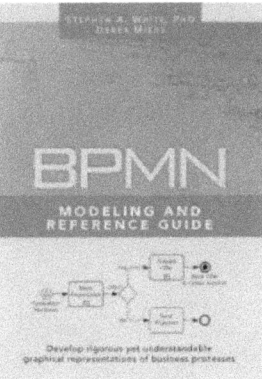

BPMN MODELING AND REFERENCE GUIDE

(see two-BPM book bundle offer on website: get BPMN Reference Guide Free)
http://www.futstrat.com/books/BPMN-Guide.php
Understanding and Using BPMN
How to develop rigorous yet understandable graphical representations of business processes.

Business Process Modeling Notation (BPMN) is a standard, graphical modeling representation for business processes. It provides an easy to use, flow-charting notation that is independent of the implementation environment.
Retail $39.95 See special 2-book offer online